New English Second

By the same author

NEW ENGLISH
a complete secondary English course

New English First
New English Second
New English Third
New English Fourth

A New English Course
Third edition for GCSE

An ABC of English Teaching
a teachers' handbook with examples taken from the New English *series*

Heinemann Short Stories edited by Rhodri Jones

One: My World
Two: Other Worlds, Other Places
Three: Facing Up to the World
Four: The World Around Us
Five: The World Ahead

Poetry Anthologies edited by Rhodri Jones

New English Second

by

Rhodri Jones

Heinemann Educational Books

Heinemann Educational Books Ltd
Halley Court, Jordan Hill, Oxford OX2 8EJ

OXFORD   LONDON   EDINBURGH
MADRID   ATHENS   BOLOGNA
MELBOURNE   SYDNEY   AUCKLAND
IBADAN   NAIROBI   GABORONE   HARARE
KINGSTON   PORTSMOUTH (NH)   SINGAPORE

ISBN 0 435 10495 0

© Rhodri Jones 1978

First published 1978
Reprinted 1979, 1980, 1982, 1984, 1986, 1987, 1989, 1990 (twice)

Designed and illustrated by Chris Gilbert
Cover designed by David Farris

Printed and bound in Great Britain by Butler and Tanner Ltd
Frome and London

Contents

vi

Introduction

For the Pupil

This course is intended to help you to a deeper understanding of what English is about. It should help you to gain pleasure and understanding from reading, and skill and fluency in writing and talking. It is not meant to be easy. If you wish to improve your ability in English, you will have to work hard. There is no getting away from that.

Included in the course are many pieces of writing, some taken from what might be called traditional examples of English literature, some from writing specifically aimed at young readers, and some which have been written by people of your own age. It is hoped that you will enjoy these for their own sake and also find in them a source of inspiration for your own writing.

For the Teacher

This course is designed for use with mixed ability classes. The material is intentionally demanding, and some pupils may find some of it difficult. But no pupil will improve his command of written and spoken English unless he is stretched and comes face to face with the challenge of new ideas, new imaginative adventures, new words and new ways of looking at and understanding words.

If pupils are to meet this challenge successfully, the teacher is, of course, essential. He must encourage and guide and be ready to adapt the material, where necessary, to the particular needs of his class and to the needs of individuals within his class. As well as providing much practice in writing and reading, the course is intended to provide much opportunity for oral work which the teacher can initiate, and to which pupils of all abilities can contribute their ideas and experiences. Since all young people also enjoy being read aloud to, it is hoped that the teacher will use his skill to bring alive the many extracts from novels used in the course and to make them more readily accessible to his pupils whatever their ability.

UNIT 1

Down My Way

 Reading and Understanding

The Jungle

Where do you live? What kind of area is it? What kind of houses, shops, streets, facilities, does it have? Do you like living where you live? Would you like to live somewhere else? If so, where?

These are questions which you have possibly never asked yourself. When you grow up in a place, you tend to take it for granted. So it is useful sometimes to take a hard look at where you live – to see it as though through the eyes of a stranger seeing it for the first time, to weigh up the good and the bad things about it. Then, perhaps, in the future, when you may have more choice over where you live, you will know the kinds of things to look for and think about.

This is where reading comes in. As you grow older, you may have the chance to travel about and see how other people live – to see other towns and perhaps even other countries. When on holiday, you might get to know other areas and become aware that they are different from your own. Not everyone has the opportunity to move about much and go to other places, and this is where the world of books comes in. Through reading, we can find out about other people and other places. We can ask ourselves whether we would want to be like them or live where they do. We can gain experience of other ways of life and learn to understand and appreciate them without having to leave our own armchair.

Here, for instance, is Kevin walking home with his sister Sandra and his friend Dick. He lives in a district which he calls 'The Jungle' in an imaginary city called Cobchester. Is it the kind of area you live in or know about?

It was a fine spring day, not warm but with a sort of hazy sunshine, and I was walking through the Jungle with my sister Sandra and my friend Dick. The Jungle isn't a real jungle, it's a district off the Wigan Road in the city of Cobchester. We call it the Jungle because all the streets are named after tropical flowers – like Orchid Grove, where we live. That may sound gay and colourful, but there's nothing colourful about the Jungle. It's a dirty old place, and one of these days the Corporation are going to pull it all down – if it doesn't fall down of its own accord first.

But on this sunny Saturday morning, as we walked home to dinner, even the Jungle seemed a cheerful place. Summer was coming, the blades of grass were showing between the stone setts, and soon the weeds would blossom on the empty sites. The days were getting longer. Next week perhaps we would be playing cricket after school. There was a dog in Mimosa Row that I was getting very friendly with. I was going to make a soap-box car for my cousin Harold. Life was full of interesting things to do.

We walked three abreast, with Sandra in the middle. And as we turned into Orchid Grove I felt happy and burst out singing.

'Hark at him!' said Sandra. 'Not a care in the world.'

'Poor old Kevin!' said Dick, with mock sympathy. 'He's got a pain. Where does it hurt, Kevin?'

'I'll hurt *you* in a minute!' I said.

'Oh yes? You and who else?'

'Do you think I couldn't?'

'Yes, I do think you couldn't.'

'Well, I'll show you.' And we started a friendly scuffle, the kind that happens a dozen times a day.

I generally get the worse of any fight with Dick. He's fourteen, a year older than I am, and quite a bit bigger. He's a cheerful red-headed boy, very good-looking, and the only thing wrong with him is that he's bossy. He thinks he's a born leader (which he may be) and he thinks he's always right (which he isn't). And now he held me off with one hand, grinning in a way that he knew would annoy me.

'Break it up, you two!' said Sandra. Small and

thin, with sharp determined face, she stepped between us. 'Fight when you're on your own, not when you're with me. Kevin, what did you start it for? It was all your fault.'

Sandra always blames me – partly because I'm her brother and partly because in her eyes Dick can do no wrong.

'Just wait a minute, Sandra,' said Dick, 'Give me time to bash his brains out. Oh no, I was forgetting, he hasn't any....'

'Oh, leave off!' said Sandra again; and then, as something caught her eyes, she added, 'Just look what's happening over there!'

Dick and I broke it up, and looked the way she was pointing.

Along the other side of the street came the two grown-ups from our house. First, Doris, in her best coat and headscarf, stalking ahead as fast as she could walk. Then Walter, with a battered suitcase, scurrying after her.

Walter is our uncle. When our parents died Sandra and I went to live with Walter and his two young children, Harold and Jean. Walter's wife had left him, and Sandra had to act as mother to the younger ones. It was hard work for her. She's only twelve herself.

When Doris, a friend of Walter's, came to live with us, it looked as though things might get better. But not for long. Doris was a blonde, bulky woman with a round, puddingy face. She was always padding about the house in slippers, a cigarette in her mouth, grousing and not getting anything done. She didn't like us children, and she tried to take it out on Walter. Every few days they'd have a row and she'd threaten to go away.

'I'm leaving you,' she'd say. 'I'm not staying in this house another minute.'

'All right, then,' Walter would say. 'Hop it, and good riddance.'

He knew she wouldn't hop it, because she'd nowhere else to go.

'You'll say that once too often, Walter Thompson,' she'd tell him, and then she'd go on grumbling: 'What with you and them brats, it's enough to drive me barmy....' But it would all die down. By evening they'd be round at the George, the pub in the next street, just as if nothing had happened. Sandra would put Harold and Jean to bed, and then she and I would sit up and do what we liked for a bit, until Walter and Doris came back.

But now, this Saturday midday, the two of them were hurrying along Orchid Grove in a very strange manner. Doris strode ahead, looking neither left nor right. Walter caught up with her and tried to say

something, but she ignored him. Neither of them took any notice of us.

JOHN ROWE TOWNSEND, *Gumble's Yard*

Why do Kevin and his friends call the area 'The Jungle'?

Do you think it is an appropriate name?

What impression do you get of it from the way Kevin describes it?

Why does Kevin find it less drab than usual?

Describe the impression you get of Dick in your own words.

What are Sandra's feelings towards Kevin and Dick?

How would you describe the kind of remarks Dick makes about Kevin?

Doris was 'stalking ahead' and Walter was 'scurrying after her'. Use your own words to describe how they were walking.

Work out the relationships between Kevin, Sandra, Harold, Jean, Walter and Doris.

What picture do you get of Walter and Doris?

What responsibilities does Sandra carry in the household? Do you think this is reasonable?

This time, it looks as though Doris is walking out for good. What do you think has happened?

Town and Country

Look at the pictures on the opposite page. What do you think it would be like to live in these places?

What would be the advantages and disadvantages of each?

 Writing

Other People

One of the ways in which we can build up an impression of an area we live in is from how other people describe it. Willy's mother in the following extract, for instance, has a very low opinion of the people who live on the other side of the street. From what is described, do you think her view is justified? Think about your own area. What do your parents, brothers or

sisters, or neighbours say about it. Do you agree or disagree with them?

Another way is to try to see your area through the eyes of someone else. Willy Overs in the extract is six years old and has not been allowed out on his own into the streets around his home. Imagine you were that age and were leaving your house to explore the streets around your home for the first time. How would you feel about the people you meet? – the older children, for instance, and shopkeepers. How would you describe the corner shop, if there is one, or the church, the main road, the park, the tower block or some other landmark in your area if you were seeing it for the first time?

Sometimes we are so familiar with where we live that we no longer look at individual houses or shops or streets. We take them all for granted. You have probably walked your route to school so often, for example, that you no longer notice the buildings and people on the way. Try next time to examine everything carefully as though you were going to be asked to make a map of your walk and to write descriptions of the buildings and people you passed.

Here is Willy describing his area, much of which he has heard about from other people and much of which he is seeing for the first time.

The first time that Willy Overs ran away from home was in the spring of 1895, when he was six years old. He was not, you would have thought, the sort of boy to plunge into an adventure of this sort. He was small and thin and shrinking – apt to be knocked about by larger boys – he always tried if possible to play at the girls' end of the school-yard.

Besides, the world outside 19 Audley Street terrified him. Even the other side of the road seemed a wild and savage place. Rough boys lived there who jeered at him and his brother George if ever they ventured out by themselves, and through open street doors he sometimes caught sight of a mess and muddle that his mother would never have allowed.

But it was much more frightening beyond Audley Street. As he went to school with his mother, or to the Co-operative shop in London Road, or when they all went to the Wesleyan chapel in Grosvenor Street on Sundays, he saw back streets that made him shrink up close to his mother, where wild-haired women screamed at each other from doorsteps and ragged children played without shoes, where washing hung out of windows and there were notices 'Mangling done here'.

'Are those slums?' he once asked his mother fearfully, remembering the word from one of the stories they had had read to them in Sunday School. But she had told him sharply that he mustn't speak so loud.

Inside his house was light and warmth and safety. There was his father in the shop to guard them from dangers in the front. If you looked through the lace-curtained window in the door between the parlour and the shop you could see Mr Overs' back standing behind the counter only a few inches away. And there lying on the shelf in front of the glass jars of sweets, although Willy could not see it, was The Stick, which could be used to threaten insolent boys (though boys who came into Mr Overs' shop usually left their insolence outside in the street). And there was his mother in the kitchen at the back of the house, cooking or sewing or doing the ironing. If Willy wanted to be particularly safe he would get under the table in the kitchen, and then with the brown plush table-cloth making walls round him on three sides, he would stare at the red coals between the bars in the stove opposite, hugging his knees, and comfortably certain that here the dangerous outside world could not possibly find him.

The outside world was Manchester, but of Manchester Willy, aged six, could form no impression at all. His father told him that Ardwick, where they lived, was part of Manchester – just a little part of it. So he thought vaguely of Manchester as a world of black little houses, just like the streets he saw about him, all stuck together in long rows with chimneys puffing up lines of yellow smoke; where you hurried past the side streets for fear of what you might see there, where the buzzer called from unseen mills for the people to come to work, and called again in the evenings to send them home. This to Willy was Ardwick, and Manchester, and the whole world.

But it was into this world, nevertheless, that Willy ran that April morning, and it probably would never have happened if he and George, his four-year-old brother, had not been sitting in the parlour.

'Need we sit in the parlour?' George had said in a whining voice, hanging on to the edge of the kitchen door as his mother swooped from dresser to table and back again, gathering up all the implements that she needed for her baking.

'You know I won't have you under my feet when I'm baking. You're very lucky to have a parlour to sit in. I've known children that were tied to the table leg when their mothers were cooking.'

'I hate the parlour, it's dark. Why do we have to live on the dark side of the street? There are always shadows on our side. There aren't none the other.'

'You be thankful you do live on this side of the

street, George Overs,' said his mother, scandalized. 'It's the respectable side. There's riff-raff the other. You look at their doorsteps and sills. And their curtains! Proper poverty-struck they are. Now give over talking and go along with Willy.'

'Can I have my soldiers, then?'

'You know quite well you can't have your soldiers in the parlour.'

'The marbles, then.'

'Nor your marbles, neither. You know that as well as I do. And if you don't behave yourself and go along this minute there'll be no cake for your tea.'

'Can I ask Father for some paper and pencils?' asked Willy, who, at six, had more mature tastes.

'If Father'll let you have those then that will be all right. But there's to be no mess on the floor, mind, and you're not to touch anything that's there.'

Willy and George finally shut the door on the bright warm kitchen, where the April sun streamed cheerfully in. The passage outside seemed cold and dark, so did the parlour. Willy had always disliked the parlour, except on Sundays when all four of them would be sitting round the fire. Only then did it take on a home-like, family look. At other times it was dark and stiff with plumped-up cushions perched on their points and every antimacassar spread starched and correct over the chair backs, and a look of disuse over it all.

'I'll go and ask Father,' said Willy. He pulled open the door into the shop. 'Father, Mother says can we have some paper and pencils?' He had to put in 'Mother says' because he and George were not supposed to show themselves in the shop.

'There's some old invoices. You can use the backs of those. You'll find two pencils in the brass pot on the sideboard. You going to be in the parlour this morning?'

'Mother's baking,' said Willy in a flat, disconsolate voice.

'You mind you're quiet then. You don't want me bringing in The Stick, do you?' Willy looked at his father's spiky ginger whiskers and his fierce blue eyes, and quailed.

'No, Father.'

'You tell George to mind what he's about, then. We won't get Mr Ramsbottom coming here for his cigars if the news gets around that there's boys racketing about behind the shop.'

The invoices and the pencils kept them quiet for a while. Then Willy gave it up and lay on his back, staring up at the ceiling and trying to imagine what the room would look like turned upside down, making a white floor with the gaslight sticking up from the middle of it. George kept interrupting his concentration. He was doing scribbles, wavy lines like hills and valleys, and showing them to Willy and asking, 'Is it proper writing now, Willy?' Willy could not read very much, and could only write in crooked capitals, but he knew that writing, grown-up writing, though difficult to read, was not like that.

'No, that's not proper writing.'

After a bit, George started to whine. 'It *is* proper writing. Father's goes like that. I *know* it's proper writing.'

'What does it say, then?'

'I don't know.'

'Writing has to say something.'

'Why does it?'

Willy had had enough. He wanted to be left alone with his thoughts. 'I'm going outside,' he said.

'Going outside' meant only one thing, a visit to the petty at the bottom of the yard. At 19 Audley Street the petty was never referred to in so many words. 'Going outside' was quite enough; usually adults did not say as much as that.

From the passage, he put his head in at the kitchen door. 'I'm going outside,' he said, looking wistfully round at the kitchen. It was his favourite room in the house, and after the murky gloom of the parlour it now looked particularly desirable. He liked the dresser with its blue and white service of plates that they never used; the black shining range with its steel knobs that his mother used to burnish with sandpaper, and the high mantelpiece with the loud-ticking clock.

His mother, flushed with the heat of the range which had been stoked up for her baking, looked up from the cake tins and bowls spread on the table in front of her. 'All right then, just this once, but don't you go on making excuses to go out. And mind you wipe your feet coming in, I scrubbed that floor yesterday. And whatever you do shut that door quiet and don't go making draughts or I'll have everything in the oven ruined.' Then she relented. 'There might be some scrapings if you and George are really good boys. You hurry up and mind what I said about the door, now.'

Willy moved off. He cast a frightened look into the dank, dark scullery on the other side of the passage, where there wasn't any gas so you had to take a candle at night when you were sent to wash. A tap was dripping now in a melancholy way into the stone sink. Then he pulled open the back door and slipped out.

It seemed so bright and sunny that he blinked. It was a fine mild morning. He and George had wanted to be outside playing, but his mother had said no, they would be in and out everlastingly through the back door making draughts and spoiling her cakes, she knew them. Besides, Father had just whitewashed the yard walls, and they would be kicking dirty balls about.

Beyond the gate in the wall Willy could hear children playing in the passage that ran the length of the row of Audley Street houses. Every house had a yard behind it, and every yard opened on to the passage. It made a good playground, though Willy and George's mother wouldn't allow them there. 'I'm not having you mixing with that nasty rough lot,' she used to say. So their games were limited to the whitewashed enclosure of the yard.

Willy went to the yard door and put his eye to the crack by the hinges. He couldn't see anything and a whistling draught made him blink. There were feet playing hopscotch outside, somebody was kicking a tin can, somebody else was bouncing a ball. The sun and the smell of the warm, rain-washed air went to Willy's head. He drew the bolt of the door, opened it, and peered out.

The hopscotch stopped at once. 'Look who's here!' yelled one of the players, a big boy of eight with a thatch of red hair. 'Little Willy Overs who's too good to play with us. Ooh, don't he look sweet, don't he just, in his little woolly stockings and his nice clean boots!'

'Bet yer old man don't know you're here!' screeched another. 'Bet he'd give you a leathering if he cotched you. Him and his old ginger whiskers!'

Willy looked warily behind him. Certainly he did not want his mother to hear any of this. He knew quite well that he was not allowed to unbolt the door.

'He's looking for his mammy,' jeered the redhead, 'Mammy's little pet in his little woolly stockings. Shall we blow his nose for him?'

'I'm going for a walk,' said Willy in a trembling voice.

'He's going for a walk!' parroted two or three voices with contemptuous disbelief.

'With his little reins to stop him falling down!' added the redhead. He was two years older than Willy and sometimes came into the shop to buy sweets. He was very different then in front of Mr Overs and within reach of The Stick.

'I'm going to the Park,' said Willy, and with legs shaking with fear, he marched down the cobbles. There were hoots and yells behind him, but nobody followed, and he got to the end of the passage, where it came out in Crown Street.

He just could not go back again, straight into the mob of boys. The only other way was down Audley Street and in at the shop door. But his father and

The Stick were there. At the thought of The Stick his legs went faster and he ran down Crown Street.

Crown Street was very like Audley Street: the same terraces of narrow black houses with lace curtains and a pot of aspidistra in the windows. But the people in Crown Street were strangers to Willy. Nobody gave him a glance, nobody asked him what he was doing, or told him to go home.

He passed the bottom of Audley Street, running still, and reached Grosvenor Street. Grosvenor Street was a wide one, noisy with carts and wagons and trams. You went down it to reach Chapel and the Co-operative, and you passed on the way a side street that Willy particularly dreaded, where he had once seen a man lying in the gutter. He turned in the opposite direction and ran on.

He was brought up short by another road at the end of Grosvenor Street, the one that ran north into the city, and south, his father had told him, into 'the country'. He did pull up here, aghast at what he had done; he had hardly ever been as far as this. But he would have to go on, because behind him lay dangers that he could not face. And then he remembered the Park, and a glimmer of daring was kindled inside him.

His father had talked about the Park and how he was going to take George and him to see it as soon as George was big enough to walk there. What was it, he had asked. Grass, said his father, and water, and flowers – hundreds of flowers. Who did it all belong to? To everybody, said his father, to everybody who paid his rates, that was. 'Do you pay your rates?' he asked his father. 'I do that,' said his father fiercely.

So the Park was something that belonged to his father and others like him and where there were flowers and grass like a picture book. For weeks now he had burned to see it. He even knew where it was. His father had pointed down this big road, Oxford Street it was called, and said you could reach the park by walking on out of Manchester. It was too dangerous to go home now, so why didn't he try to find the Park? And here Willy discovered for the first time that if you make a move, however timid, in a certain direction, events, like a wheel, can sweep you along with them and take you up, to a point further than you had ever dreamed.

GILLIAN AVERY, *A Likely Lad*

What are the unpleasant things about the area Willy lives in?

Why does his mother disapprove of the people who live on the other side of the street?

What do the older boys think of Willy?

Are there things about the extract which suggest that they are wrong?

Point out some of the things about the homes and streets described here that are different from today.

Other Children

Probably the people in your area you come into contact with most, apart from your parents, are other children. Are there any other children in your street? What are they like? Are they friendly or not? This poem describes some children who are hostile.

My parents kept me from children who were
    rough
And who threw words like stones and who wore
    torn clothes.
Their thighs showed through rags. They ran in the
    street
And climbed cliffs and stripped by the country
    streams.

I feared more than tigers their muscles like iron
And their jerking hands and their knees tight on
    my arms.
I feared the salt coarse pointing of those boys
Who copied my lisp behind me on the road.

They were lithe, they sprang out behind hedges
Like dogs to bark at our world. They threw mud
And I looked another way, pretending to smile.
I longed to forgive them, yet they never smiled.
                            STEPHEN SPENDER

What similarities are there between this poem and the extract from A Likely Lad?

Why do you think the poet's parents wouldn't let him play with these children?

What impression do you get from the poem of what the poet was like when young?

What are his feelings towards the other children?

People Down My Street

Think of the people who come down your street. There may be regular ones like the paper boy, the milkman, the postman or a policeman. There may be buses or people on their way to and from work. Do you see them regularly? Can you describe what they are like? Have you ever thought about the kind of lives they lead?

Here is an account of one of these people.

The Postman

Satchel on hip
the postman goes
from doorstep to doorstep
and stooping sows

each letterbox
with seed. His right
hand all the morning makes
the same half circle. White

seed he scatters,
a fistful of
featureless letters
pregnant with ruin or love.

I watch him zig-
zag down the street
dipping his hand in that big
bag, sowing the cool, neat

envelopes which
make *twenty-one*
unaccountably rich,
twenty-two an orphan.

I cannot see
them but I know
others are watching. We
stoop in a row

(as he turns away),
straighten and stand
weighing and delaying
the future in one hand.
                            JON STALLWORTHY

Why does the poet describe the letters as 'featureless'?

What does he imagine all the people in the houses doing?

What does the use of the word 'delaying' suggest?

Have you ever waited and watched for the postman? When?

New Arrival

How long have you lived where you are living now? All your life? Or have you just moved in? Have you watched new people arrive at a house or flat nearby and wondered who they are and what they will be like? Talk about examples you can remember.

Moving into a new area can be an unsettling experience. You probably don't know the area well and you have to get to know it and your new neighbours. New experiences like this can often fill people with fear and uncertainty. How do you think Martin copes in this extract?

At half past six Mr Singer got back from the engineering works where he was a draughtsman, gave a doubtful look at the outside of Songberd's Grove and rang his own doorbell. Martin opened the door, but before he got caught up in the rush of welcome to his father he was aware once more of movements and watchers outside, and quick withdrawals into other doorways. Feeling as though he were pulling up the drawbridge of a besieged fortress, he drew his father in quickly and across the hall into the safety of their own room.

'Well!' said Mr Singer and rubbed his hands. A large fire was now crackling away in the elegant fireplace, for although it was summer, Mrs Singer had wanted to disperse the musty, unused atmosphere of the rooms, and to air out their chairs and sofa which had been so long in store. She had found a blue-checked cloth from somewhere among the luggage, and on the table which this now adorned pilchards, tomatoes and a new loaf of bread were spread out.

'The old things, eh?' Her husband looked round the room with satisfaction and then sank down comfortably into the dent in the old sofa which he had made a long time ago, before the war. 'Sorry I couldn't get over to clean it up a bit for you, but I've been working overtime. They delivered the wood and coal all right, I see. It's not much of a place outside, I'm afraid, but this is a bit of all right!' He looked round the friendly room once again and lit his pipe.

'It's all right, love,' said Mrs Singer, giving him a pat on the knee as she passed, 'though it's shocking dirty.' Happiness and relief at being in her own place and away from her sister-in-law had made her fluff out and glow like a wet hen that had just been dried off in front of a fire, but at the moment she was preoccupied, searching again for something elusive in her bag.

'I do believe I've gone and lost the key of the suitcase that's got the aired sheets in it; run out, Martin, and see if I dropped it outside in the fuss of coming in? A little silly key, you know the one,' and the thing that Martin dreaded had come upon him. Like the newly arrived voyager to the moon that he imagined himself to be, he had to step out of the security of his space-ship and tread on the unknown territory; the things that lurked behind the trees and the stones of the moonscape, or in other words

behind the pillars and doorways of Songberd's Grove, would be able to get him. Squaring his shoulders and whistling a little, settling his glasses firmly in their place, he moved away from the safe Singer territory and out of the door.

The low sun was slanting across the trodden mud waste in front of the houses and turned them into a sort of Sahara desert, in which the shallow pools that were left from yesterday's rain gleamed like pieces of metal. Martin blinked for a moment in the orange glow and then was aware once more of the silent, watching children.

'Hallo, kids,' he said jauntily, but there was no reply, except for a faint giggle that ran through them like the wind through barley. Only the younger ones seemed to be out at this moment. Turning his back on them Martin started to examine the ground in front of No. 7 systematically, kicking the little pool in each depression with his toe-cap till the water spurted up, but he could find no key. Well, it wasn't here, they would just have to break open the suitcase, that was all. He straightened and half-turned to go in again when he was aware that two larger boys had come up behind him, as silently as though they had been playing grandmother's steps, or like two greased natives through the jungle.

One of them, who had muddy-coloured hair and a muddy-coloured face to match, and light, expressionless eyes the colour of dirty bath-water, handed him a bit of paper. The other was rusty haired and heavily freckled, with bright blue eyes. He wore a blue and white striped tee-shirt and he looked nervous and rather cowed. Martin stared at them.

'Message from No. 1,' said Mudface shortly. 'Wants to see you to-morrow, 9.30 sharp.'

Still Martin looked at them, from the bottom step of No. 7, and realised now that the small fry had come back again and were grouped about behind the two larger ones, listening with interest. The fact that he was on his own doorstep gave him courage.

'Who's No. 1?' he asked, in his most off-hand voice, 'I don't know that I particularly want to see him,' and as he gazed down loftily into Mudface's eyes the small crowd behind him gasped.

'No. 1 lives in No. 1 and he's called No. 1 because he is No. 1!' said Mudface fiercely, all on one tone, as though repeating a lesson, 'and you'd better come!' and turning on his heel he grabbed the rusty one and marched away. It seemed to Martin that the latter gave him a fleeting look of interest and almost of sympathy as he went, leaving Martin and the curious crowd to stare at one another.

'Good night', he said casually, as he mounted the

last step, and as though his defiance had given them courage, a faint, uncertain answering murmur came from one or two of his watchers. He closed the front door behind him and leant against it for a moment inside, He had a strong feeling that somehow and somewhere war had been declared.

'Found it, love!' said his mother, flushed and beaming, as he went in, for her husband had just given her a smacking kiss; she held the key up in one hand and all the aired and home-smelling sheets over the other arm. 'Sorry to have sent you out on a fool's errand, but there, I expect you've been getting to know some of the others and seen a likely friend or two. Supper's ready when I've just put these down.'

With a look of affectionate pity at her total, grown-up lack of comprehension, Martin smoothed down his hair again and slipped the piece of paper into his pocket; then he went over to the table and sat down.

ANNE BARRETT, *Songberd's Grove*

Why does Martin feel 'as though he were pulling up the drawbridge of a besieged fortress' when he draws his father into the house?

Why does Martin square his shoulders and whistle a little as he goes to the door?

Why does the small crowd of children gasp when Martin replies to Mudface?

Why does Martin give his mother 'a look of affectionate pity'?

Are there signs in the passage that Martin will cope? What are they?

Town Life

This picture of town life is by L. S. Lowry. Imagine you have moved into an area like this. Studying the picture, describe what the area is like.

Sandra Street

Sometimes there can be rivalry between people who live in one part of a town and those who live in another. One group of people will look down on another group because of where they live. This is what happens in the complete short story that follows. It is by the Trinidadian writer Michael Anthony. But notice, too, how because of the insults made about Sandra Street the narrator Steve is made to see it afresh as though for the first time and to realize the merits of where he lives, and how the teacher makes him use his eyes. Mr Blades stresses the importance of observation. If you want to write well, you have to use your powers of observation and see things as they really are.

This is a very thoughtful story that repays study. It is about how people feel about where they live. It is about two people, Steve and Mr Blades, coming to understand each other better. It is about how to write. Perhaps you could come back to it again later and re-read it.

Mr Blades, the new teacher, was delighted with the compositions we wrote about Sandra Street. He read some aloud to the class. He seemed particularly pleased when he read what was written by one of the boys from the other side of the town.

'Sandra Street is dull and uninteresting,' the boy wrote. 'For one half of its length there are a few houses and a private school (which we go to) but the other half is nothing but a wilderness of big trees.' Mr Blades smiled from the corners of his mouth and looked at those of us who belonged to Sandra Street. 'In fact,' the boy wrote, 'it is the only street in our town that has big trees, and I do not think it is a part of our town at all because it is so far and so different from our other streets.'

The boy went on to speak of the gay attractions on the other side of the town, some of which, he said, Sandra Street could never dream of having. In his street, for instance, there was the savannah where they played football and cricket, but the boys of Sandra Street had to play their cricket in the road. And to the amusement of Mr Blades, who also came from the other side of the town, he described Sandra Street as a silly little girl who ran away to the bushes to hide herself.

Everyone laughed except the few of us from Sandra Street, and I knew what was going to happen when school was dismissed, although Mr Blades said it was all a joke and in fact Sandra Street was very fine. I did not know whether he meant this or not, for

he seemed very much amused and I felt this was because *he* came from the other side of town.

He read out a few more of the compositions. Some of them said very nice things about Sandra Street, but those were the ones written by ourselves. Mr Blades seemed delighted about these, too, and I felt he was trying to appease us when he said that they showed up new aspects of the beauty of Sandra Street. There were only a few of us who were appeased, though, and he noticed this and said, 'All right, next Tuesday we'll write about the other side of the town.'

This brought fiendish laughter from some of us from Sandra Street, and judging from the looks on the faces of those from the other side of the town, I knew what would happen next Tuesday, too, when school was dismissed. And I felt that whatever happened it wasn't going to make any difference to our side or to the other side of the town.

Yet the boy's composition was very truthful. Sandra Street was so different from the other streets beyond. Indeed, it came from the very quiet fringes and ran straight up to the forests. As it left the town there were a few houses and shops along it, and then the school, and after that there were not many more houses, and the big trees started from there until the road trailed off to the river that bordered the forests. During the day all would be very quiet, except perhaps for the voice of one neighbour calling to another, and if some evenings brought excitement to the schoolyard, these did very little to disturb the calmness of Sandra Street.

Nor did the steel band gently humming from the other side of the town. I had to remember the steel band because although I really liked to hear it, I had to put into my composition that it was very bad. We had no steel bands in Sandra Street, and I thought I could say that this was because we were decent, cultured folk, and did not like the horrible noises of steel bands.

I sat in class recalling the boy's composition again. Outside the window I could see the women coming out of the shops. They hardly ever passed each other without stopping to talk, and this made me laugh. For that was exactly what the boy had written – that they could not pass without stopping to talk, as if they had something to talk about.

I wondered what they talked about. I did not know. What I did know was that they never seemed to leave Sandra Street to go into the town. Maybe they were independent of the town! I chuckled a triumphant little chuckle because this, too, would be good to put into my composition next Tuesday.

Dreamingly I gazed out of the window. I noticed

how Sandra Street stood away from the profusion of houses. Indeed, it did not seem to belong to the town at all. It stood away, not proudly, but sadly, as if it wanted peace and rest. I felt all filled up inside. Not because of the town in the distance but because of this strange little road. It was funny, the things the boy had written; he had written in anger what I thought of now in joy. He had spoken of the pleasures and palaces on the other side of the town. He had said why they were his home sweet home. As I looked at Sandra Street, I, too, knew why it was my home sweet home. It was dull and uninteresting to him but it meant so much to me. It was . . .

'Oh!' I started, as the hand rested on my shoulder.

'It's recess,' said Mr Blades.

'Oh! Yes, Sir.' The class was surging out to the playground. I didn't seem to have heard a sound before.

Mr Blades looked at me and smiled. 'What are you thinking of?' he said.

He seemed to be looking inside me, inside my very mind. I stammered out a few words which, even if they were clear, would not have meant anything. I stopped. He was still smiling quietly at me. 'You are the boy from Sandra Street?' he said.

'Yes, Sir.'

'I thought so,' he said.

* * *

What happened on the following Tuesday after school was a lot worse than what had ever happened before, and it was a mystery how the neighbours did not complain or Mr Blades did not get to hear of it. We turned out to school the next morning as if all had been peaceful, and truly, there was no sign of the battle, save the little bruises which were easy to explain away.

We kept getting compositions to write. Mr Blades was always anxious to judge what we wrote, but none gave him as much delight as those we had written about Sandra Street. He had said that he knew the other side of the town very well and no one could fool him about that, but if any boy wrote anything about Sandra Street the boy would have to prove it. And when he had said that, he had looked at me and I was very embarrassed. I had turned my eyes away, and he had said that when the mango season came he would see the boy who didn't speak the truth about Sandra Street.

Since that day I was very shy of Mr Blades, and whenever I saw him walking towards me I turned in another direction. At such times there would always be a faint smile at the corners of his mouth.

I stood looking out of the school window one day, thinking about this and about the compositions, when again I felt a light touch and jumped.

'Looking out?' Mr Blades said.

'Yes, Sir.'

He stood there over me, and I did not know if he was looking down at me or looking outside, and presently he spoke: 'Hot, eh?'

'Yes,' I said.

He moved in beside me and we both stood there looking out of the window. It was just about noon and the sun was blazing down on Sandra Street. The houses stood there tall and rather sombre-looking, and there seemed to be no movement about save for the fowls lying in the shadows of the houses. As I watched this a certain sadness came over me and I turned to Mr Blades, but I changed my mind and did not speak. He had hardly noticed that I looked up at him. I saw his face looking sad as his eyes wandered about the houses. I felt self-conscious as he looked at the houses, for they were no longer new and the paint had been washed off them by the rains and they had not been repainted. Then, too, there were no gates and no fences around them as there were in the town, and sometimes, with a great flurry a hen would scamper from under one house to another leaving dust behind in the hot sun.

I looked at Mr Blades. He was smiling faintly. He saw me looking at him. 'Fowls,' he said.

'There are no gates,' I apologized.

'No, there are no gates.' And he laughed softly to himself.

'Because . . .' I had to stop. I did not know why there were no gates.

'Because you did not notice that before?'

'I noticed that before,' I said.

Looking sharply at me he raised his brows and said slowly: 'You noticed that before. Did you put that in your composition? You are the boy from Sandra Street, are you not?'

'There are more from Sandra Street.'

'Did you notice the cedar grove at the top?' he went on. 'You spoke of the steel band at the other side of the town. Did you speak of the river? Did you notice the hills?'

'Yes.'

'Yes?' His voice was now stern and acid. His eyes seemed to be burning up from within.

'You noticed all this and you wrote about Sandra Street without mentioning it, eh? How many marks did I give you?'

'Forty-five.'

He looked surprised. 'I gave you forty-five for writing about the noises and about the dirty trams of the town? Look!' he pointed, 'do you see?'

'Mango blossoms,' I said, feeling I wanted to cry out: 'I wanted to show it to you!'

'Did you write about it?'

'No.' I just wanted to break out and run away from him. He bent down to me. His face looked harder now, though kind, but I could see there was fury inside him.

'There is something called observation, Steve,' he said. '*Observation*. You live in Sandra Street, yet Kenneth writes a composition on your own place better than you.'

'He said Sandra Street was soppy,' I cried.

'Of course he said it was soppy. It was to his purpose. He comes from the other side of the town. What's he got to write on – gaudy houses with gates like prisons around them? High walls cramping the imagination? The milling crowd with faces impersonal as stone, hurrying on buses, hurrying off trams? Could he write about that? He said Sandra Street was soppy. Okay, did you prove it wasn't so? Where is your school and his, for instance?'

I was a little alarmed. Funny how I did not think of that point before. 'Here,' I said. 'In Sandra Street.'

'Did you mention that?'

Mercifully, as he was talking, the school bell sounded. The fowls, startled, ran out into the hot sun across the road. The dust rose, and above the dust, above the houses, the yellow of mango blossom caught my eye.

'The bell, Sir.'

'Yes, the bell's gone. What is it now – Geography?'

'Yes, Sir.' And as I turned away he was still standing there, looking out into the road.

It was long before any such thing happened again, though often when it was dry and hot I stood at the window looking out. I watched the freedom of the fowls among the tall houses, and sometimes the women talked to each other through the windows and smiled. I noticed, too, the hills, which were now streaked with the blossoms of the poui, and exultantly I wondered how many people observed this and knew it was a sign of the rains. None of the mango blossoms could be seen now, for they had already turned into fruit, and I knew how profuse they were because I had been to the hills.

I chuckled to myself. *There is something called observation, Steve.* And how I wished Mr Blades would come to the window again so I could tell him what lay among the mango trees in the hills.

I knew that he was not angry with me. I realized that he was never angry with any boy because of the part of town the boy came from. We grew to like him, for he was very cheerful, though mostly he seemed dreamy and thoughtful. That is, except at composition time.

He really came to life then. His eyes would gleam as he read our compositions, and whenever he came to a word he did not like he would frown and say any boy was a sissy to use such a word. And if a composition pleased him, he would praise the boy and be especially cheerful with him, and the boy would be proud and the rest of us would be jealous and hate him.

I was often jealous. Mr Blades had a passion for compositions, and I was anxious to please him to make up for that day at the window. I was anxious to show him how much I observed, and often I noted new things and put them into my compositions. And whenever I said something wonderful I knew it because of the way Mr Blades would look at me, and sometimes he would take me aside and talk to me. But many weeks ran out before we spoke at the window again.

I did not start this time because I had been expecting him. I had been watching him from the corner of my eye.

'The sun's coming out again,' he said.

'It's cloudy,' I said.

It had been raining but now the rains had ceased although there were still great patches of dark cloud in the sky. When the wind blew they moved slowly and cumbersomely, but if the sun was free of one cloud there would soon be another. The sun was shining brightly now, although there was still a slight drizzle of rain, and I could smell the steam rising from the hot pitch and from the galvanized roofs.

'Rain falling, sun shining,' Mr Blades said. And I remembered that they said at such times the Devil fought his wife, but when Mr Blades pressed me to tell what I was laughing at, I laughed still more and would not say. Then thoughtfully he said, 'You think they're all right?'

'What, Sir?'

'In the immortelle root.'

I was astonished. I put my hands to my mouth. How did he know?

He smiled down at me: 'You won't be able to jump over now.' And the whole thing came back. I could not help laughing. I had put into my composition how I had gone into the hills on a Sunday evening, and how the mango trees were laden with small mangoes, some full, and how there were banana trees among the immortelle and poui. I had written, too, about the bunch of green bananas I had placed to ripen in the immortelle roots and how afterwards I had jumped across the river to the other bank.

'They're all right,' I said, and I pretended to be watching the steam rising from the hot pitch.

'I like bananas,' said Mr Blades. I was sure that he licked his lips as he looked towards the hills.

I was touched. I felt at one with him. I liked bananas too and they always made me lick my lips. I thought now of the whole bunch which must be yellow by now inside the immortelle roots.

'Sir . . .' I said to him, hesitating. Then I took the wild chance. And when he answered, a feeling of extreme happiness swept over me.

I remember that evening as turning out bright, almost blinding. The winds had pushed away the heavy clouds, and the only evidence of the rains was the little puddles along Sandra Street. I remember the hills as being strange in an enchanted sort of way, and I felt that part of the enchantment came from Mr Blades being with me. We watched the leaves of the cocoa gleaming with the moisture of the rains, and Mr Blades confessed he never thought there was so much cocoa in the hills. We watched the cyp, too, profuse among the laden mango trees, and the redness of their rain-picked flowers was the redness of blood.

We came to the immortelle tree where I had hidden the bananas. I watched to see if Mr Blades licked his lips but he did not. He wasn't even watching.

'Sir,' I said in happy surprise, after removing the covering of trash from the bunch. Mr Blades was gazing across the trees. I raised my eyes. Not far below, Sandra Street swept by, bathed in light.

'The bananas, Sir,' I said.

'Bananas!' he cried, despairingly. 'Are bananas all you see around you, Steve?'

I was puzzled. I thought it was for bananas that we had come to the hills.

'Good Heavens!' he said with bitterness. 'To think that *you* instead of Kenneth should belong to Sandra Street.'

MICHAEL ANTHONY

 Assignments

Choose several of the following to write about:

1. Write about where you live – your house, your street, your neighbours and neighbourhood.
2. Moving In. Write a story about someone moving house and his first impressions of a new area.
3. Write about the people who come to your street – the paper boy, the milkman, the postman, the visitors, etc.
4. Write an account of your street or area from the point of view of a milkman or a postman doing his daily round.
5. Write a story in which you become involved in a row with a neighbour.
6. Playing in the Street. Write a story about the rivalry between two gangs of children.
7. The atmosphere on Sunday mornings in an area is usually different from that of other mornings. Write about Sunday morning in your street.
8. Think about the buildings in your neighbourhood. Describe one that you think is attractive and one that you find ugly.
9. Write about the advantages and disadvantages of living in the country or in a town.
10. Describe a busy town centre or a quiet village high street.
11. Write about the advantages and disadvantages of living in a flat as opposed to living in a house.
12. Write about your walk to school, describing the places and people you pass on the way.

 Language

A. Parts of Speech

If you have studied Book One of this course, you ought to remember what parts of speech are, and you ought to be able to name and describe the different parts of speech and give

13

examples of them. See if you can do this now before looking at what follows.

Just in case you have forgotten, this section will revise the different parts of speech, and in later sections we shall be studying some of them in more detail than we did in Book One. **Remember that parts of speech are those different categories into which we group words according to the jobs they do in sentences.** In the sentence, 'The shop on the corner was closed', the word 'shop' is the name of something. It belongs to that group of words that includes the names of things; it is therefore a noun. Here is a summary of the eight different parts of speech for you to check.

PART OF SPEECH	DESCRIPTION	EXAMPLES
noun	the name of something	cat, orange, Muriel, theatre, sprinter
pronoun	a word that can take the place of a noun	she, them, me, it, that
adjective	a word that describes a noun or pronoun	small, lively, blue, tall, thin
adverb	a word that modifies or describes a verb	slowly, feebly, warily, very, so
verb	a word that tells us the action someone or something is performing; the state he or it is in; the process of change he or it is going through	run, speak, act, look be, seem become, grow
conjunction	a word that joins other words or statements	and, but, since, until
interjection	a word that expresses an exclamation	oh, ah, alas
preposition	a word that shows the relationship between one word and another	from, towards, above, before

State what part of speech each of the words in italics is in the following sentences.

1. The *tree in* our *garden is tall and slender*.
2. The *houses across* the *road* have been condemned.
3. *You can* set your *watch by* the *time* the *postman calls*, *he is so regular*.
4. The *next-door neighbours play* their *radio loud* all day.
5. The *pond in* the *park was* frozen *over on* Christmas Day.
6. The *children* who *live in* the *house on* the *corner went on holiday last week*.
7. *After* the *long hot summer*, the *lawns* were *parched and brown*.
8. The *queue at* the *bus-stop waited patiently as* the *rain grew heavier*.
9. The *battered car was parked for so many days outside* our *house that we assumed it* had been *abandoned*.
10. The *children* playing *football in* the *street dashed for* the *pavement as* the *car sped past*.

B. Figures of Speech

Can you remember what figures of speech are? Perhaps the words 'simile', 'metaphor', 'personification', 'onamatopoeia' and 'alliteration' may remind you. Can you remember what these words refer to? Try to describe them and give examples before reading what follows.

Figures of speech are devices used in writing and speech to make what you are saying more vivid and precise; they are ways of saying things so that the meaning is clearer or presented in a more colourful way. Here is a summary of the figures of speech we studied in Book One for you to revise.

FIGURE OF SPEECH	DESCRIPTION	EXAMPLES
simile	a comparison in which we say one thing is *like* another	His words were like balm to his wounded feelings.
metaphor	a comparison in which we say one thing *is* another (which it literally cannot be)	His eyes were opened by his friend's disclosures.
personification	a metaphor in which an inanimate object or an animal is given the qualities of a human being	The table groaned under the weight of the food.
onomatopoeia	the use of a word or words whose sound suggests the sense	pitter-patter; sizzle
alliteration	the use of the same letter or sound in a number of words to produce a particular effect	a scintillating spectacle; a melodious murmur

Give further examples of each of these figures of speech.

Vocabulary

A. Dictionary

It is important that you should try to extend your vocabulary. The more words you understand and are able to use, the more ideas you will be able to express and the more clearly you will be able to express those ideas. It is helpful to keep a vocabulary notebook in which you write new words and their meanings so that you can later use these words in your own writing. The value of the dictionary cannot be overstressed in this connection. It should be by your side all the time, and you should refer to it frequently: that is the only way in which you can increase your command of words. When you come across a word in your reading whose meaning you don't understand, look it up in your dictionary and make a note of it in your notebook.

Look again at the extract from A Likely Lad *in the 'Writing' section. Are there any words whose meaning you don't understand? What do the following words mean? Try to guess by studying them in their context and then check with your dictionary.*

plunge	scandalized
shrinking	invoices
ventured	concentration
jeered	murky
insolent	burnish
whining	dank
implements	glimmer

Use each of these words in sentences of your own.

B. House/Home

Study the following sentences:

My house is the one on the corner.

This desirable three-bedroom house is for sale.

He took his petition to the House of Lords.

It is time you all went home.

Take this dog to the home for stray animals.

Comment on the difference in meaning between the words 'house' and 'home'.

C. Habitations

'House' is a name we give to the place we live in, but there are many kinds of houses or habitations. Here are some of them.

Can you distinguish between them and say precisely what kind of living-place each describes?

cabin	pavilion
shack	hotel
chalet	manor-house
croft	palace
mansion	bungalow
villa	flat
cottage	tower block
lodge	maisonette
castle	penthouse

D. Streets

What is the difference between a road and a street? Could these words be used to refer to the same thing or do they suggest different kinds of thoroughfares?

Here are some more examples of names given to streets. *What would you expect to find if a street or place was called one of the following?*

place	passage
terrace	square
parade	circus
row	crescent
walk	arcade
lane	gardens
alley	grove
close	avenue

Invent an appropriate place-name for each of these. For example, Primrose Lane, Station Road.

E. -ette

'Maisonette' is an interesting word. It comes from the French word 'maison' meaning a house and the suffix '-ette' meaning little, so 'maisonette' literally means 'little house'. As we saw in Book One, a suffix is an element added to the root or main part of a word in order to indicate the part of speech it is or to modify the meaning of the word. A suffix like '-ette' which indicates a smaller version of something is called a diminutive suffix.

Make a list of other words which end in the suffix '-ette' and give their meanings.

The suffix '-kin is also a diminutive suffix. For example, the word 'manikin' means 'a little man'. *Can you find any more words which have the suffix '-kin'?*

 Spelling

A. Your Own Work

Spelling correctly can be difficult. To be able to do it requires care and practice. Not everyone makes the same spelling mistakes. It is important that you come to recognize the words that *you* get wrong. Then, because you know the spelling of a particular word is difficult for you, you will take especial pains to get it right next time or you will learn some personal trick to help you spell the word correctly. For instance, the word 'separate' is often mis-spelled. If you get it wrong, perhaps by pronouncing it to yourself in an exaggerated way (with two 'a's) you will remember how to spell it correctly next time.

It will help if you keep a spelling notebook in which you enter those words in your own work which your teacher has corrected. Add to the list every time your own written work is marked, and if you are in doubt, refer to the list. You will find that the same words tend to come up again and again.

Look at the written work you have done in this unit. Copy the correct versions of words you have mis-spelled into your notebook.

B. Capital Letters

Street names have capital letters because they are the names of places. Each element of a street name has a capital letter. For example:

Leicester Square
North Circular Road
West Nile Street
Piccadilly

Write down ten street names, making sure you give each element of the name a capital letter.

The same is true for the names of geographical places – each element has a capital letter. For example:

Pentland Hills
River Thames
English Channel
Gulf of Mexico

(Note, however, that unimportant words like 'of' do not have capitals.)

Write down ten examples of geographical place-names.

Here are some points about the use of capital letters for you to revise:

1. 'I' is always a capital letter when it is written by itself except when it refers to the letter in the alphabet.
2. Proper names and titles begin with capital letters.
3. The first word of a sentence has a capital letter.
4. The first word of a quotation and the first spoken word have a capital letter.
5. Days of the week and months begin with capital letters.
6. The names of seasons and points of the compass do not begin with capital letters.
7. Titles such as duke, headmaster, chairman, prime minister have a capital letter when one particular individual is referred to and when that individual's name can be inserted as an alternative to the title.
8. In titles of films, plays, novels, etc., only the first word and following important words have capital letters.

Give examples to illustrate each of these points.

 Activities

A. 1. In groups, work out a scene in which a newcomer to the area comes into contact with other children and makes friends or is not accepted. What kind of person is your newcomer – shy, conceited, overbearing, snobbish? What are the other children like – friendly, stand-offish, bullying?

2. Use the poem 'My Parents Kept Me from Children Who Were Rough' as the basis for an improvisation.

3. The Row. In groups, work out a situation where your neighbours complain to your parents about you. What is the cause – stealing apples, chasing their cat, climbing on their wall, playing football in front of their house? Do your parents stand up for you or cover up for you or tell you off? Do they tell you off in front of the neighbours or wait until they have gone? How do you get your own back on the neighbours?

17

4. New neighbours have moved in. Work out a situation where you try to find out who they are and what they do. You suspect they may be criminals or up to no good. What makes you think this?

5. Imagine you live in a street that is going to be pulled down by the council – perhaps to make way for a new road. Work out scenes that show how the people in the street react. Would some organize a petition? Would there be a protest meeting? Would a representative from the council come and explain the situation? Would some of the inhabitants of the houses refuse to move?

B. 1. Make a street map of the immediate area round your home, indicating points of interest.

2. Find out and make lists of bus numbers and routes, hospitals, stations, fire stations, schools, parks and green areas in your neighbourhood.

3. Find out the history of your area, including how it got its name.

4. Find out from your parents or neighbours how the place you live in has changed over the past twenty or thirty years. Perhaps you could record their comments on a cassette recorder and play them to the rest of the class. Discuss whether it is better or worse now.

5. Discuss how your area could be improved.

John Rowe Townsend, *Gumble's Yard*
   Widdershins Crescent
Mark Twain, *The Adventures of Tom Sawyer*
Eve Garnett, *The Family from One End Street*
   Further Adventures of the Family from One End Street
Eric Allen, *The Latchkey Children*
Gillian Avery, *A Likely Lad*
Roy Brown, *A Saturday in Pudney*
Pierre Berna, *A Hundred Million Francs*
Elizabeth Enright, *The Saturdays*
Eleanor Graham, *The Children Who Lived in a Barn*
Elizabeth Stucley, *Magnolia Buildings*
Alison Uttley, *The Country Child*
Jenifer Wayne, *The Day the Ceiling Fell Down*
Leon Garfield, *Smith*
   The Strange Affair of Adelaide Harris
Margaret Stuart Barry, *Tommy Mac*
Bill Naughton, *The Goalkeeper's Revenge*
F. Hodgson Burnett, *The Secret Garden*
Louisa M. Alcott, *Little Women*
Meindert deJong, *The Wheel on the School*

Reading List

One of the most valuable ways of learning how other people live is by reading about them. The following books are fiction, but that does not mean that what they describe is untrue. Often it is through the imagination of a writer that we can come to a closer understanding of reality. Try to read one or more of the following books which are about families and the area where they live. The books are very varied in style and approach, and they may not all appeal equally to you. Don't be put off if the one you choose is not to your taste: try another one. It is only by experiencing different types of books that you can find out which ones appeal to you.

UNIT 2

The Sea

 Reading and Understanding

Alone at Sea

Like fire, the sea has its good side and its bad side. It can provide man with food. It can provide him with employment. It can help him to move from place to place. It can offer him opportunities for sport and pleasure. But it can also be wild and destructive. It can sweep in and flood the land, devastating towns and drowning people. Life at sea is never free from the danger of shipwreck and disaster.

It is not surprising, therefore, that the sea can inspire great fear and awe. Some people, for instance, are afraid to go on boats or to swim in the sea. How do you feel about the sea? If you live inland, when did you first see the sea, and what were your feelings? How many of you can swim? How did you learn to swim? Did you learn easily, or were you afraid to start with?

Perhaps you can understand then how Mafatu feels in this extract. He lives on one of the Polynesian Islands, and all his life he has been afraid of the sea. Now, to prove himself, he has ventured on the sea alone except for Kivi, his pet albatross, and Uri, his dog.

Day broke over a grey and dismal world. The canoe lifted and fell idly on the glassy swells. Mafatu looked back over his shoulder, searching the horizon for a last glimpse of Hikueru; but the atoll had vanished, as if to hide itself forever from his concern.

The matting sail slatted uselessly. But there seemed to be no need of a sail: the little canoe was riding one of the mysterious ocean currents that flow in their courses through the length and breadth of the Pacific, the *Ara Moana*, Paths of the Sea, as the Ancients called them. They were the ocean currents that had carried the Polynesian navigators from island to island in the childhood of the world. Mafatu was drifting farther and farther away from his homeland.

With wide-flapping wings Kivi rose from the bow of the canoe. In ascending spirals the bird climbed higher and higher, until at last he was no more than a grey speck against the lighter grey of the sky. Mafatu watched his albatross disappear and felt a desolation flood his heart. Now there was only Uri to keep him company in this hostile world of sky and sea. Uri.... The yellow dog lay curled up in the shadow of the bow, opening one eye from time to time to look at his master. Wherever Mafatu went, Uri, too, would go.

All around, as far as the eye could reach, were wastes of leaden water. The canoe was the moving centre of a limitless circle of sea. The boy shuddered. His fingers gripped the paddle convulsively. He thought of Kana and the other boys – what would they say when they learned that he had disappeared? And Tavana Nui – would there be sorrow in his father's heart? Would he believe that Moana, the Sea God, had claimed his son at last?

It was an ominous, oppressive world at this season of storm. Half a mile distant a whale heaved its varnished hulk to the surface, to throw a jet of vapoury mist high into the air; then it submerged, leaving scarcely a ripple to mark its passage. A shoal of flying fishes broke water, skimming away in a silver shimmer of flight. A dolphin sped after them, smooth-rolling in pursuit, so close that the boy could hear the sound of its breathing. This world of the sea was ruled by Nature's harsh law of survival. Mafatu knew the sea with an intimacy given to few. He had seen fleets of giant mantas whipping the lagoon of Hikueru to a boiling fury; he had seen the mighty cachalot set upon by killer-whales and torn to ribbons almost in the blink of an eye; once he had seen an octopus as large as the trunk of a tamanu, with tentacles thirty feet long, rise from the mile-deep water beyond the barrier-reef.... *Ai*, this sea!

Mafatu opened one of the green drinking nuts and tilted back his head to let the cool liquid trickle down his parched throat; more refreshing than spring water, cool on the hottest days, and as sustaining as food. The boy scooped out the gelatinous meat for Uri and the dog ate it gratefully.

The ocean current which held the canoe in its grip seemed to have quickened. There was a wind rising, too, in little puffs and gusts. Now the canoe heeled over under the sudden attack, while Mafatu scrambled on to the outrigger to lend his weight for ballast; then the wind dropped as suddenly as it appeared, while the canoe righted itself and the boy breathed freely once again. He searched the skies for Kivi. His albatross might have been one of a thousand sea birds flying against the roof of the sky, or he might have vanished utterly, leaving his friends here in solitary space. The bird had led Mafatu out through the reef-passage at Hikueru into the open ocean, and now, it seemed, had deserted him.

A storm was making, moving in out of those mysterious belts which lie north and south of the equator, the home of hurricanes. The wind shifted a point, bringing with it a heavy squall. Mafatu lowered the sail on the run and gripped the steering paddle with hands that showed white at the knuckles. All around him now was a world of tumbling water, grey in the hollows, greenish on the slopes. The wind tore off the combing crests and flung the spray at the sky. Like advance scouts of an oncoming army, wind gusts moved down upon the canoe, struck at it savagely. So busy was Mafatu with the paddle that there was no time for thought. He called a prayer to Maui, God of the Fishermen:

'*Maui è! E matai tu!*'

Somehow the sound of his own voice reassured him. Uri lifted his head, cocked his ears, thumped his tail for a second. The canoe rose to the swells as lightly as a gull and coasted like a sled down the frothing slopes. What skill had wrought this small canoe! This dugout, hewn from the mighty tamanu tree. It swooped and yielded, bucked and scudded, one with the fierce element whose back it rode.

The sky darkened. A burst of lightning lit up the sea with supernatural brilliance. An instantaneous crack of thunder shattered the world. Lightning again, striking at the hissing water. Mafatu watched it with fascinated eyes. Now it was all about him. It ran to the end of the boom in globes of fire that exploded and vanished, and in the awful moment of its being it revealed mountain shapes of dark water, heaving, shouldering.... How long could this frail craft of wood and sennit resist? Under the combined attack of wind and sea it seemed that something must inevitably give way. The wind shrilled a fiercer note. Spray stung the boy's flesh, blinded his eyes, chilled his marrow.

The sail went first – with a split and a roar. Fragments swept off on the back of the wind. The cords that held the mast hummed like plucked wires. Then with a rending groan the mast cracked. Before Mafatu could leap to cut it clear, it snapped off and disappeared in a churn of black water. The boy clung to the paddle, fighting to keep his canoe from turning broadside. Water swept aboard and out again. Only the buoyancy of tamanu kept the craft afloat. Uri cowered in the bow, half submerged, his howls drowned by the roar of the elements. Mafatu gripped his paddle for very life, an unreasoning terror powering his arms. This sea that he had always feared was rising to claim him, just as it had claimed his mother. How rightly he had feared it! Moana, the Sea God, had been biding his time.... 'Some day, Mafatu, I will claim you!'

The boy lost all sense of time's passage. Every nerve became dulled by tumult. The wind howled above his head and still Mafatu clung to the lashed steering paddle; clung fast long after strength had vanished and only the will to live locked his strong fingers about the shaft. Even death would not loose the grip of those fingers. He held his little craft true to the wind.

There was a wave lifting before the canoe. Many the boy had seen, but this was a giant – a monster livid and hungry. Higher, higher it rose, until it seemed that it must scrape at the low-hanging clouds. Its crest heaved over with a vast sigh. The boy saw it coming. He tried to cry out. No sound issued from his throat. Suddenly the wave was upon him. Down it crashed. *Chaos!* Mafatu felt the paddle torn from his hands. Thunder in his ears. Water strangling him. Terror in his soul. The canoe slewed round into the trough. The boy flung himself forward, wound his arms about the mid-thwart. It was the end of a world.

ARMSTRONG SPERRY, *The Boy Who Was Afraid*

What signs are there that Mafatu was reluctant to leave home?

How does he feel when Kivi flies away?

When the author describes the sea as 'wastes of leaden water', what does he mean?

Describe the sea creatures that Mafatu observes.

How does the sea change when the wind gets up?

What does Mafatu think about his canoe?

What are Mafatu's thoughts when the lightning occurs?

What effect does the storm have on the canoe?

What does Mafatu think will be the outcome of the storm?

How does the storm compare with others the boy has known?

Shipwrecked

Matafu in fact manages to survive this storm and to prove that he can conquer the power of the sea. But others are not so lucky. The story of Robinson Crusoe, for instance, is well known – how he was shipwrecked on a desert island and made a life for himself there, first alone, and then with the help of Man Friday, whom he rescued from cannibals. Here is the account of Crusoe's escape from the shipwreck.

With this design we changed our course, and steered away N.W. by W. in order to reach some of our English islands, where I hoped for relief; but our voyage was otherwise determined; for a second storm came upon us, which carried us away with the same impetuosity westward, and drove us so out of the very way of all human commerce, that had all our lives been saved, as to the sea, we were rather in danger of being devoured by savages than ever returning to our own country.

In this distress, the wind still blowing very hard, one of our men early in the morning cried out, 'Land!' and we had no sooner ran out of the cabin to look out, in hopes of seeing whereabouts in the world we were, but the ship struck upon a sand, and in a moment, her motion being so stopped, the sea broke over her in such a manner, that we expected we should all have perished immediately; and we were immediately driven into our close quarters, to shelter us from the very foam and spray of the sea.

It is not easy for any one, who has not been in the like condition, to describe or conceive the consternation of men in such circumstances. We knew nothing where we were, or upon what land it was we were driven, whether an island or the main, whether inhabited or not inhabited; and as the rage of the wind was still great, though rather less than at first, we could not so much as hope to have the ship hold many minutes without breaking in pieces, unless the winds, by a kind of miracle, should turn immediately about. In a word, we sat looking one upon another, and expecting death every moment, and every man acting accordingly, as preparing for another world; for there was little or nothing more for us to do in this. That which was our present comfort, and all the comfort we had, was that, contrary to our expectation, the ship did not break yet, and that the master said the wind began to abate.

Now, though we thought that the wind did a little abate, yet the ship having thus struck upon the sand, and sticking too fast for us to expect her getting off, we were in a dreadful condition indeed, and had nothing to do but to think of saving our lives as well as we could. We had a boat at our stern just before the storm, but she was first staved by dashing against the ship's rudder, and in the next place, she broke away, and either sunk, or was driven off to sea, so there was no hope from her; we had another boat on board, but how to get her off into the sea was a doubtful thing. However, there was no room to debate, for we fancied the ship would break in pieces every minute, and some told us she was actually broken already.

In this distress, the mate of our vessel lays hold of the boat, and with the help of the rest of the men they got her slung over the ship's side; and getting all into her, let go, and committed ourselves, being eleven in number, to God's mercy, and the wild sea; for though the storm was abated considerably, yet the sea went dreadful high upon the shore.

And now our case was very dismal indeed, for we all saw plainly that the sea went so high, that the boat could not live, and that we should be inevitably drowned. However, we committed our souls to God in the most earnest manner; and the wind driving us towards the shore, we hastened our destruction with our own hands, pulling as well as we could towards land.

What the shore was, whether rock or sand, whether steep or shoal, we knew not; the only hope that could rationally give us the least shadow of expectation was, if we might happen into some bay or gulf, or the mouth of some river, where by great chance we might have run our boat in, or got under the lee of the land, and perhaps made smooth water. But there was nothing of this appeared; but as we made nearer and nearer the shore, the land looked more frightful than the sea.

After we had rowed, or rather driven, about a league and a half, as we reckoned it, a raging wave, mountain-like, came rolling astern of us, and plainly bade us expect the *coup de grâce*. In a word, it took

us with such a fury, that it overset the boat at once; and separating us, as well from the boat as from one another, gave us not time hardly to say. 'O God!' for we were all swallowed up in a moment.

Nothing can describe the confusion of thought which I felt when I sunk into the water; for though I swam very well, yet I could not deliver myself from the waves so as to draw breath, till that wave having driven me, or rather carried me, a vast way on towards the shore, and having spent itself, went back, and left me upon the land almost dry, but half dead with the water I took in. I had so much presence of mind, as well as breath left, that seeing myself nearer the mainland than I expected, I got upon my feet, and endeavoured to make on towards the land as fast as I could, before another wave should return and take me up again. But I soon found it was impossible to avoid it; for I saw the sea come after me as high as a great hill, and as furious as an enemy, which I had no means or strength to contend with. My business was to hold my breath, and raise myself upon the water, if I could; and so, by swimming, to preserve my breathing, and pilot myself towards the shore, if possible; my greatest concern now being, that the sea, as it would carry me a great way towards the shore when it came on, might not carry me back again with it when it gave back towards the sea.

The wave that came upon me again, buried me at once 20 or 30 feet deep in its own body, and I could feel myself carried with a mighty force and swiftness towards the shore a very great way; but I held my breath, and assisted myself to swim still forward with all my might. I was ready to burst with holding my breath, when, as I felt myself rising up, so, to my immediate relief, I found my head and hands shoot out above the surface of the water; and though it was not two seconds of time that I could keep myself so, yet it relieved me greatly, gave me breath and new courage. I was covered again with water a good while, but not so long but I held it out; and finding the water had spent itself, and began to return, I struck forward against the return of the waves, and felt ground again with my feet. I stood still a few moments to recover breath, and till the water went from me, and then took to my heels and ran with what strength I had farther towards the shore. But neither would this deliver me from the fury of the sea, which came pouring in after me again, and twice more I was lifted up by the waves and carried forwards as before, the shore being very flat.

The last time of these two had well near been fatal to me; for the sea, having hurried me along as before, landed me, or rather dashed me, against a piece of a rock, and that with such force, as it left me senseless, and indeed helpless, as to my own deliverance; for the blow taking my side and breast, beat the breath as it were quite out of my body; and had it returned again immediately, I must have been strangled in the water. But I recovered a little before the return of the waves, and seeing I should be covered again with the water, I resolved to hold fast by a piece of the rock, and so to hold my breath, if possible, till the wave went back. Now as the waves were not so high as at first, being near land, I held my hold till the wave abated, and then fetched another run, which brought me so near the shore, that the next wave, though it went over me, yet did not so swallow me up as to carry me away, and the next run I took I got to the mainland, where, to my great comfort, I clambered up the cliffs of the shore, and sat me down upon the grass, free from danger, and quite out of the reach of the water.

DANIEL DEFOE, *The Adventures of Robinson Crusoe*

What does Robinson Crusoe mean when he says 'our voyage was otherwise determined'?

What happens to the ship?

Describe the state the men are in when the ship strikes sand.

What signs of hope are there?

What do the men do when they fear the ship will break up?

Why is launching the boat likely to be of no use?

What does the author mean when he says 'we hastened our destruction with our own hands'?

What is the only hope the men in the boat have?

What happens to the boat?

Why is Robinson Crusoe not able to swim?

How is it that he makes land?

What danger does he still have to contend with?

How is it that he is nearly killed?

How is he able to save himself?

Describe the impression you get of Robinson Crusoe's feelings in this passage and the way he faces this experience.

What are your own feelings on reading the passage?

Robinson Crusoe *was first published in 1719. Can you find ways in which the author Daniel Defoe writes or uses words that are different from today's usage?*

 Writing

Making a Living

Many men make their living from what they can win from the sea. The life of a fisherman must be as hazardous as that of a miner, each trying to earn a living from nature itself. Compare the two. What dangers do they undergo?

It is not only fish that man gains from the sea. Here is an account of diving for pearls. Manta Diablo is a sea monster that people believed kept guard over the cave where the pearls were found.

Near the mouth of the cave the water was very clear. I picked up my basket and sink stone, took a deep breath, and slipped over the side of the canoe, remembering all that the old man had taught me.

I reached the bottom after about a fathom and a half. I looped my foot in the rope tied to the sink stone and waited until the bubbles that had risen behind me disappeared and I could find the bed of shells I had noticed from above. The bed was five steps away towards the mouth of the cave. I walked carefully in the sand as I had learned to do.

The shells were the largest I had ever seen. They were half the length of my arm and thick through as my body and covered with weed that looked like a woman's hair. I chose the nearest one, which seemed to be easier to get at than the others. I took out my knife and worked quietly, but a school of small fish kept swimming in front of my eyes, so I failed to pry the shell loose before my lungs began to hurt and I had to go up.

On my second dive I had no sooner reached the bottom than a shadow fell across the bed where I was working. It was the shadow of a grey shark, one of the friendly ones, but by the time he had drifted away my breath was gone.

I dived six times more and worked quickly each time I went down, hacking away with my sharp knife at the base of the big shell where it was anchored to the rock. But it had been growing there for many years, since long before I was born I suppose and it would not come free from its home.

By this time it was late in the afternoon and the light was poor. Also my hands were bleeding and my eyes were half-blind with salt from the sea. But I sat in the canoe and thought of all the hours I had spent for nothing. And I thought too of the Sevillano and the great pearl he had found, or said he had found, in the Gulf of Persia.

I filled my lungs and took the sink stone and went down again. With the first stroke of my knife, the shell came free. It toppled over on one side, and I quickly untied the rope from the sink stone and looped it twice around the shell and swam back to the surface. I pulled up the shell, but it was too heavy for me to lift into the canoe, so I tied it to the stern and paddled out of the cave.

Across the lagoon I could see the old man standing among the trees. From time to time during the day I had caught glimpses of him standing there with his eyes fixed on the cave. I knew that I could drown and he would not try to save me, and that he was telling El Diablo all the while that he had not wanted me to go to the cave and that he therefore was not to blame. But I also felt that if I found a pearl he would be willing to take his share because he had nothing to do with finding it.

He came out from the trees as I paddled across the lagoon and strolled down to the beach as if he did not care whether I had found a pearl or not. I suppose this was to show El Diablo and his friends the fish and the long, grey shark that Soto Luzon was without blame.

'A big one,' he said when I dragged the shell ashore. 'In my life I have never seen such a monster. It is the grandfather of all oysters that live in the sea.'

'There are many in the cave bigger than this one,' I said.

'If there are so many,' he answered, 'then the Manta Diablo cannot be mad that you have taken only one of them.'

'Perhaps a little mad,' I said and laughed, 'but not much.'

The mouth of the oyster was closed and it was hard to put my blade between the tight edges of the shell.

'Lend me your knife,' I said. 'Mine is blunted from use.'

The old man placed his hand on the hilt of his knife and pulled it from the sheath and then slipped it back again.

'I think it is better if you use your own knife,' he said and his voice began to tremble as he spoke.

I wrestled a long time with the oyster. At last the hard lips began to give a little. Then I could feel the knife sink through the heavy muscles that held them together and suddenly the lips fell apart.

I put my finger under the frilled edge of the flesh as I had seen my father do. A pearl slid along my finger and I picked it out. It was about the size of a pea. When I felt again, another of the same size rolled out and then a third. I put them on the other half of the shell so they would not be scratched.

The old man came and leaned over me, as I knelt there in the sand, and held his breath.

Slowly I slid my hand under the heavy tongue of the oyster. I felt a hard lump, so monstrous in size that it could not be a pearl. I took hold of it and pulled it from the flesh and got to my feet and held it to the sun, thinking that I must be holding a rock that the oyster had swallowed somehow.

It was round and smooth and the colour of smoke. It filled my cupped hand. Then the sun's light struck deep into the thing and moved in silver swirls and I knew that it was not a rock that I held but a pearl, the great Pearl of Heaven.

'Madre de Dios,' the old man whispered.

I stood there and could not move or talk. The old man kept whispering over and over, 'Madre de Dios.'

Darkness fell. I tore off the tail of my shirt and wrapped the pearl in it.

'Half this is yours,' I told him.

I handed the pearl to him, but he drew back in fear.

'You wish me to keep it until we reach La Paz?' I said.

'Yes, it is better that you keep it.'

'When shall we go?'

'Soon,' he said hoarsely. 'El Diablo is away but he will come back. And his friends will tell him then about the pearl.'

SCOTT O'DELL, *The Black Pearl*

Describe the process of diving for pearls.

Why does the old man not let the narrator use his knife?

Do you think the chance of finding a pearl is worth the effort?

Disaster at Sea

One of the most famous disasters at sea was the sinking of the *Titanic* in 1912. There was great pride in the building of this ship which was considered unsinkable. Then, on its maiden voyage, it collided with an iceberg and was sunk with great loss of life. In this poem, Thomas Hardy meditates on the tragedy.

The Convergence of the Twain

In a solitude of the sea
Deep from human vanity,
And the pride of Life that planned her, stilly
couches she.

Steel chambers, late the pyres
   Of her salamandrine fires,
Cold currents thrid, and turn to rhythmic tidal
      lyres.

   Over the mirrors meant
   To glass the opulent
The sea-worm crawls – grotesque, slimed, dumb,
      indifferent.

   Jewels in joy designed
   To ravish the sensuous mind
Lie lightless, all their sparkles bleared and black
      and blind.

   Dim moon-eyed fishes near
   Gaze at the gilded gear
And query: 'What does this vaingloriousness
      down here?' ...

   Well: while was fashioning
   This creature of cleaving wing,
The Immanent Will that stirs and urges every-
      thing

   Prepared a sinister mate
   For her – so gaily great –
A Shape of Ice, for the time far and dissociate.

   And as the smart ship grew
   In stature, grace and hue,
In shadowy silent distance grew the Iceberg too.

   Alien they seemed to be:
   No mortal eye could see
The intimate welding of their later history,

   Or sign that they were bent
   By paths coincident
On being anon twin halves of one august event,

   Till the Spinner of the Years
   Said 'Now!' And each one hears,
And consummation comes, and jars two hemis-
      pheres.
                THOMAS HARDY

How does the poet first picture the ship?

What does he imagine has happened to the engines?

How does he describe the past and the present state of the mirrors?

How are the past and present state of the jewels compared?

What does the poet imagine the fish think as they swim about the wreck?

What does he imagine was happening at the same time as the ship was being planned and built?

Why is the word 'seemed' important in the statement 'alien they seemed to be'?

What idea is the poet putting forward about the ship and the iceberg?

What does he mean when he says the collision 'jars two hemispheres'?

Moods of the Sea

Finally, here are some poems describing different moods of the sea. Do they evoke memories in your own mind about the sea and your experience of it?

Sound of the Sea on a Still Evening

It comes through quietness, softly crumbling in
Till it becomes the quietness; and we know
The wind to be will reach us from Loch Roe.
From the receding South it will begin
To stir, to whisper; and by morning all
The sea will lounge North, sloping by Clach-toll.

Gentlest of prophecies. The most tottering grass
Stands still as a stiff thorn, as though its root
Groped not in sand but in sand's absolute
And was itself disqualified to pass
Into a shaking world where it must be
Not grass but grasses waving like the sea.

Three heifers slouch by, trailing down the road
A hundred yards of milky breath: they rip
The grasses sideways. Waterdrops still drip
From the turned tap and tinily explode
On their flat stone. An unseen bird goes by,
Its little feathers hushing a whole sky.

And yet a word is spoken. When the light
Gives back its redness to the Point of Stoer
And sets off cocks like squibs, pebbles will roar
At their harsh labour, grinding shells to white
And glittering beaches, and tall waves will run
Fawning on rocks and barking in the sun.
                NORMAN MACCAIG

Pick out the words used in this poem which describe the sound of the sea.

Try to say exactly what impression each gives.

What other words could you use to describe the noise the sea makes?

The Great Wave

Study this picture entitled 'The Great Wave' by the Japanese artist Hokusai. What impression of the sea does it present? What words describing the sea does it suggest?

The Deserted Beach

Quietly the waves lap on the shore,
Clear, cool and blue,
Rippling over soft, brown sand.
Slap, slap, as the little waves reach the beach.
But
Dark clouds come,
Waves grow high,
And the quiet beach is transformed to
A wild frenzy of waves and wind.

JUDITH MARSLAND

Describe the contrast in the moods of the sea portrayed in this poem.

The Sea Shore

I walk along the pebbly shore
And throw food for the gulls,
But they cry for more.
The driftwood floats in on the morning tide.
Some crabs scamper past me
Then hide.
The glistening starfish in the sun lies.
A wave rushes up
Then dies.
The wet pebbles glint in the sun.
I pick one up
Then run
Away to the chalk cliffs
Where I study my treasure.
It's beautiful oval
And has a grey tint.
It looks brand new
Fresh from the mint.
I walk back along the shore.
Tin cans, sweet wrappers, bits of glass:
The beach is not clean anymore.

TERESA LANE

What contrast is made in this poem?
Have you ever walked along the sea shore?
What kinds of things have you found?

Assignments

Choose several of the following to write about:

1. On being Sea-sick.
2. Storm at Sea.
3. Crossing the Channel.
4. The Shipwreck.
5. Write a sea shanty.
6. Write a description, perhaps as a poem, about what it feels like to swim in the sea, or under the sea.
7. Write a description or a poem about a deserted beach.
8. Write a story about a trawler which goes out fishing.
9. Write a story or a poem from the point of view of someone on the shore waiting for the return of a fishing trawler during a storm.
10. Write a story about smugglers or wreckers.
11. Rescue at Sea. Write a story about a lifeboat or another ship coming to the rescue of another vessel that is in difficulties.
12. Describe the life and thoughts of a lighthouse-keeper or a coastguard.

 Language

A. Punctuation

Using punctuation marks correctly is very important if what you write is to be clearly understood. Remember particularly to write in sentences and to use full stops. Otherwise, it becomes difficult for a reader to separate one statement from another when all your ideas are jumbled together.

Here are the main punctuation marks we studied in Book One for you to revise.

PUNCTUATION MARK	DESCRIPTION	EXAMPLES
full stop	1. used to show the end of a sentence 2. used to show an abbreviation	The waves crashed against the rocks. a.m., p.m., etc.
comma	1. used to separate different statements in a sentence 2. used to separate the different items of a list 3. used after words or phrases added to a sentence	The boat, which I did not consider safe, put out to sea. Remember to take your towel, soap, comb and toothbrush with you. However, you must not be late.
exclamation mark	used to indicate strong feeling	Fire! Good heavens!
question mark	used to indicate a question	How are you today?

Write down further examples for each use of these punctuation marks.

Write out this passage correctly punctuated:

No one was ready when the first wave struck everyone and everything was thrown into confusion how could we have known that such storms were possible in the Mediterranean we had been used to clear skies calm seas brilliant piercing sun and pale romantic moon the idea that the sea had a fury all its own never occurred to us and what fury the boat was tossed up and down on the suddenly gigantic waves as though it were no more than a cork as the water crashed over the bows the passengers clung desperately to anything they could find rigging bulkhead the steering wheel the sides we were all drenched in stinging sea-water with the taste of salt in our mouths hanging on for dear life to anything that would save us from being swept overboard the only one who passed through the storm unaware was Tommy of course who was asleep below like a new-born babe after being violently sea-sick as he had been nothing else mattered.

B. Nouns

Let's look more closely at nouns. We were reminded in Unit 1 that **nouns form that part of speech which includes the names of things.** But we can further subdivide nouns into various groups according to the kind of noun it is. **Nouns can be divided into four different categories: abstract, collective, common and proper.**

An abstract noun is the name given to an idea which we can think about but which we cannot, strictly speaking, feel, taste, see, smell or hear. It usually denotes a quality or state. For example, weakness, cowardice, childhood, hatred. The suffixes '-ness', '-hood' and '-ship' usually indicate abstract nouns. All nouns which refer to objects that have a physical existence are said to be concrete.

A collective noun is the name given to several persons or things of the same kind regarded as one group. For example, a class, a committee, a crew, a crowd.

28

A common noun is the name that belongs to all members of a class of persons or things of the same kind. The names of most ordinary everyday objects are common. For example, girl, table, sea, sky, pencil, floor.

A proper noun is the name given to one particular person or thing only. Names of people, towns, geographical locations and titles are proper nouns. They require capital letters. For example William Wallace, the Royal Opera House, Leeds United, the Moray Firth.

Write down ten more examples each of abstract, collective, common and proper nouns.

Say what kind of noun each of the following is:

army	strength
progress	seat
work	team
spade	moon
Benjamin	condition
cardigan	quotation
spelling	flock
singing	influenza
the Straits of	string
Magellan	art
sleep	the Guardian
covey	battalion
eye	protest
sight	coffee
site	Wembley
mob	Stadium

Vocabulary

A. The Sea

Here are some sentences describing the effects of the sea. *Study them and say what impression each of them is trying to put across.*

The waves pounded the beach.
The waves roared in towards the shore.
The waves crashed against the cliffs.
The boat was tossed by the waves.
The boat bobbed up and down.
The boat swayed to the movement of the waves.

The waves crept up the sand.
The waves sidled on to the beach.
The water sighed against the side of the boat.
The boat was dashed on the rocks.
The waves swept the boat from stem to stern.
The rise and fall of the waves made him feel sea-sick.
The swell of the sea made his stomach feel queasy.
The boat foundered beneath the weight and force of the waves
The water shimmered in the moonlight.

B. Marine

The word 'marine' comes from the Latin word 'mare' meaning the sea and the suffix '-ine' meaning to do with. 'Marine' therefore means 'to do with the sea' as in the sentence 'He is studying marine insurance'. *See if you can work out or discover the meaning of the following words which are connected with 'marine'.*

mariner
submarine
maritime
aquamarine
marina

Use these words in sentences.

C. Sea-

Explain the difference between the following:

urchin	sea-urchin
dog	sea-dog
green	sea-green
horse	sea-horse
anemone	sea-anemone
lion	sea lion
mile	sea mile
weed	seaweed

Spelling

A. Sea/See

Some words like 'sea' and 'see' are pronounced the same but they have very different meanings and are spelled differently. Other examples are 'son' and 'sun', and 'bean' and 'been'. The technical name given to a word which is pronounced the same as another but which has a different sense and a different spelling is homophone. In Book One, we looked at a number of words which are very similar and which require care in distinguishing between them. Here are some further words for you to learn. Use some of them in sentences.

idle, idol, idyll
incidence, incidents
knave, nave
knead, need
know, no
larva, lava
lea, lee
leak, leek
lessen, lesson
lets, let's
lightening, lightning
lineament, liniment
liqueur, liquor
loath, loathe
loose, lose
mail, male
main, mane
maize, maze
manikin, mannequin
manner, manor
meat, meet
medal, meddle
meter, metre
miner, minor
moan, mown
moral, morale
muscle, mussel

Note that not all these words are true homophones. *Pick out the pairs of words which are in fact pronounced the same.*

B. The Hyphen

The hyphen is a sign (-) used to join two or more words or to separate the different parts of a word (for instance, when the word runs over from one line to the next). It is important to know about the hyphen because its use or omission can sometimes alter the meaning of a word or can prevent your meaning from being clear.

The hyphen is used:

1. to join two or more words that are to be considered as one unit or one part of speech. For example,

log-book
built-up
fire-alarm
man-made
self-propelled
dining-room
passer-by

2. to make a word more easily read or understood. For example,

pre-eminent
co-operative
de-ice
re-cover
lamp-post

3. to add a prefix to a proper name. For example,

un-American
pro-Labour
anti-Communist

Find more examples of these three uses for yourself.

Sometimes the omission of a hyphen can lead to confusion. *Say what the difference in meaning is between the following:*

an ill educated man	an ill-educated man
a hard working man	a hard-working man
forty odd inhabitants	forty-odd inhabitants
recover the armchair	re-cover the armchair
old fashioned stockings	old-fashioned stockings
a man eating tiger	a man-eating tiger
a little used car	a little-used car
two year-old cats	two-year-old cats

Write sentences containing the following words:

old-fashioned
ill-used
de-ice
pre-eminent
built-up
five-year-old
make-shift
on-looker
dog-like
man-made
semi-detached

 Activities

A. 1. In groups, work out a situation where there is a mutiny at sea. What is the cause of it? What kind of person is the captain? Who is leading the mutiny? What are his motives for doing so? What is the outcome?

2. The father of a family has been drowned at sea. Work out what happens when the eldest son announces that he wants to go to sea too.

3. One of you prepare a speech to recruit the others to become a fisherman or to join the Royal Navy. The rest can prepare awkward questions to ask.

4. Imagine a situation where a group of smugglers is being questioned by a customs officer. What information does the officer have? How can the smugglers cover up or explain it away?

B. 1. Find out what you can about some of the mysteries of the sea such as the *Marie Celeste*. Report back to the rest of the class.

2. Make a collection of poems about the sea. Perhaps the members of the class could find one poem each. Read them out and put them in a booklet.

3. Find out about the life-boat service. Give an account of it to the rest of the class.

4. If you can, visit a fishing port or a life-boat station and write about it.

5. Listen to the radio ballad 'Fishing the Herring' which is available on record.

6. Try to listen to some music describing the sea such as the 'Sea Interludes' from Benjamin Britten's *Peter Grimes*, *La Mer* by Debussy or the Overture to Wagner's *The Flying Dutchman*. Write about what the music suggests to you.

7. Collect objects from the sea and make an exhibition of them in your classroom – things like sea-shells, corks from fishing-nets, sea-urchins or dried starfish, pebbles from the beach, dried seaweed.

Reading List

The sea is a popular subject for stories for young people. Try to read some of the following novels.

R. L. Stevenson, *Treasure Island*
Daniel Defoe, *Robinson Crusoe*
Theodore Taylor, *The Cay*
Armstrong Sperry, *The Boy Who Was Afraid*
Leon Garfield, *Jack Holborn*
Scott O'Dell, *The Black Pearl*
Willard Price, *Underwater Adventure*
    South Sea Adventure
C. Walter Hodges, *Columbus Sails*
J. Meade Falkner, *Moonfleet*
Patrick O'Brian, *The Golden Ocean*
Michael Brown (Ed.), *A Book of Sea Legends*
Charles Vipont, *Blow the Man Down*
K. M. Peyton, *The Maplin Bird*
    Windfall
Peter Dawlish, *Dauntless Sails Again*

UNIT 3

Fireworks and Bonfires

 Reading and Understanding

Penny for the Guy

The drawing-in of the evenings in October and November brings to mind the approach of Guy Fawkes' Night and all the fun of fireworks and bonfires. It is strange to think that an event long ago when a group of conspirators tried to blow up the Houses of Parliament should be remembered now as an occasion for children to have a night out and enjoy themselves. The date on which the attempt was to occur – November the Fifth – is one of the most famous in the calendar. Everyone knows what November the Fifth stands for. But preparations start long before then with children gathering material for their bonfires or taking up their stand in the streets with a stuffed dummy of a guy in a make-shift cart or an old pram accosting passers-by 'to spare a penny for the guy'. Some people disapprove of this demanding of money – especially when it occurs during the first week in October! – and regard the children who do it as little better than scroungers. What do you think?

Have you ever gone out with a guy asking people for money? Or collected odd pieces of furniture or rubbish for a bonfire? Or can you remember a particular Guy Fawkes' Night when something special happened? Talk about it.

Henry Mayhew published his *London Labour and the London Poor*, a collection of interviews with people he met, in the middle of the nineteenth century. Compare the experiences of this young exploiter of the Guy Fawkes tradition with your own.

I always go out with a Guy Fawkes every year. I'm seventeen years old, and I've been out with a guy ever since I can remember, except last year; I didn't then, because I was in the Middlesex Hospital with an abscess, brought on by the rheumatic fever. I was in the hospital a month. My father was an undertaker; he's been dead four months: mother carries on the trade. He didn't like my going out with guys, but I always would. He didn't like it at all, he used to say it was a disgrace. Mother didn't much fancy my doing it this year. When I was a very little 'un, I was carried about for a guy.

I couldn't have been more than seven years old when I first began. They put paper-hangings round my legs – sometimes they bought, and sometimes they got it given them; but they gave a rare lot for a penny or twopence. After that they put on me an apron made of the same sort of paper – showy, you know, then they put a lot of tinsel bows, and at the corners they cut a sort of tail... it looked stunnin'; then they put on my chest a tinsel heart and rosettes; they were green and red because it shows off. All up my arms I had bows and things to make a showoff. Then I put on a black mask with a little red on the cheek, to make me look like a devil: it had horns, too. Always pick out a devil's mask with horns: it looks fine and frightens the people most. The boy that dressed me was a very clever chap, and made a guy to rights. Why, he made me a little guy about a foot high, to carry in my lap – it was pieces of quilting, like, a sort of patch-work all sewn together – and then he filled it with sawdust and made a head of shavings. He picked the shavings small, and then sewed them up in a little bag; and then he painted a face, and it looked very well; and he made it a little tinsel bob-tail coat, and a tinsel cap with two feathers on the top. It was made to sit in a chair; and there was a piece of string tied to each of the legs and the arms; and a string came behind; and I used to pull it, and the legs and arms jumped up.

I was put in a chair, and two old broom-handles were put through the rails, and then a boy got in front, and another behind; and carried me off round

Holborn way in the streets and squares. Every now and then they put me down before a window; then one of 'em used to say the speech, and I used all the time to keep pulling the string of my little guy, and it amused the children at the windows. After they'd said the speech we all shouted hurrah! and then some of them went and knocked at the door and asked 'Please to remember the Guy;' and the little children brought us ha'pence and pence; sometimes the ladies and gentlemen chucked money out of the window. At last they carried me into Russell Square. They put me down before a gentleman's house and began saying the speech: while they were saying it, up comes a lot of boys with sticks in their hands. One of our chaps knew what they were after, and took the little guy out of my hand, and went on saying the speech. I kept on sitting still.

After a bit one of these boys says 'Oh, it's a dead guy; let's have a lark with it!' and then one of 'em gives me a punch in the eye with his fist and then snatched the mask off my face, and when he pulled it off he says, 'Oh, Bill, it's live 'un!' We were afraid that we should get the worst of it, so we ran way round the Square. The biggest boy of the lot carried the chair. After we'd run a little way they caught us up again and says, 'Now then, give us all your money.' With that, some ladies and gentlemen that saw it all came up and says, 'If you don't go, we'll lock you up;' and so they let us go away. And so we went to another place where they sold masks and we bought another.

Then they asked me to be guy again, but I wouldn't for I'd got a black eye through it already. So they got another to finish out the day. When we got home at night we shared two shillings apiece. There were five of us altogether; but I think they chiselled me. I know they got a deal more than that, for they'd had a good many sixpences and shillings. People usedn't to think much of a shilling at that time of day, because there weren't any but little guys about then; but I don't know but what people encourage little guys most now, because they say that the chaps with the big ones ought to go out to work.

Next year I was out with a stuffed guy. They wanted me to be guy again, because I wasn't frightened easily, and I was lightish; but I told 'em, 'No, I've had enough of being guy; I won't be guy any more; besides I had such fine money for getting a whack in the eye!' We got on pretty well that year; but it gets worse and worse every year. We got hardly any this year; and next I don't suppose we shall get anything at all. These chaps that go about pitchin' into guys we call 'guy-smashers'; but they don't only do it for the lark of smashing the guys; they do it for the purpose of taking the boys' money away, and sometimes the clothes. If one of 'em has hole in his boots, and he sees a guy with a good pair on, he pretty soon pulls 'em off the guy and hooks it off with 'em.

After I'd been out with guys for three or four years, I got big enough to go to work, and I used to go along with my brother and help him at a coal-shed, carrying out coals. I was there ten months, and then one night – a bitter cold night, it was freezing hard – we had a naphtha lamp to light in the shop; and as me and my brother were doing it, either a piece of the match dropped in or else he poured it over, I can't say which, but all at once it exploded and blew me across the road and knocked him in the shop all a-fire; and I was all a-fire, too – see how it's burnt my face and the hand I held the lucifer in. A woman run out of the next shop with some wet sacks, and throw'd them upon me, but it flared up higher then: water won't put it out, unless it's a mass of water like an engine. Then a milkman ran up and pulled off his cape and throw'd it over me, and that put it out; then he set me up, and I ran home, though I didn't know how I got there; and for two days I didn't know anybody. Another man ran into the shop, and pulled out my brother, and we were both taken to the University Hospital. Two or three people touched me, and the skin came off on their hands ... I was seven months before I got well. But I've never been to say well, since, and I shall never be fit for hard work any more.

The next year I went out with a guy again, and I got on pretty well; and so I've done every year, except last. I've had several little places since I got burnt, but they haven't lasted long.

This year I made a stunning guy. First of all I got a pair of my own breeches – black 'uns – and stuffed 'em full of shavings. I tied the bottoms with a bit of string. Then I got a black coat – that belonged to another boy – and sewed it all round to the trousers; then we filled that with shavings, and gave him a good corporation. Then we got a block, such as the milliners have, and shoved that right in the neck of the coat, and then we shoved some more shavings all round, to make it stick in tight; and when that was done it looked just like a dead man. I know some-thing about dead men, because my father was always in that line. Then we got some horsehair and some glue, and plastered the head all round with glue, and stuck the horsehair on to imitate the hair of a man; then we put the mask on: it was a twopenny one – they're a great deal cheaper than they used to be, you can get a very good one now for a penny – it had a great big nose, and it had two red horns, black eyebrows, and red cheeks. I like devils, they're so ugly. I bought a good-looking 'un two or three years ago, and we didn't get hardly anything, the people said, 'Ah! it's too good-looking; it don't frighten us at all.' Well then, after we put on his mask we got two gloves, one was a woollen 'un, and the other a kid 'un, and stuffed 'em full of shavings, and tied 'em to the chair. We didn't have any lantern, 'cos it keeps falling out of his hands. After that we put on an old pair of lace-up boots. We tied 'em to the legs of the breeches. The feet mostly twist round, but we stopped that; we shoved a stick up the leg of his breeches, and the other end into the boot, and tied it, and then it wouldn't twist round very easily.

After that we put a paper hanging cap on his head; it was silk-velvet kind of paper, and decorated all over with tinsel bows. His coat we pasted all over with blue and green tinsel bows and pictures. They were painted theatrical characters, that we buy at the shop a ha'-penny a sheet plain, and a penny a sheet coloured: we bought them plain, and coloured 'em ourselves. A-top of his hat we put an ornament. We got some red paper, and cut it into narrow strips, and curled it with the scissors, the same as his feather, and decorated it with stars, and bows, and things, made out of paper, all manner of colours, and pieces of tinsel. After we'd finished the guy we made ourselves cocked hats, all alike, and then we tied him in a chair, and wrote on his breast, *Villainous Guy*. Then we put two broomsticks under the chair and carried him out.

There were four of us, and the two that weren't carrying, they had a large bough of a tree each, with a knob at the top to protect the guy. We started off at once, and got into the squares, and put him in front of the gentlemen's houses, and said this speech:

Pray, gentlefolk, pray
Remember this day,
At which kind notice we bring
This figure of sly
Old villainous Guy,
He wanted to murder the King.

With powder in store,
He bitterly swore
By him in the vaults to compare,
By him and his crew,
And Parliament, too,
Should all be blow'd up in the air.

So please to remember
The fifth of November,
The gunpowder treason and plot,
I see no reason

Why gunpowder treason
Should ever be forgot.

So hollo, boys! Hollo boys!
Shout out the day!
Hollo boys! Hollo boys!
Hollo! Hurray!

When we got home I opened the money-box and shared the money: one had 5d, and two had $4\frac{1}{2}$d each; and I had 7d because I said the speech. At night we pulled him all to pieces, and burnt his stuffing, and let off some squibs and crackers. I always used to spend the money I got guying on myself. I used to buy sometimes fowls, because I could sell the eggs. There are some boys that take out guys that do it for the sake of getting a bit of bread and butter, but not many that I know of.

It doesn't cost much to make a guy. The clothes we never burn – they're generally too good: they're our own clothes, that we wear at other times; and when people burn a guy they always pull off any of the things that are of use first; but mostly the guy gets pulled all to pieces, and only the shavings get burnt.

HENRY MAYHEW, *London Labour and the London Poor*

Why do you think the narrator's father disapproved of his going out with a guy?

When he was a child he was himself dressed up as a guy. How was he dressed? How does this compare with the appearance of guys today?

Why was the narrator reluctant to be a guy a second time?

Why were people less generous to the big guys?

Why did gangs attack the people with guys?

Describe the guy the narrator made this year.

What advice would he give about the kind of face to give a guy?

Why did the narrator get the largest share of the money?

Why did these young people go guying?

Henry Mayhew wrote down what people told him in their own words. How can you tell this from the way this passage is written?

Guy Fawkes

Here are some engravings made of the conspiracy and the execution of Guy Fawkes and his companions. Look at the pictures and then tell the story of the gunpowder plot.

Bates — Robert Winter — Christopher Wright — Iohn Wright — Thomas Percy — Guido Fawkes — Robert Catesby — Thomas Winter

 Writing

Guy Fawkes' Night

In your own writing, it is not enough just to say what happened. You must also try to describe it in a way that is interesting to the reader. Look at how William Mayne describes things in this extract. He doesn't, for instance, just describe the appearance of the guy; he makes a mystery and a character of it. The opening sentence begins a small mystery which is soon unravelled, but it gives the reader a tiny shock as he reads which is then resolved. And the idea that the guy might in fact be alive is continued later in the passage. Notice too the way in which the characters behave. They do things and say things which are typical of the different kinds of people they are. For instance, why does the author say 'Amy stayed at the back of the line'?

Then there is the firing of the big rocket. William Mayne doesn't just say they fired the big rocket. He invents complications and difficulties which have to be solved so that the firing of the big rocket becomes more of an event, appropriate to its importance as the largest firework to be lit. It is by creating unusual and unexpected detail like this that the story is made lively and interesting. Perhaps he is remembering an occasion when something like this happened, but more likely he is imagining what it might have been like and creating situations where unusual things happen. Think about this when you come to your own writing. After you have read the passage, go through these introductory notes again.

John came down in the morning to find a stranger in the hall. Mother had started when he had gone to bed, and made a guy before she went herself. It was standing on a stick at the bottom of the stairs. Amy would not come down at first, until Mother explained that it was only a big doll. Amy was still not quite pleased, and came down with her back to the rail, facing the tall thing with its staring eyes. Mother said that Amy's eyes were no smaller than the guy's.

John shook hands with it, and thought it was too real for comfort. It might suddenly breathe, he thought.

He was in the middle of his breakfast when a face he knew began to come up to the front door. It was under a school hat and above a school coat, but it was L for Leader. He swallowed a spoonful of corn-flakes without cracking them all first, and they clung to his throat on the way down. Before L for Leader had touched the doorbell he was carrying the guy into the kitchen.

Then he opened the door. Amy was saying, loudly in the room, so that anyone could hear, 'Why has that bad doll man gone into the kitchen? Mother, will he come in here?'

L for Leader had an urgent message for him. 'Don't forget about the guy,' was all she said.

'No, O.K.,' said John, and shut the door on her. He could hear Mother approaching.

'Why didn't you show it to her?' said Mother.

'Because I'm not supposed to do it until today,' said John. 'She's never pleased unless you do exactly what she says. Even then she might say something beastly.'

'She's a strange friend,' said Mother.

'She's a leader,' said John. 'That's different.'

During the day they went shopping and bought fireworks. There were sparklers for Amy. She did not think they were much of a present when she first saw them, but Mother lit her one at the fire when they came home, and held it over the hearth. The sharp smell of it filled the room long after the glittering life had died and it was a black wire on top of the coke.

Daddy came home with a big rocket. The stick of it was as long as a walking stick. He laid it on the window ledge.

After tea, which was a long meal for John, because he could eat only one biscuit, and he had to wait for the others and do nothing but keep still, the guy came back into the hall, to be ready as soon as it was properly dark. Amy would not come through to get her coat on. The coat had to be taken to her.

Then L for Leader rapped on the door. John let her in. Behind her was Andy.

'Ready?' said L for Leader. 'Then be sharp, we haven't got long.'

'Why?' said John.

'Just haven't,' said L for Leader, and came in to look at the guy. She looked at it very quickly, and said nothing about it.

'She's in a terrible mood,' said Andy, quietly to John. 'I don't know why. She was all right at school.'

'Are we going?' said Mother.

'Yes,' said John. 'Is it all right them coming?' he asked L for Leader.

'Of course,' said L for Leader. 'We have to have

them or we can't have fireworks. Anyone knows that.'

L for Leader went in front, carrying the guy. Behind her walked Andy, and then John. Amy stayed at the back of the line ...

Then there was no more talking, because a Roman Candle was shooting up its fire and bursting it overhead.

The banging fireworks were taken to one side of the fire, and a little way off, and the gentle ones, for the smaller children, were lit on the other side, so there were two parties.

'Mothers and kids for the pretty ones,' said Andy. 'And gangs and dads for the loud ones over here.'

At first Amy jumped at all the bangs. Mother asked her whether she would like to go home. But she couldn't go, because she had to see the silver and golden fountains, and the green and red lights. When she saw the fountains she thought they were water. She had once seen real fountains. She wanted to know why the water in the taps at home was plain and not coloured.

The bonfire grew smaller, and its heat grew larger. People had to go further and further away from it. It was like a small sun flaming in the night.

John found Daddy and asked him whether he had brought the big rocket. Daddy said he was keeping it to end the show with. He was wondering what to stand it in. Small rockets could be stood in bottles, but this one was so big that it would pull a bottle over. If it did that it would streak across the ground, and might even get out into the road and attack a bus.

Catherine wheels were the best favourite. They had a bad habit of coming off the pin, but when they worked they lasted longest and changed colour all the time. They had come with a little stick, with a pin all ready in the end of it, so that you could hold it. Amy held one, with her eyes tight closed and her face turned away. After that she even came and asked for a banger to be thrown at her. She stood about a yard away, and jumped into the air when it blew up, and ran back to Mother feeling she was the bravest person there.

Some people shriek. Sylvia did. Andy said that L for Leader would have shut her up long ago, but tonight they were having no leaders, so he let her carry on.

Mary got by herself, and exploded her fireworks one by one until they were all gone. Then she picked up the bodies and threw them in the fire. One of them was still alive, and spat back a red blob, then a green blob before wrinkling itself up black in the embers.

Andy shared out his fireworks with Nick's gang, who had used theirs up in the last few days. Now they were hungry for them. They took great care to ask Andy to watch his own bangers being lit and his own rockets being sent into space.

The big rocket had to wait until they were all on the way home. There was nothing to stand it in near the bonfire. The only place in the park was the hollow gatepost beside the lane. It was just right. People had filled it half full of stones and gravel, dropping a piece in now and then over the years to see what happened. Now it was just the right depth to hold the bottom of the stick and leave the part that had to be lit over the side.

John helped Daddy stand the rocket in the right place, so that it would go over the park and not over the houses. Then Daddy touched a flame to the blue paper, and it began to glow.

The little red glow took a long time to work. Then it spat once. It glowed more, coughed out some smoke, and then a long tail of flame. The rocket seemed to stand on the flame for a long time. It wasn't really a long time, but just long enough for you to think it hadn't gone yet. Then there was a roar, and the rocket had gone. Before it went it had got itself ready, like a runner, and when it did go it was out to break the record. It looked as if it would never stop. It went up in a curve of fire, then thudded softly, and there was nothing to be seen. Then there was a shower of new bright stars in the sky, dropping, dropping, with smoke above them, and fading as they came. Then each one went out, as if it had gone behind something. In the silence that followed, there was a tumbling sound, and the shell of the rocket, and its stick, rattled in the branches of a tree in the park.

WILLIAM MAYNE, *Plot Night*

Look at each individual character's part in the evening. Say how what he or she says or does builds up our impression of the character.
Read the introductory notes again.

Warning

Study this poster.
Are the instructions clear?
Do you think it would persuade people to use fireworks properly?

Poems

Here is a brief anthology of poems about fireworks and Guy Fawkes' Night. While reading them, keep a look out for hints on how to make your own writing more interesting. It may be the way the poet uses particular words. It may be the way he expresses a feeling. It may be the unusual or unexpected point of view he takes up. Even if you don't notice anything on the surface that could be useful in your own writing, simply by studying the poems carefully, something of the skill these poets have employed will come through to you and come out in your own writing without your even being aware of it!

November Story

The evening had caught cold;
   Its eyes were blurred.
It had a dripping nose
   And its tongue was furred.

I sat in a warm bar
   After the day's work;
November snuffled outside
   Greasing the sidewalk.

But soon I had to go
   Out into the night
Where shadows prowled the alleys,
   Hiding from the light.

But light shone at the corner
   On the pavement where
A man had fallen over
   Or been knocked down there.

His legs on the slimed concrete
   Were splayed out wide;
He had been propped against a lamp-post;
   His head lolled to one side.

A victim of crime or accident,
   An image of fear,
He remained quite motionless
   As I drew near.

Then a thin voice startled silence
   From a doorway close by
Where an urchin hid from the wind:
   'Spare a penny for the guy!'

I gave the boy some money
   And hastened on.
A voice called, 'Thank you, guv'nor!'
   And the words upon

The wincing air seemed strange
   So hoarse and deep –
As if the guy had spoken
   In his restless sleep.
          VERNON SCANNELL

What does the poet think the figure sprawling on the ground is at first?
   Why is he disconcerted by the boy's words?

Gunpowder Plot

For days these curious cardboard buds have lain
In brightly coloured boxes. Soon the night
Will come. We pray there'll be no sullen rain
To make these magic orchids flame less bright.

Now in the garden's darkness they begin
To flower: the frenzied whizz of Catherine wheel
Put forth its fiery petals and the thin
Rocket soars to burst upon the steel

Bulwark of a cloud. And then the guy,
Absurdly human phoenix, is again
Gulped by greedy flames: the harvest sky
Is flecked with threshed and glittering golden
   grain.

'Uncle! A cannon! Watch me as I light it!'
The women helter-skelter, squealing high,
Retreat; the paper fuse is quickly lit,
A cat-like hiss, and spit of fire, a sly

Falter, then the air is shocked with blast.
The cannon bangs and in my nostrils drifts
A bitter scent that brings the lurking past
Lurching to my side. The present shifts,

Allows a ten-year memory to walk
Unhindered now; and so I'm forced to hear
The banshee howl of mortar and the talk
Of men who died, am forced to taste my fear.

I listen for a moment to the guns,
The torn earth's grunts, recalling how I prayed.
The past retreats. I hear a corpse's sons –
'Who's scared of bangers!' 'Uncle! John's afraid!'
          VERNON SCANNELL

What does the cannon remind the poet of?

On the next page there are two poems in which the figure of Guy Fawkes speaks. *Which do you prefer and why?*

39

Guy Fawkes' Day

I am the caught, the cooked, the candled man
With flames for fingers and whose thin eyes foun-
tain,
I send on the stiff air my shooting stare
And at my shoulder bear the burning mountain.

I open on the dark my wound of speeches,
With stabs, with stars its seven last words wear,
My tongue of torches with the salamander
Breeds conversaziones of despair.

Milled in the minted light my skin of silver
Now curls, now kindles on the thicket's bone,
And fired with flesh in sepulchres of slumber
Walks the white night with sparks and showers
sown.

At my fixed feet soldiers my coat of carbon
Slit with the speared sky. Their sacked eyes scan
My mask of medals. In bright mirrors of breath
Our faces fuse in death. My name is man.

CHARLES CAUSLEY

Please to Remember

Here am I,
A poor old Guy:
Legs in a bonfire,
Head in the sky.

Shoeless my toes,
Wild stars behind,
Smoke in my nose,
And my eye-peeps blind;

Old hat, old straw –
In this disgrace;
While the wildfire gleams
On a mask for face.

Ay, all I am made of
Only trash is;
And soon – soon,
Will be dust and ashes.

WALTER DE LA MARE

Finally, here are two poems about fireworks.
Look at the way they describe them.

November the Fifth

And you, big rocket,
I watch how madly you fly
Into the smoky sky
With flaming tail;
Hear your thin wail.

Catherine wheel,
I see how fiercely you spin
Round and round on your pin;
How I admire
Your circle of fire.

Roman candle,
I watch how prettily you spark
Stars in the autumn dark
Falling like rain
To shoot up again.

And you, old guy,
I see how sadly you blaze on
Till every scrap is gone;
Burnt into ashes
Your skeleton crashes.

And so,
The happy ending of the fun,
Fireworks over, bonfire done;
Must wait a year now to remember
Another fifth of November.

LEONARD CLARK

Fireworks

They rise like sudden fiery flowers
That burst upon the night,
Then fall to earth in burning showers
Of crimson, blue, and white.

Like buds too wonderful to name,
Each miracle unfolds,
And Catherine wheels begin to flame
Like whirling marigolds.

Rockets and Roman candles make
An orchard of the sky,
Whence magic trees their petals shake
Upon each gazing eye.

JAMES REEVES

Children's Writing

While it is valuable to read what other people
have written because it can give you ideas and
show you the way, this does not mean that you
have to copy them. It is still possible to have
new ideas and to see things in a light that no one
else has thought of before. Here are four poems
written by schoolchildren of your own age. *Are
there ideas here which haven't been expressed in
the other pieces about fireworks and Guy
Fawkes' Night that you have read?*

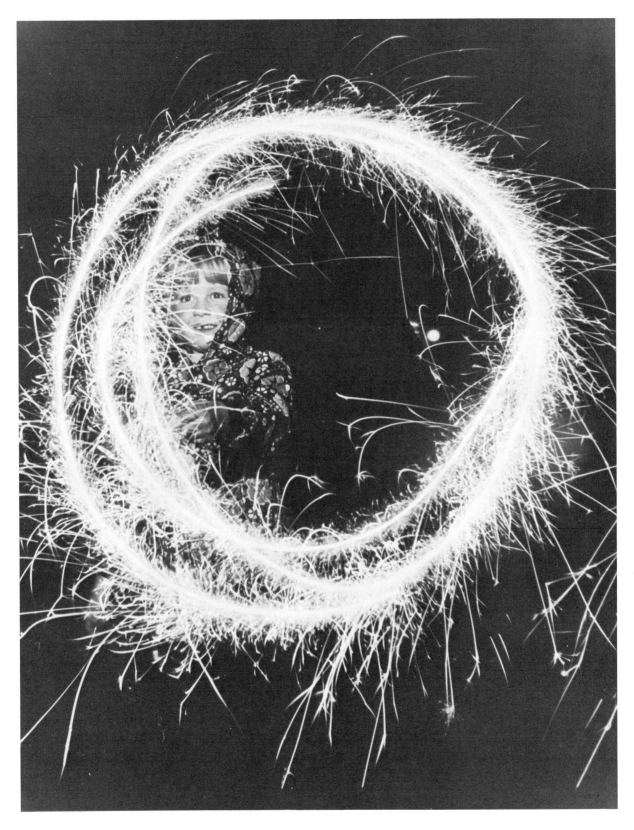

41

Parents call them a waste of money,
Children call them a load of fun,
Police call them troublemakers,
The fire-brigade call them a menace.
The hospital staff work overtime because of them.
They are good fun ...
But only if they are used properly.
Imagine it as money
Going up in smoke and flames.
How many people would buy them then?

MICHAEL

A Catherine wheel spins round
Seeming to say something you can't quite catch.
Swish! – a Golden Rocket cuts through the air
And explodes where the stars seek refuge.

SHEILA

Rockets zoom high in the air,
Painting the heavens with stars;
Like roaring dragons the fireworks spurt
As if in a furious temper.

TIMOTHY

Bang!
Everyone jumps as the silence is broken.
Was that the last?
Swoosh!
No!
Is that the last?
No!
Yes!
No!'
Oh! Yes it is!

JACQUELINE

Assignments

Choose several of the following to write about:

1. Describe a Guy Fawkes' Night that you remember.
2. Write a story about going out with a guy to collect money.
3. The Prank. Write a story about someone who takes a firework to school and gets into trouble.
4. The Bonfire. Write a story about preparations for bonfire night and how it goes off.
5. The Accident. Write a story about what happens when a firework goes wrong or is incorrectly lit.
6. Fireworks. Write a poem describing what fireworks look like.
7. Write a poem about Guy Fawkes.
8. Write a poem about a firework, using the words to create the shape of the firework itself on the page.
9. Imagine you are the guy. What are your thoughts while being displayed to collect money and when you are on the bonfire.
10. After the Bonfire. Write an account of visiting the scene of a bonfire the morning after. What do you see? What can you smell?

Language

A. Adjectives

Adjectives are words that describe nouns and pronouns. Just as nouns can be divided into different categories according to the particular kinds of nouns they are – abstract, collective, common or proper – so can adjectives. It is not important to remember these different categories of adjectives, but it is useful to have a look at them. It is a way of studying and thinking about words more closely so that we really see them and understand them better and so use them more effectively.

Here are some of the different jobs adjectives do. Adjectives can:

1. point out, e.g., *those* papers, *such* ideas;
2. show possession, e.g., *my* opinion, *their* ball;
3. ask questions, e.g., *which* coat? *what* table?
4. indicate number, e.g., *each* article, *four* potatoes;
5. express an indefinite number or amount, e.g., *any* money, *some* sugar;
6. indicate order, e.g., the *second* door;
7. indicate the kind of person or object we are writing or talking about, e.g., the *thin* man, the *red* apple.

Most adjectives belong to category 7.

Find more examples of adjectives belonging to each of the categories given above and write them down in sentences.

Use each of the following adjectives in sentences, saying which particular job each is doing according to the categories given above.

its	fourth
following	angry
fat	our
whichever	many
green	every
this	lively
all	that
much	

B. Comparison of Adjectives

Adjectives are said to have three degrees – positive, comparative and superlative. The positive is the form of the adjective used to describe the basic quality, e.g., tall, weak. If we compare this with an object or person that has more of this quality, we use the comparative form, e.g., taller, weaker. If we compare it with a third object or person with even more of this quality, we use the superlative form, e.g., tallest, weakest. Here are some more examples:

POSITIVE	COMPARATIVE	SUPERLATIVE
strong	stronger	strongest
strange	stranger	strangest
lucky	luckier	luckiest
big	bigger	biggest
thin	thinner	thinnest
grey	greyer	greyest

As you can see, the commonest way of forming the comparison of adjectives is to add -er to the positive to form the comparative degree and -est to the positive to form the superlative degree.

Where the addition of -er or -est would result in a clumsily shaped or sounding word, the comparative degree is formed by adding 'more' before the positive, and the superlative by adding 'most'.

POSITIVE	COMPARATIVE	SUPERLATIVE
beautiful	more beautiful	most beautiful
merciful	more merciful	most merciful
cunning	more cunning	most cunning
languid	more languid	most languid

A few adjectives have irregular comparisons. You probably know them already. If you don't, learn them.

POSITIVE	COMPARATIVE	SUPERLATIVE
bad	worse	worst
far	farther	farthest
	further	furthest
fore	former	foremost
		first
good	better	best
little	less	least
much or many	more	most

'Elder' and 'eldest' are used as the comparative and superlative of 'old' when they refer to the members of a family, e.g.

My eldest sister is getting married.

Otherwise, 'older' and 'oldest' are used.

Beware of using a double comparative, e.g., say either

It was the prettiest hat I had ever seen.

Or

It was the most pretty hat I had ever seen.

Write down the comparative and superlative forms of these adjectives. Be careful with the spelling. If in doubt, check the 'Spelling' section A first.

lovely	sad
stubborn	handsome
woolly	noisy
dangerous	plain
grim	pleasant
stupid	glad
odd	joyful
weird	

C. Punctuation of Speech

When in writing we quote the actual words spoken by someone, we put these words into quotation marks (also called inverted commas), e.g.

He said, 'Come at five o'clock.'

Note the following points:

1. The first spoken word has a capital letter whether it comes at the beginning of the sentence or not. See the example above.

2. The verb of saying is separated from the spoken words by a comma or commas, e.g.

He said, 'Wait for me.'
'Where are you going,' he asked, 'on such a cold morning?'

3. Punctuation marks connected with the spoken words come *inside* the quotation marks, e.g.

'Why do you want me?' he asked.
He said, 'Stop there.'

4. Quotation marks come before the first spoken word and after the last in a speech except where they are interrupted by a verb of saying. You should not use separate quotation marks for each sentence, e.g.

'Come and see me on Thursday,' he said. 'I shall be at home then. My parents are going out to visit friends.'

Not

'Come and see me on Thursday,' he said. 'I shall be at home then.' 'My parents are going out to visit friends.'

5. Begin a new paragraph for each new speaker, e.g.

'Come and see me on Thursday,' he said.
'I can't,' I replied. 'I have to go and see my piano teacher.'

6. If a quoted speech continues for more than one paragraph, quotation marks appear at the beginning of each paragraph but not the end of the paragraphs except for the final one, e.g.

'Today I want to talk to you about the dangers of fireworks,' he began. 'This is a subject on which I am an expert. At the age of eight, I nearly lost the sight of an eye because of a carelessly lit rocket.

'Then when I was twelve, one of my friends put a lighted match into the pocket of another boy, and the fireworks exploded. The boy was lucky to escape with only a burned jacket.

'Now I know better than to play with fireworks. They have been banned in my household.'

7. Quotation marks can be either single or double, depending on the preference of the writer or the printer. It doesn't matter which you use so long as you keep to one type. When words are quoted within a quotation or speech, the alternative type of quotation marks should be used, e.g.

Either 'Did Mary say, "Come here"?' he asked.
Or "Did Mary say, 'Come here'?" he asked.

There are a lot of instructions here, and punctuating speech correctly is quite difficult. *Read the notes through again and see that you understand them. Then try to put them into practice.* You are almost certain to want to use speech in your own stories and writing, so it is worth making the effort to learn the rules. When you are reading a book or a newspaper, notice how speech is punctuated, and this will help you. *Have a look again at the extract from* Plot Night *paying particular attention to the punctuation of the spoken words.*

Rewrite the following passage, punctuating it correctly. Remember to begin a new paragraph for each new speaker.

Have you got the bangers ready asked Mary yes said Tim I've got them in this box be careful what you do with them said Patrick you know how dangerous they can be if you mishandle them rubbish said Tim you always exaggerate I don't said Patrick you remember what happened last year oh don't remind me said Mary I was frightened out of my life poor Mittens was terrified out of her skin who's Mittens Tim asked our cat said Mary who cares about cats said Tim I do said Mary defiantly don't you dare upset her.

Write a dialogue between one of the following pairs:

a milkman and a housewife
a park attendant and an old-age pensioner
a bus conductor and a difficult customer
a deck-chair attendant and a bather
an ice-cream seller and a cheeky child

 ## Vocabulary

A. Words from Proper Names

Have you ever thought why a Catherine wheel is so called? The name of this whirling firework comes from the martyrdom of St Catherine who was put to death on a spiked wheel. There are a large number of words which have come from the names of people. Can you say or find out the derivation of the following words and explain their meanings?

boycott	poinsettia
quisling	nicotine
wellington boot	silhouette
guillotine	volt
mesmerism	watt
Tasmania	forsythia
Louisiana	loganberry
camellia	pasteurize
zeppelin	raglan
shrapnel	saxophone

Can you think of any other words which have come into the language from the names of people who are associated with the object so named?

B. Bonfire

The English language is rich in words that have come into the language from many different sources. There are the words which have been adapted from people's names as in the previous section. There are the words which have come from different languages – from Greek and Latin, French, Italian, German, Hindu and other Asiatic languages. Words have a history all their own, and it is interesting to trace this history and find out their derivation or origin. The word 'bonfire', for instance, was originally 'bonfire' because the main material for fires like this was once bones (from burning martyrs or heretics at the stake). (At least, that is one explanation – other experts say differently.)

What can you find out about the origins of the following words?

alphabet	good-bye
anorak	humour
Bible	magazine
bungalow	marmalade
bus	oasis
cereal	piano
circus	ski
dandelion	television
diamond	umbrella
electric	yoghurt

C. Whoosh!

Whoosh!
Bang!
Zoom!

These are some of the words used to describe the sounds made by fireworks. What is the technical name given to words of this kind? (If in doubt, see the summary of figures of speech in the 'Language' section of Unit 1.)

Write down as many other words as possible which could be used to describe the noises made by fireworks.

 ## Spelling

A. Comparison of Adjectives

When forming the comparison of adjectives (that is, adding -er or -est to the ordinary form) there are two particular types of words where care is needed. These are:

1. adjectives ending in -y. If the adjective ends in -y preceded by a consonant, change the 'y' to 'i' before adding -er or -est, e.g.

lovely	lovelier	loveliest
lively	livelier	liveliest
merry	merrier	merriest

But

grey	greyer	greyest
gay	gayer	gayest

45

Find other examples of adjectives ending in -y and write out the comparative and superlative forms.

2. adjectives which double the final consonant before adding -er or -est, e.g.

big	bigger	biggest
sad	sadder	saddest
thin	thinner	thinnest
fat	fatter	fattest
fit	fitter	fittest

Find other examples of adjectives which double the final consonant before adding -er and -est.

B. Possessive

Note the spelling of Guy Fawkes' Night.

In Book One, we learned that the apostrophe is used to show that a letter has been omitted from a word, e.g., 'don't' for 'do not', 'can't' for 'cannot', 'I'm' for 'I am'. (*For revision, write down twenty more words where the apostrophe is used in this way.*)

The apostrophe has another use. It can indicate the possessor or owner of something, e.g.

the boy's bat
the girl's glove

In these examples, boy and girl are possessing something, bat and glove respectively, and to show this the 's is added.

Here are the rules for forming the possessive.

1. If the possessor is singular, add 's, e.g., the man's leg, the sun's rays.
Note: some proper names ending in 's' add only ', e.g. Achilles' heel, Charles' pen, Guy Fawkes' Night. Other exceptions like this are 'for goodness' sake', 'for peace' sake'.

2. If the possessor is plural, add ', e.g., ladies' scarves, the trees' roots.
Note: if the plural possessor does not end in 's', then the possessive is formed by adding 's, e.g. men's coats, children's toys.

In order to find out whether the possessor is singular or plural, turn the phrase around. For instance, there could be confusion about where the apostrophe comes in a phrase like 'the old people's home'. If you turn the phrase around into 'the home belonging to the old people', you can see that 'people' is a plural possessor not ending in 's'. The possessive is therefore formed according to the rules by adding 's.

Write down further examples of possessive phrases.

Turn the following into possessive phrases, inserting the apostrophe in the correct place. (For example, 'the work done during two hours' becomes 'two hours' work'.)

1. the outfitter for gentlemen
2. the tea you are having today
3. the match that was played yesterday
4. the roofs belonging to the houses
5. the car belonging to Frank
6. the car belonging to Francis
7. the holiday lasting six weeks
8. the knock belonging to the postman
9. the glow belonging to the fire
10. the siren belonging to the ship
11. the hat belonging to Mary
12. the waddle belonging to the goose
13. the games played by the children
14. the tricks played by the monkeys
15. the cots belonging to the babies

Now go back and learn the rules for forming the possessive again. Make sure you understand them and use them. But use them only when possession or belonging is indicated. Sometimes people put in apostrophes before every 's' at the end of a word. Make sure you don't do this.

 Activities

A. 1. In groups, work out the situation of children going out asking for 'a penny for the guy'. One of you could be the guy or it could be a stuffed one. Others could be different kinds of passers-by – friendly, suspicious, hostile.

2. You are letting off your fireworks. One of you is being silly and playing about. What happens? Do you tell him to behave himself? Is there an accident?

3. You are having a bonfire. Show the preparations for it, how you build it up, how you light it, how you react to the flames and add more fuel. Perhaps there is someone who gets in the way or behaves dangerously.

4. Enact the story of the Gunpowder Plot.

B. 1. Find out about Guy Fawkes. Give an account of the Gunpowder Plot to the rest of the class.

2. Find out about the origin of fireworks. Tell the rest of the class what you have found out.

3. Try to listen to Handel's 'Fireworks Music'. Find out the story of how it came to be written and of its first performance.

4. Make a survey of the class to find out which are the most popular fireworks.

5. Some people think that fireworks should be banned except for properly organized public displays. Discuss this view.

Reading List

Try to read one or more of the following books which are about or contain episodes dealing with November the Fifth.

William Mayne, *Plot Night*
Margaret Stuart Barry, *Tommy Mac*
Helen Cresswell, *The Winter of the Birds*
Leon Garfield, *The Pleasure Garden*
 The Ghost Downstairs
Nina Bawden, *A Handful of Thieves*
Dylan Thomas, *Quite Early One Morning*

CONSOLIDATION I

In these sections, we shall be revising and consolidating what has been learned earlier. Look again at the relevant sections of Units 1, 2 and 3 and see if you have understood and remembered the points made. Then try to answer these questions. This is an opportunity for you to find out how much you have learned. If there are questions you cannot answer, it means that you will have to go back and spend extra time revising the relevant sections.

A. Language

1. What is a pronoun?
2. Give five examples of pronouns.
3. What is a preposition?
4. Give five examples of conjunctions.
5. Say what kind of verb 'grow' is in this sentence: 'He finds it difficult to grow potatoes.'
6. What is a simile?
7. Write a sentence containing a metaphor.
8. Distinguish in meaning between a part of speech and a figure of speech.
9. Give an example of onomatopoeia.
10. Give an example of alliteration.
11. What is personification?
12. Say what figure of speech is found in this sentence and explain the meaning: 'The sun made giant strides across the sky.'
13. When do we use a full stop?
14. When do we use a comma?
15. What is a common noun?
16. What is a concrete noun?
17. Give five examples of abstract nouns.
18. Name four different kinds of jobs adjectives can do.
19. What job do most adjectives do?
20. How do most adjectives form the comparative and superlative forms?
21. Give five examples of adjectives with their comparatives and superlatives.
22. What are the comparative and superlative forms of the adjective 'good'?
23. When do we use quotation marks?

24. What do we have to remember about the first spoken word when written down?
25. When do we use single inverted commas and when do we use double inverted commas?
26. Why is it useful to be able to use single and double inverted commas?
27. Do we put punctuation connected with spoken words inside or outside the quotation marks?
28. Write down this sentence correctly punctuated:
    Why are you so late he demanded.

B. Vocabulary

1. What is a bungalow?
2. What is a maisonette?
3. What is a circus when applied to a place-name?
4. What is a crescent when applied to a place-name?
5. What is a suffix?
6. Give three examples of suffixes.
7. What does the suffix '-ette' mean?
8. What does the suffix '-kin' mean?
9. What does 'cigarette' mean literally?
10. Give three words which could be used to describe how waves land on the shore.
11. What does 'marine' mean literally?
12. What is a marina?

13. What do we mean by the derivation of a word?
14. What does 'boycott' mean?
15. What is the derivation of 'pasteurize'?
16. What is the derivation of 'saxophone'?
17. What is the derivation of 'dandelion'?
18. What is the derivation of 'umbrella'?
19. What is onomatopoeia?
20. Give five examples of words that are onomatopoeic.

C. Spelling

1. Write down a street name.
2. What does the first word of a sentence always begin with?
3. Do the names of the seasons have capital letters?
4. What is a homophone?
5. Give three pairs of words that are homophones.
6. Explain the difference in meaning between 'know' and 'no'.
7. Explain the difference in meaning between 'lets' and 'let's'.
8. Explain the difference in meaning between 'manner' and 'manor'.
9. Explain the difference in meaning between 'muscle' and 'mussel'.
10. What is a hyphen and when is it used?
11. Explain the difference between 'old fashioned' and 'old-fashioned'.
12. Write down the comparative and superlative forms of the adjective 'sad'.
13. What is the rule for words ending in -y if a suffix is added?
14. Why is 'Guy Fawkes' Night' so spelled?
15. What are the rules for forming the possessive?
16. Explain two uses of the apostrophe and give five examples of each use.

UNIT 4

Ghosts

 ### Reading and Understanding

The Ghosts Appear

Have you ever had any experiences like these?
– You are sitting in a room at night by yourself
when you hear a noise outside. You open the
door but there is no one there. Or you are
sitting in a room when the door slowly opens.
Again, when you investigate, there is no one
there. Or you put something down and go out
and when you come back it isn't there any more
– it has vanished. Talk about these experiences.

Things like these happen to most of us, and
usually there is a sensible reason for them. It
might be the wind blowing, or a cat, or an object
which has disappeared has been taken by
someone else. But sometimes there seems to be
no explanation, and it is at times like these that
we may think there are ghosts about.

Or imagine another situation. You have
woken up suddenly in the middle of the night. It
is pitch dark all around you. Then you hear a
noise – it is thin and squeaky like a floorboard
creaking, but it isn't a floorboard. You listen
intently – and there it is again. Would it ever
cross your mind that it might be a ghost?

Or you have been reading a weird ghost story
or been watching an eerie film on television,
and it is time to go to bed. Have you ever been
afraid to go upstairs? Why?

Some people believe strongly that there are
no such things as ghosts. Others believe equally
strongly that ghosts exist. What are your views?
What evidence do you have? Do you know of
anyone who has seen a ghost?

Look again at the situations and experiences
suggested above. When do people expect
ghosts to appear? What factors about the situations and experiences above would almost
lead you to expect to see a ghost?

With that in mind, read the following extract
from *The Amazing Mr Blunden*.

The wet daffodils shone in a golden heap in the grey
trug as Lucy came up the path from the lake. The
gravel that crunched beneath her feet was full of
sprouting weeds and moss grew in the shady
patches. The whole garden was badly neglected but
it still had a wild beauty. Now that the summer is
coming, thought Lucy, I'll get Jamie to help me tidy
it up a bit.

She took a short cut through the overgrown ruins
at the east end of the house and stopped to look up at
the pointed window arches that stood out like bones
against the sky. Like the bones of the bird in the
gutter, she thought; all that is left of a long-dead
building. She could see that it had once been a wing
of the house, but the soaring arches seemed to be of
some older style, perhaps some old abbey, destroyed by Henry the Eighth. Clumps of herbs had
spread from the garden into the ruins: thyme and
marjoram which gave off a sweet, wet scent under-
foot. There were wallflowers too, high up on the
stonework, and she added to her basket the few that
were within reach.

Beyond the ruins, a gravel path wound its way into
the shrubbery and she went on in search of the
rhododendron. She smelt it before she saw it, a
thick, honey scent filling the air, and then round a
corner she found the big pale-pink blossoms against
dark leaves.

She picked half-a-dozen and then stood idly,
breathing in the rich perfume. The air was noisy with
birds and she could see through a gap in the bushes
the bright green of the lawns with the crowding trees
beyond. The heat of the spring sunshine was drying
up the heavy rainfall which rose in patches of mist
above the grass.

Lucy began to feel strangely drowsy as though the
scent of the rhododendron were a sweet, heavy
drug. Her mind seemed to be growing still and
empty almost as if it had stuck in a groove from

which she was unable to move it. Her eyes seemed to focus somewhere short of the point she was looking at. She felt that she ought to make some movement, to break the growing sense of stillness that was creeping over her, but the effort was too great. A blackbird was calling, a single note repeated, a warning note; but she could not turn her head to look at him. It was as if she were concentrating all her mind upon one thing, but against her will and upon something that she did not understand.

Then she sensed that there was something moving through the mist on the lawn, just beyond the point at which her eyes were focused. She could not see very clearly, but it seemed to be two pale figures and they were moving towards her, slowly and with purpose.

Fear gripped her. She dropped the basket and her mind leaped from its groove. She looked wildly around her but there was nothing there. The columns of mist were dissolving above the lawn; the blackbird was singing, a full, bubbling song, as though he might burst at any moment.

Everything was perfectly normal and yet she was afraid. She felt convinced that she had narrowly escaped something. With swift, nervous movements, she gathered up the scattered flowers. Then she ran as fast as she could towards the house only to crash headlong into Jamie who was coming the other way.

'Now then,' said Jamie soothingly when he had regained his balance, 'what's the matter with you? You look as if you'd just seen a ghost.'

Lucy hesitated for a moment before she said, 'I thought I had, or rather, two ghosts.'

Jamie was delighted. 'Where?' he asked. 'What were they like? What were they doing?'

Lucy tried to explain but it sounded pretty feeble and Jamie was clearly disappointed.

'Is that all?' he said. 'Just the mist over the grass?'

'It wasn't only that . . .' Lucy struggled for words. 'It wasn't so much what I saw as how I felt: as if something else had taken charge of me. Oh, I can't tell you what it was like but I was frightened. And somehow I was sure that they were ghosts.'

She shuddered and, watching her, Jamie was irritated. Why should something interesting like a ghost happen to Lucy, when she only got into a state and ran away? He had been looking for some sign of a white shadowy figure ever since they had come to the house and he hadn't seen a thing yet.

'Now look, Lucy,' he said firmly, 'if you did see some ghosts, it was a bit mean to run away. After all, we did tell the old man we wouldn't be afraid. He

explained all about them needing help. Now let's go back and you can show me where it happened and I'll see if I can see anything.'

Lucy had already begun to feel foolish. So, after a moment's hesitation, she took Jamie back along the path until they stood beside the heavy, scented pink blossoms.

'It was just here,' she said. 'I thought I saw them over there on the lawn.'

But everything had changed. The sun was warm and bright and the mist had almost gone. Lucy stood by the bush and watched Jamie as he hunted around for any sign of footprints and grew increasingly scornful when he found none. As if ghosts would leave footprints anyway, she thought crossly.

And then it happened again.

A cloud passed in front of the sun and it was suddenly cold. Lucy became aware of the monotonous single note of the blackbird, the warning call, and again she sensed that her mind was slipping out of her grasp. She heard Jamie chattering as he hunted near by, but she could no longer make out what he was saying. She called his name suddenly, in fear, and reached out her hand to him.

Jamie jumped at her unexpected cry and turning saw his sister's pale frightened face and staring unfocused eyes. Suddenly the whole thing ceased to be a game and he ran to her and took hold of her hand. It was very cold and as he grasped it, he too seemed to be caught in the spell, like the people in the fairy-tale who touched the golden goose.

As they stood motionless, side by side, they became aware of two figures which they sensed rather than saw, passing across the lawn just beyond the line of their vision. Lucy was afraid and clutched at her brother's hand. But Jamie, whose only fear was that she might break the spell, clasped her hand tighter to give her courage. Then they stood without moving until the figures passed into focus: a tall girl in an old-fashioned dress and a little boy, who came walking quite naturally along the path towards them.

ANTONIA BARBER, *The Amazing Mr Blunden*

What does the author mean when she says the garden still had 'a wild beauty'?

The painted window stood out 'like bones against the sky'. Say why this is an appropriate comparison.

Look at the passage up to the moment when Lucy sensed something moving. Pick out the things which appeal to the senses of hearing, seeing and smelling.

In your own words describe the gardens and the ruins.

How does the description of these prepare the reader for what is to come?

What impression do you get of the figures when the author says they were moving towards Lucy 'slowly and with purpose'?

Why does Jamie say, 'You look as if you'd just seen a ghost'?

The author says 'Jamie was delighted'. What can you deduce from this?

What kind of ghosts was Jamie expecting?

What do you understand by the expression 'they sensed rather than saw'?

Contrast the reactions of Lucy and Jamie to the two figures.

Getting Rid of Ghosts

There are different kinds of ghosts. There are the faint misty ones that materialize and can walk through doors and walls, and there are poltergeists which you can't see but which throw things and make noises. In this extract from *The Ghost of Thomas Kempe*, James is trying to get rid of a poltergeist, a seventeenth-century sorcerer called Thomas Kempe, with the help of Bert Ellison, a jobbing builder who has come on the pretext of putting up some shelves, but he has to keep it a secret from the rest of the family.

Bert began to measure, and cut pieces of wood. 'So he played up when the Vicar was here, this bloke?'

'I'll say,' said James. 'It was one of the worst times. Knocked things over, and banged.'

'Then it's not worth trying bell, book and candle,' said Bert, 'if he's got no respect for the Church. I'd just be wasting my time. Nor's it worth getting twelve of them.'

'Twelve what?'

'Vicars,' said Bert briefly.

James had a delightful, momentary vision of twelve enormous Vicars following one another up the stairs, hitting their heads on the beams and apologizing in chorus. But Bert was not just being fanciful. He was not a man given to fancy. Apparently ghosts were normally exorcized by twelve priests in the old days. Or seven, sometimes. Or just one, if skilled in such matters.

'But that won't do with this blighter,' said Bert. He lit the cigarette from behind his ear, made some token noises with hammer and nails, and looked round the room reflectively. James waited for him to come to a decision, anxious, but at the same time deeply thankful to be thus sharing the burden of responsibility for Thomas Kempe. He felt relieved of a heavy weight, or at least partly relieved.

'No,' said Bert. 'We won't try anything like that. Nor talking to him, neither, since you say you've already had a go. You know what I think? I think we'll try bottling him.' He put a plank of wood across the chair, knelt on it, and began to saw it in half, whistling through his teeth.

'Bottling him?' said James, wondering if he could have heard correctly.

'That's right. I'll be wanting a bottle with a good firm stopper. Cork 'ud be best. And seven candles.'

'Now?'

'Might as well get on with it, mightn't we?'

James raced downstairs. On the landing he slowed up, remembering the need for discretion. He crept down the next flight, and tiptoed into the larder. He could hear his mother and Helen talking in the kitchen, and from overhead came reassuringly ordinary sawing and hammering noises made by Bert. He felt nervous on several counts: there was the problem of someone asking him what he wanted, and also he kept expecting the sorcerer to manifest himself in some way. What was he doing? Could he be scared of Bert Ellison? Or was he biding his time, before launching some furious counter-attack? From what Thomas Kempe had revealed of his character hitherto he didn't seem the kind of person to be all that easily routed, even by as phlegmatic an opponent as Bert Ellison.

There were various empty medicine bottles on the larder shelf. He selected the one with the tightest-fitting cork and began to look for candles. There was a box of gaily coloured birthday-cake ones, complete with rose-shaped holders, but they seemed inappropriate. He hunted round and unearthed a packet of uncompromisingly plain white ones – an emergency supply for electricity cuts. They were just right: serviceable and not frivolous. He was just putting them under his arm when the door opened.

'Mum says if you're picking at the plum tart you're not to,' said Helen. 'What *are* you doing with those candles?'

'The builder needs them,' said James. 'He's got to solder the shelves with something, hasn't he? He can't solder the rivets without a candle, can he? Or the sprockets.' He stared at her icily: Helen's ignorance of carpentry was total, he knew.

She looked at the candles suspiciously. 'I don't see ...' she began.

'You wouldn't,' said James, wriggling past her. 'I

should go and ask Mum to explain. Very slowly and carefully so you'll be able to follow her all right. Or if you like I will later on.' He shot up the stairs without waiting to hear what she had to say.

Bert had cleared the table and moved it to the centre of the room.

'Ah,' he said, 'that'll do fine. We'll have it in the middle, the bottle, and the candles in a circle round, like. He seems to be keeping himself to himself, your chap. I thought we'd have heard something from him by now.'

'So did I,' said James.

'Maybe he's lying low to see what we've got in mind. Is that his pipe on the shelf there?'

'Yes.'

Bert walked over and picked it up. As he did so the window slammed shut.

'There. He don't like having his property interfered with. Well, that signifies.'

'Can we get on,' said James uneasily, 'with whatever we're going to do.'

'No good rushing a thing like this,' said Bert. 'You've got to take your time. Make a good job of it.' He fiddled around with the bottle and candles, arranging them to his liking. Then he struck a match and lit the candles. The flames staggered and twitched for a moment, then settled down into steady, oval points of light.

'We'd best draw the curtains,' said Bert. 'We don't want people looking in from outside. Then pull up a chair and sit down.'

With the curtains drawn, the room was half dark, the corners lost in gloom, everything concentrated on the circle of yellow lights on the table. Bert and James sat opposite one another. The candles made craggy black shadows on Bert's face, so that it seemed different: older, less ordinary. Downstairs, a long way away, the wireless was playing and someone was running a tap.

Bert took out a handkerchief and wiped his forehead. 'Right, then.' He cleared his throat and said ponderously, 'Rest, thou unquiet spirit!'

There was dead silence. Bert, catching James' eye, looked away in embarrassment and said, 'I don't hold with thee-ing and thou-ing, as a rule, but when you're dealing with a bloke like this – well, I daresay he'd expect it.'

James nodded. They sat quite still. Nothing happened.

'Return from whence thou come – came,' said Bert. 'Begone!'

Two of the candles on James' side of the table guttered wildly, and went out.

'Ah!' said Bert. 'Now he's paying us a bit of attention.'

They waited. James could hear his mother's voice, distantly, saying something about potatoes from the sack in the shed. Uneasy, he leaned across towards Bert and whispered, 'Will it take long?'

'Depends,' said Bert. 'It's no good chivvying these characters. You've got to let them take their time.'

A draught whisked round the table. Three more candles went out.

'Cheeky so-and-so, isn't he?' said Bert.

'Does he know what he's supposed to do?' whispered James.

'He knows all right.'

But how would *they* realize it if and when Thomas Kempe did decide to conform and get into the bottle, James wondered? He wanted to ask, but felt that perhaps too much talk was unsuitable. Presumably Bert, as an experienced exorcist, would just know in some mysterious way.

'Come on, now,' said Bert. 'Let's be 'aving you.'

The last two candle-flames reached up, long and thin, then contracted into tiny points, went intensely blue, and vanished.

'That's it!' said Bert. He got up and drew the curtains.

James looked round anxiously. 'Didn't it work?'

'No. He wasn't having any. When the candles go out, that's it.'

'Couldn't we try again?'

'There wouldn't be any point to it. If he don't fancy it, then he don't fancy it, and that's that. He's an awkward cuss, no doubt about it.'

PENELOPE LIVELY, *The Ghost of Thomas Kempe*

What does 'exorcizing' mean?

What two methods does Bert pronounce ineffectual against Thomas Kempe? Why?

Bert 'was not a man given to fancy'. What kind of person is he then?

Why does James choose the bottle with the tightest-fitting cork?

Why do you think the birthday-cake candles are inappropriate whereas the plain white ones are just right?

How does James manage to keep his real purpose from his sister?

Describe how Bert sets about exorcizing the ghost.

Why is Bert embarrassed?

What signs are there that Thomas Kempe is present?

What impression do you get of Thomas Kempe from the passage?

List the ordinary events and sounds that are going on while James and Bert are trying to exorcize the ghost. What effect do these have?

True or False?

This photograph was taken in 1974 in Gawsworth graveyard near Macclesfield. *Do you think it is a photograph of a ghost? If not, what other explanation can you give?*

 Writing

Creating an Atmosphere

When writing a ghost story, it is important to make the reader believe in what you are telling him. One of the most valuable ways of doing this is by creating the right atmosphere. In the extract in 'Reading and Understanding' from *The Amazing Mr Blunden*, the description of the garden and the ruins, the sounds and scents and Lucy's feeling of being drugged, all help to put the reader into the right frame of mind to accept the ghosts when they appear. A strange, still atmosphere has been built up by the writer into which the ghosts can step naturally and be believed in by the reader. In your own writing you must try to give plenty of realistic detail so that the unusual events you are describing appear perfectly possible. You must try to create an atmosphere which makes the reader ready to believe in what you want to tell him.

Here is another passage in which atmosphere is important. Notice how the two long paragraphs at the beginning set the scene. The author takes his time over filling in the details of the room and creating the mood of stillness, darkness and loneliness so that everything seems to be held immobile. Then when things start to happen, they seem to happen with a tremendous speed which carries the reader along with it. The narrator has laughed at the idea of the Red Room being haunted and has decided to spend the night there to prove how unfounded this idea is.

I entered, closed the door behind me at once, turned the key I found in the lock within, and stood with the candle held aloft, surveying the scene of my vigil, the great red room of Lorraine Castle, in which the young duke had died. Or, rather, in which he had begun his dying, for he had opened the door and fallen headlong down the steps I had just ascended. That had been the end of his vigil, of his gallant attempt to conquer the ghostly tradition of the place, and never, I thought, had apoplexy better served the ends of superstition. And there were other and older stories that clung to the room, back to the half-credible beginning of it all, the tale of a timid wife and the tragic end that came to her husband's jest of frightening her. And looking around that large sombre room, with its shadowy window bays, its recesses and alcoves, one could well understand the legends that had sprouted in its black corners, its germinating darkness. My candle was a little tongue of light in its vastness, that failed to pierce the opposite end of the room, and left an ocean of mystery and suggestion beyond its island of light.

I resolved to make a systematic examination of the place at once, and dispel the fanciful suggestions of its obscurity before they obtained a hold upon me. After satisfying myself of the fastening of the door, I began to walk about the room, peering round each article of furniture, tucking up the valances of the bed, and opening its curtains wide. I pulled up the blinds and examined the fastenings of the several windows before closing the shutters, leant forward and looked up the blackness of the wide chimney, and tapped the dark oak panelling for any secret opening. There were two big mirrors in the room, each with a pair of sconces bearing candles, and on the mantelshelf, too, were more candles in china candlesticks. All these I lit one after the other. The fire was laid, an unexpected consideration from the old housekeeper – and. I lit it, to keep down any disposition to shiver, and when it was burning well, I stood round with my back to it and regarded the room again. I had pulled up a chintz-covered armchair and a table, to form a kind of barricade before me, and on this lay my revolver ready to hand. My precise examination had done me good, but I still found the remoter darkness of the place, and its perfect stillness, too stimulating for the imagination. The echoing of the stir and crackling of the fire was no sort of comfort to me. The shadow in the alcove at the end in particular had that undefinable quality of a presence, that odd suggestion of a lurking, living thing, that comes so easily in silence and solitude. At last, to reassure myself, I walked with a candle into it, and satisfied myself that there was nothing tangible there. I stood that candle upon the floor of the alcove, and left it in that position.

By this time I was in a state of considerable nervous tension, although to my reason there was no adequate cause for the condition. My mind, however, was perfectly clear. I postulated quite unreservedly that nothing supernatural could happen, and to pass the time I began to string some rhymes together, Ingoldsby fashion, of the original legend of the place. A few I spoke aloud, but the echoes were not pleasant. For the same reason I also abandoned, after a time, a conversation with myself upon the impossibility of ghosts and haunting. My mind reverted to the three old and distorted people downstairs, and I tried to keep it upon that topic. The sombre reds and blacks of the room troubled me; even with seven candles the place was merely dim. The one in the alcove flared in a draught, and the fire-flickering kept the shadows and penumbra perpetually shifting and stirring. Casting about for a remedy, I recalled the candles I had seen in the passage, and, with a slight effort, walked out into the moonlight, carrying a candle and leaving the door open, and presently returned with as many as ten. These I put in various knick-knacks of china with which the room was sparsely adorned, lit and placed where the shadows had lain deepest, some on the floor, some in the window recesses, until at last my seventeen candles were so arranged that not an inch of the room but had the direct light of at least one of them. It occurred to me that when the ghost came, I could warn him not to trip over them. The room was now quite brightly illuminated. There was something very cheery and reassuring in these little streaming flames, and snuffing them gave me an occupation, and afforded a helpful sense of the passage of time.

Even with that, however, the brooding expectation of the vigil weighed heavily upon me. It was after midnight that the candle in the alcove suddenly went out, and the black shadow sprang back to its place there. I did not see the candle go out; I simply turned and saw that the darkness was there, as one might start and see the unexpected presence of a stranger. 'By Jove!' said I aloud; 'that draught's a strong one!' and taking the matches from the table, I walked across the room in a leisurely manner to re-light the corner again. My first match would not strike, and as I succeeded with the second, something seemed to blink on the wall before me. I turned my head involuntarily, and saw that the two candles on the little table by the fireplace were extinguished. I rose at once to my feet.

'Odd!' I said. 'Did I do that myself in a flash of absent-mindedness?'

I walked back, re-lit one, and as I did so, I saw the candle in the right sconce of one of the mirrors wink and go right out, and almost immediately its companion followed it. There was no mistake about it. The flame vanished, as if the wicks had been suddenly nipped between a finger and a thumb, leaving the wick neither glowing nor smoking, but black. While I stood gaping, the candle at the foot of the bed went out, and the shadows seemed to take another step towards me.

'This won't do!' said I, and first one and then another candle on the mantelshelf followed.

'What's up?' I cried, with a queer high note getting into my voice somehow. At that the candle on the wardrobe went out, and the one I had re-lit in the alcove followed.

'Steady on!' I said. 'These candles are wanted,' speaking with a half-hysterical facetiousness, and scratching away at a match the while for the mantel candlesticks. My hands trembled so much that twice I missed the rough paper of the matchbox. As the mantel emerged from darkness again, two candles in the remoter end of the window were eclipsed. But with the same match I also re-lit the larger mirror candles, and those on the floor near the doorway, so that for the moment I seemed to gain on the extinctions. But then in a volley there vanished four lights at once in different corners of the room, and I struck another match in quivering haste, and stood hesitating whither to take it.

As I stood undecided, an invisible hand seemed to sweep out the two candles on the table. With a cry of terror, I dashed at the alcove, then into the corner, and then into the window, re-lighting three, as two more vanished by the fireplace; then, perceiving a better way, I dropped the matches on the iron-bound deedbox in the corner, and caught up the bedroom candle-stick. With this I avoided the delay of striking matches; but for all that the steady process of extinction went on, and the shadows I feared and fought against returned, and crept in upon me, first a step gained on this side of me and then on that. It was like a ragged storm-cloud sweeping out the stars. Now and then one returned for a minute, and was lost again. I was now almost frantic with the horror of the coming darkness, and my self-possession deserted me. I leaped panting and dishevelled from candle to candle in a vain struggle against that remorseless advance.

I bruised myself on the thigh against the table, I sent a chair headlong, I stumbled and fell and whisked the cloth from the table in my fall. My candle rolled away from me, and I snatched another as I rose. Abruptly this was blown out, as I swung it off the table by the wind of my sudden movement, and immediately the two remaining candles followed. But there was light still in the room, a red light that staved off the shadows from me. The fire! Of course I could still thrust my candle between the bars and re-light it!

I turned to where the flames were still dancing between the glowing coals, and splashing red reflections upon the furniture, I made two steps towards the grate, and incontinently the flames dwindled and vanished, the glow vanished, the reflections rushed together and vanished, and as I thrust the candle between the bars darkness closed upon me like the shutting of an eye, wrapped about me in a stifling embrace, sealed my vision and crushed the last vestiges of reason from my brain. The candle fell from my hand. I flung out my arms in a vain effort to thrust that ponderous blackness away from me, and, lifting up my voice, screamed with all my might – once, twice, thrice. Then I think I must have staggered to my feet. I know I thought suddenly of the moonlit corridor, and, with my head bowed and my arms over my face, made a run for the door.

But I had forgotten the exact position of the door, and struck myself heavily against the corner of the bed. I staggered back, turned, and was either struck or struck myself against some other bulky furniture. I have a vague memory of battering myself thus, to and fro in the darkness, of a cramped struggle, and of my own wild crying as I darted to and fro, of a heavy blow at last upon my forehead, a horrible sensation of falling that lasted an age, of my last frantic effort to keep my footing, and then I remember no more.

H. G. WELLS, *The Red Room*

Describe the room and its furniture in your own words.

Show how darkness and sounds and stillness are emphasized in the opening paragraphs.

How does the narrator try to keep up his spirits?

What is the first sign that the narrator is frightened when the candles start going out?

Do you find the rest of the story exciting? Try to give reasons for your opinion.

Stories in Verse

Here are three poems each of which tells a ghost story. See whether you enjoy them. *Discuss the different attitudes of the characters involved towards ghosts.*

Two's Company

The sad story of a man who didn't believe in ghosts

They said the house was haunted, but
He laughed at them and said, 'Tut, tut!
I've never heard such tittle-tattle
As ghosts that groan and chains that rattle;
And just to prove I'm in the right,
Please leave me here to spend the night.'

They left him just as dusk was falling
With a hunchback moon and screech-owls calling.

But what is that? Outside it seemed
As if chains rattled, someone screamed!

Come, come, it's merely nerves, he's certain
(But just the same, he draws the curtain).
The stroke of twelve – but there's no clock!
He shuts the door and turns the lock
(Of course, he knows that no one's there,
But no harm's done by taking care!);
Someone's outside – the silly joker,
(He may as well pick up the poker!).
That noise again! He checks the doors,
Shutters the windows, makes a pause
To seek the safest place to hide –
(The cupboard's strong – he creeps inside).
'Not that there's anything to fear!'
He tells himself, when at his ear
A voice breathes softly, 'How do you do!
I am a ghost. Pray, who are you?'

RAYMOND WILSON

Colonel Fazackerley

Colonel Fazackerley Butterworth-Toast
Bought an old castle complete with a ghost,
But someone or other forgot to declare
To Colonel Fazack that the spectre was there.

On the very first evening, while waiting to dine,
The Colonel was taking a fine sherry wine,
When the ghost, with a furious flash and a flare,
Shot out of the chimney and shivered, 'Beware!'

Colonel Fazackerley put down his glass
And said, 'My dear fellow, that's really first class!
I just can't conceive how you do it at all.
I imagine you're going to a Fancy Dress Ball?'

At this, the dread ghost gave a withering cry.
Said the Colonel (his monocle firm in his eye),
'Now just how you do it I wish I could think.
Do sit down and tell me, and please have a drink.'

The ghost in his phosphorous cloak gave a roar
And floated about between ceiling and floor.
He walked through a wall and returned through a pane
And backed up the chimney and came down again.

Said the Colonel, 'With laughter I'm feeling quite weak!'
(As trickles of merriment ran down his cheek).
'My house-warming party I hope you won't spurn.
You *must* say you'll come and you'll give us a turn!'

At this, the poor spectre – quite out of his wits –
Proceeded to shake himself almost to bits.
He rattled his chains and he clattered his bones
And he filled the whole castle with mumbles and moans.

58

But Colonel Fazackerley, just as before,
Was simply delighted and called out, 'Encore!'
At which the ghost vanished, his efforts in vain,
And never was seen at the castle again.

'Oh dear, what a pity!' said Colonel Fazack.
'I don't know his name, so I can't call him back.'
And then with a smile that was hard to define,
Colonel Fazackerley went in to dine.

CHARLES CAUSLEY

The Old Wife and the Ghost

There was an old wife and she lived all alone
   In a cottage not far from Hitchin:
And one bright night, by the full moon light,
   Comes a ghost right into her kitchen.

About that kitchen neat and clean
   The ghost goes pottering round,
But the poor old wife is deaf as a boot
   And so hears never a sound.

The ghost blows up the kitchen fire,
   As bold as bold can be;
He helps himself from the larder shelf,
   But never a sound hears she.

He blows on his hands to make them warm,
   And whistles aloud 'Whee-hee!'
But still as a sack the old soul lies
   And never a sound hears she.

From corner to corner he runs about,
   And into the cupboard he peeps;
He rattles the door and bumps on the floor,
   But still the old wife sleeps.

Jangle and bang go the pots and pans,
   As he throws them all around;
And the plates and mugs and dishes and jugs,
   He flings them all to the ground.

Madly the ghost tears up and down
   And screams like a storm at sea;
And at last the old wife stirs in her bed –
   And it's 'Drat those mice,' says she.

Then the first cock crows and morning shows
   And the troublesome ghost's away.
But oh! what a pickle the poor wife sees
   When she gets up next day.

'Them's tidy big mice,' the old wife thinks,
   And off she goes to Hitchin,
And a tidy big cat she fetches back
   To keep the mice from her kitchen.

JAMES REEVES

Assignments

Choose several of the following to write about:

1. You wake up in the middle of the night and hear a strange noise. Describe what happens when you go to investigate.
2. The Haunted House.
3. Imagine you are a ghost and write about your thoughts and adventures.
4. Most ghosts tend to be sad unhappy creatures. Write a story about a happy ghost.
5. Write a story about a ghost that comes back to haunt someone who has wronged him when he was alive.
6. Write a factual account or a story about how to get rid of a ghost.
7. Write a story about someone pretending to be a ghost in order to frighten someone else – but something goes wrong.
8. Write a poem which creates a ghostly atmosphere.
9. Write a story about someone who doesn't believe in ghosts involved in events that make him change his mind.

Language

A. Active and Passive

This has been called the shortest ghost story ever written:

> He put out his hand for the matches; the matches were put into his hand.

Do you get the point?

In this section we shall be looking at a number of aspects of the verb, probably the most complex part of speech. In Book One, we studied one difficult point about the verb and that was its mood. Can you remember? **The mood of a verb expresses the state of mind of the verb. There are four moods.**

MOOD	DESCRIPTION	EXAMPLES
indicative	used for factual statements and questions	The sun *is shining* brightly. How *are* you today?
imperative	used for orders, commands, requests, entreaties	*Fire!* *Help* me with this crate.
subjunctive	used to express a wish or uncertainty, hesitation or possibility	*May* you do well. If I *were* rich, I should certainly visit Greece.
conditional	used to express actions which are conditional (that is, depend on) something else	It *would be* sad if you were to leave. I *should run* if I were you.

Write further examples for each of these moods.

You may also remember that we said that the moods of verbs are difficult to understand and that it was not essential for you to know about them. The same is true about the other aspects of the verb we shall be studying in this section. But try to understand them. Have a go. If you can manage them, they will give you a deeper understanding of how words work and of the richness and complexity of words.

The first new aspect we shall be examining is the voice of a verb. Look again at the example given at the beginning of this section, and particularly at the verbs. First of all, 'he' is doing something ('put out his hand') and then something is done to him ('the matches were put into his hand'). The first verb is active, and the second is passive.

A verb is said to be in the active voice if the subject of the verb is actually performing the action of the verb, e.g.

Linda dropped the glass.
The dog chased the cat.

A verb is said to be in the passive voice if the action of the verb is being done to the subject by someone or something else, e.g.

The glass was dropped by Linda.
The cat was chased by the dog.

(Remember the normal meanings of the words 'active' and 'passive'. If you are 'active', it implies that you are lively and doing something. If you are 'passive', it implies that something is being done to you.)

Write down five sentences each containing an active verb and five sentences each containing a passive verb.

State which of the verbs in the following sentences are active and which are passive.

1. The wind howled eerily round the ramparts.
2. The stranger was taken by surprise by the sudden appearance of the dark figure.
3. The door slowly creaked open.
4. The windows rattled in their frames.
5. The light of the candles began to waver in the draught.
6. He had been told to expect strange noises.
7. The curtains were quivering in the alcove.
8. He was quaking in his shoes.
9. All the keys had been taken by someone.
10. There was no way he could lock the door.

Rewrite the following sentences changing the verbs from the active to the passive or from the passive to the active.

1. The mouse was pursued by the cat.
2. The prize marrow was grown by an amateur.
3. The disco was organized by the Sixth Form.
4. The class put on an exhibition of their work.
5. The street was crowded with shoppers.
6. His friend opened the door.
7. The girl threw the book out of the window.
8. The ball was kicked into the air by the boy.

60

9. The gardener cut the grass.
10. The litter was picked up by the park-keeper.

B. Tenses

Verbs work in time. They can refer to the past, the present or the future. **The forms of the verb which tell us the time of an action and whether this action is continuing or completed are called tenses.** The three simple tenses are:

present	I see	I come
past	I saw	I came
future	I shall see	I shall come

These are the most common tenses.

If the action is in progress for some time, the tenses are:

present continuous	I am seeing	I am coming
past continuous (or *imperfect*)	I was seeing	I was coming
future continuous	I shall be seeing	I shall be coming

If the action is completed, the tenses are:

present perfect (or *perfect*)	I have seen	I have come
past perfect (or *pluperfect*)	I had seen	I had come
future perfect	I shall have seen	I shall have come

These are the tenses of the indicative mood. The conditional and subjective moods also have tenses. It is not important to know all these variations of tenses. What is important is to be able to recognize when a tense refers to the past, the present or the future.

Sometimes, pupils get mixed up with their tenses and begin in the past and then go on to the present as in the following example.

He opened the door and went in. The lights are on and everything seems quiet. Then suddenly the lights go out.

What is wrong with this? Remember that, on the whole, it is safer to keep to the same tense throughout a story or a composition.

Another fault some pupils develop is the use of the present continuous tense when the straightforward present is all that is needed, e.g.

I am opening the door when my friend knocks.

Instead of

I open the door when my friend knocks.

State whether the tense of the verbs in the following sentences is past, present or future.

1. I think you should have told the truth.
2. When you have finished making the beds, sweep the floor.
3. After he had finished speaking, everyone went home.
4. Will you please stop making that noise?
5. As there was nothing else to watch on television, he went to bed.
6. I want to be an architect when I grow up.
7. Let's go for a walk after everyone has gone to bed.
8. I shall be only too pleased to give you the results of the examination, if you will only be quiet.
9. Stop behaving like an idiot.
10. Do you remember when you were very young?

C. Finite Verb

A finite verb is a verb that forms a tense and has a subject (that is, the noun or pronoun about which a statement is being made). For example, in the following sentence,

He is singing at the top of his voice.

'is singing' is the present tense and 'he' is the

pronoun referring to the person about whom the statement is being made. 'Is singing' is therefore a finite verb. Generally speaking, every sentence must have at least one finite verb because it is finite verbs which give 'sense' to sentences.

State which of the verbs in the following statements are finite.
1. The last shall be first.
2. Playing in the garden.
3. To walk to London.
4. His parents were very worried because he arrived home so late.
5. Stop running in and out of the house.
6. Are you able to finish the exercise?
7. The clock stopped at half-past eight.
8. Made in England.
9. The flowers have withered through lack of water.
10. Put the light on.

Finite verbs also have person and number. Can you remember from Book One what person and number are? Here is a summary to remind you.

PERSON	DESCRIPTION	EXAMPLES
1st	the person speaking	I, me, we
2nd	the person spoken to	you
3rd	the person or thing spoken about	he, she, it, dog, sky, desk

NUMBER	DESCRIPTION	EXAMPLES
singular	when one person or object is referred to	he, it, desk, cart, glove
plural	when more than one person or object is referred to	they, us, dogs, hats, tables

The person and number of a finite verb depend on and are determined by its subject, e.g., in the sentence

He walked down the street.

'walked' is third person and singular because 'he' is third person and singular.

State the person and number of the finite verbs in the following sentences.

1. I shall be asking for your homework in a minute.
2. They moved to the other side of the room.
3. We shouted at the top of our voices.
4. Send me a postcard.
5. The last sentence was difficult.
6. Have you booked your ticket yet?
7. The horses raced across the field.
8. When shall I see you again?
9. Let me know if you have any problems.
10. Today is the last day for sending in your request.

You were told that the verb is a complex part of speech. Look back over this section and revise the points made. We haven't finished yet. There is more in the next Unit!

Vocabulary

A. Riddles

Here are some word riddles for you to solve. Each of the lines reveals a letter and the letters add up to a word. Can you discover what the word is?

> My first is in tow but not in cow.
> My second is in sew but not in sow.
> My third is in now but not in blow.
> What am I?

> My first is in bought but not in sought.
> My second is in flight but not in fought.
> My third is in cake but not in dough.
> My fourth is in slack but not in slow.
> My whole is a colour. Now you should know.
> What am I?

> My first is in scene but not in need.
> My second is in shed but not in seed.
> My third is in bright but not in bought.
> My fourth is in light but not in sought.
> My fifth is in deal but not in lean.
> My whole is something we have all been.
> What am I?

Now devise some riddles of your own on the same pattern.

B. Clerihews

Clerihews are four-line verses which are like pocket autobiographies. The first line should end with the name of a character or historical person, and the lines should rhyme in pairs. There should be a rhythmic shape to the stanza, but there is no definite metrical pattern. The shorter the lines, the neater the effect. The rhyme of the last line should punch the point home. Here are some examples written by schoolchildren which should make the form clear.

> Robin Hood
> Ran through the wood,
> But Friar Tuck
> Always stuck.
>
> > BRIAN

> Oliver Twist
> With a flick of his wrist
> Removed a locket
> From Fagin's pocket.
>
> > GEORGE

> Samuel Pepys
> Never sleeps:
> He writes his diary
> In Westminster Priory.
>
> > SAM

> The Emperor Nero
> Was no hero:
> He played the lyre
> All through the fire.
>
> > BRIAN

Now try to write some clerihews yourself. If you can't think of a subject, try Alfred the Great, Richard of Bordeau, Anne of Cleves, Anne Boleyn or Charles the First.

Find out where clerihews get their name from.

C. Limericks

Everyone has heard of limericks. They are five-line verses with lines one, two and five rhyming, and lines three and four rhyming. Lines three and four are shorter than the other lines. They usually begin 'There was a ...' But a few examples will soon show you the pattern. Here are some written by schoolchildren.

> There was a young boy at the zoo
> Who said he saw Winnie the Pooh
> With Christopher Robin
> Riding on Dobbin
> And the rest of that Pooh Corner crew.
>
> > IAN

> There was a young man from the Rhine
> Whose father called him Frankenstein.
> When out for the day
> Meeting people he'd say
> 'I much prefer oil to wine.'
>
> > BARRY

63

There was a young man from Peru
Who believed that a secret he knew.
The secret was flight
So he flew like a kite,
And now he's star turn in a zoo.

BARRY

Now try to write some limericks of your own. Make sure they are your own work and not ones that you vaguely remember hearing.

What is the derivation of the word 'limerick'? Some people think it is connected with the town in Ireland, but no one is quite sure.

pale, pall
pore, pour
pray, prey
precede, proceed
premises, premisses
prise, prize

Use some of these words in sentences.

 Spelling

A. 'gh'

Note the spelling 'gh' in the following words.

aghast	ghost
ghastly	ghostly
gherkin	ghoul
ghetto	

Make sure you know what these words mean. Use each of them in a sentence.

B. More Homophones

Here are some more words whose sounds are the same or similar and whose meanings and spellings you must know. See if you can distinguish between them.

oar, ore
ordinance, ordnance
pail, pale
pain, pane
pair, pare, pear
passed, past
peace, piece
peal, peel
pedal, peddle
peer, pier
personal, personnel
place, plaice
plain, plane
plum, plumb

 Activities

A. 1. In groups, work out what happens when you are exploring an old deserted mansion and a ghost appears. What does the ghost do? How does it behave? Does it want your help or is it trying to frighten you? How do you make contact?

2. You and your friends have made a bet to sleep in a room that is reputed to be haunted. What happens?

3. In order to get your own back on your friends, you disguise yourself as a ghost. How do your friends react? Do they see through your disguise?

4. To play a trick on your friends, you pretend to be a ghost. What happens when a real ghost joins in?

B. 1. Make a survey of the class to find out how many believe in ghosts and why.

2. Find out about some famous cases of ghosts in the past. Perhaps there are some in your area. Give an account of them to the rest of the class.

3. Find out about the different kinds of ghosts that are supposed to exist and about methods used to exorcise them.

4. Discuss ways people claim to have of getting in touch with the spirits of the dead. Do you believe they work?

5. Find a ghost story which you have enjoyed reading and retell it to the rest of the class.

6. Find out about werewolves, vampires, Dracula, Frankenstein's monster, or any other fiendish spirit, and tell the rest of the class about it.

7. Try to listen to a record of Moussorgsky's *A Night on the Bare Mountain* and write about what the music suggests to you.

8. What do you know about E.S.P. (Extra Sensory Perception)? Find examples and discuss whether you believe in it or not.

Reading List

Here are some novels about ghosts. Try some of them and see if you like them.

Leon Garfield, *Mister Corbett's Ghost*
    The Ghost Downstairs
Philippa Pearce, *Tom's Midnight Garden*
Antonia Barber, *The Amazing Mr Blunden*
Penelope Lively, *The Ghost of Thomas Kempe*
Stephen Chance, *Septimus and the Minster*
    Ghost
William Mayne, *Earthfasts*
Penelope Farmer, *Charlotte Sometimes*
Charles Dickens, *A Christmas Carol*

There are many collections of ghost stories. Some of the stories in the following anthologies may appeal.

Ghostly Gallery: ed. Alfred Hitchcock
The House of Nightmare: ed. Kathleen Lines
The Restless Ghost: ed. Susan Dickinson
Ghosts and Hauntings: ed. Aidan Chambers
Ghosts: ed. Aidan Chambers
Ghosts 2: ed. Aidan Chambers
Ghosts: ed. William Mayne
Ghosts, Spooks and Spectres:
    ed. Charles Molin

UNIT 5

Winter

Reading and Understanding

Sent Home

What does winter mean to you? Does it mean getting out of bed in a cold bedroom and rushing into your clothes? Does it mean washing in cold water – or not washing at all because the pipes have frozen? Does it mean a shivering walk to school, your ears burning with cold and your toes growing numb? Does it mean having to stay in because it gets dark so soon and because the weather is too bad for you to go out? These are some of the discomforts and drawbacks of winter. Can you think of any others?

Winter has another side to it. We enjoy a warm cosy room all the more when we can hear the wild wind howling outside. Hot soup never tastes so good as when we have just come in from the cold. Without snow and ice there would be no snowmen, snowball fights, skating or sledging. What other pleasures can winter bring?

Sometimes, the weather can be so bad in winter that people can't get to work, and offices are undermanned or have to be closed. Have there ever been times when you have not been able to get to school or when you have been sent home early because of the weather? Talk about them.

In the following passage, Amy comes home from school knowing that she is unlikely to be able to go to school next morning because of the snow.

Amy Bowen, bending and shuffling, climbed out from the back of Mrs Rhys's van into the snowy wind and banged the doors shut, turning the handle on what was now an empty shelter for she was the last to be dropped of the eight children Mrs Rhys brought back from school each day, just as in the mornings she was the first to be picked up. Only tomorrow there would surely be no picking up; no school tomorrow, thought Amy, as she stood by the road-side holding her collar tight together under her chin and watching Mrs Rhys turn the van. The windscreen wipers were beginning to be clogged, she noticed. Busily working to and fro they cleared a smaller space at every wipe.

Mrs Rhys manoeuvred her van until it was point-ing round the way it had come, for the road finished here: it was a dead end. The village of Melin-y-Groes was two miles further back, and school itself five miles beyond that in the larger village of Colva.

'You get from here, Amy, just as quick as you can,' said Mrs Rhys. She had wound her window down and put out her head. The snow beat into both their faces. 'It's coming in thicker every minute and there's quite a step for you to go – will you be all right, do you think?'

'Oh, I'll be all right, Mrs Rhys – I like it,' said Amy, stretching up to scoop snow off the windscreen so as to give the wipers a better chance.

'You'll be saying something different time you get home – I know I shall. Never mind about that snow, Amy – let it alone – you'll only get your fingers wet before you start,' said Mrs Rhys, putting her gear lever into first but keeping her foot on the clutch as though reluctant to leave her last charge there on her own with not another soul in sight, and the storm increasing. 'I don't have to ask if your Granny's well stocked up with food, I suppose – she always is – she's wonderful that way.'

'Do you think it's going to last long, then?'

'Well, I shouldn't be surprised, indeed – I always say it's bad when it comes on this time of day. Maybe I should have put you down with young Ivor, Din-tirion – the Protheroes would have been glad enough for you to stop with them.'

'I wouldn't have wanted to,' said Amy. 'Sup-posing we do get snowed in I'd rather be up the Gwyntfa with Granny – she wouldn't enjoy it half so much on her own.'

'One's not much company, that's true,' said Mrs Rhys. 'Well, you make haste then – the sooner you're home the better.'

Amy watched the van drive away. It left two black lines on the white road. Then she pulled off a glove and unbuttoned enough of her coat to be able to shove her cotton shoe-bag inside against her jersey where it would keep dry.

There was a box fastened to the post of the five-barred gate. It had a strip of roofing-felt nailed on top and a door in front. Amy opened the door and took out a blue enamel milk-can with a lid. Then she looked hopefully into the little square interior, but there were no letters.

Years ago, according to legend, a certain giant drover called Casswell, being set upon by cattle-thieves, had lifted the gate then hanging here clean off its hinges and brought it smashing down on the heads of his attackers, defeating them. Whether true or not this story was the reason why the present boundary-gate between road and valley was known as Casswell's Gate even though there were now no Casswells living in these parts.

Usually Amy clambered over it but today, so as to avoid getting her skirt wet with the snow already lying thick on the top bar, she unhooked it and went through, dropping the hook behind her. The flakes were big and loose, soft white lumps of snow blow-ing across sideways on the wind as though they too were in haste to get home. Amy had tied her scarf round her head before she left school and was glad now to have her ears covered. She bent her head, turning it so as to protect her face, and trudged on.

Snow, she thought, was a marvel – it was indeed! Snow was like nothing else: it changed the world, the whole of life, in a matter of moments. Not only the shapes of trees and grasses were changed but daily habits – even laws lost their power and had no mean-ing when snow fell.

That morning lessons had been uncertain. Mr Wil-liams, the schoolmaster, looked out of the window often and doubtfully, as though the low grey sky held a message of warning. And outside it was very still. No birds were flying about; nothing moved.

'I don't like the look of it,' said Mr Williams, twice.

At half past twelve they had their dinner and immediately afterwards he went into the play-ground, not pausing to put on his overcoat, and stood there for some time staring towards the north where the sky above the hills was dark and seemed to be getting darker. Even as he watched the dark-ness came down and hid the tops of the hills, and then the whole of them. They were swallowed by the sky. And in place of the stillness that had lasted so ominously all morning, a great draught of air rushed forward: the wind was rising. Crowded together at the window the children could see their school-master's trousers flap and branches begin to sway and bend, and a bevy of small birds burst suddenly out from the cover of a holly-tree opposite and scattered in all directions. Mr Williams came inside in a hurry.

'You've got snow on your coat, sir,' said Danny Price.

Five minutes later snow was sweeping across the playground and Mr Williams was at the telephone ringing up the various members of School Transport to tell them to come at once.

'It's only going to get worse,' they heard him say, 'and we'd better have them away from here as soon as we can – if we don't, we'll never be able to get them away at all by the look of it.'

There were thirty-nine children in the school and each of them felt it was a special treat to be let off two hours of schooling on a Tuesday, as good as a party almost, even though most of them, living on Radnorshire hill-farms, knew well enough how disastrous a heavy fall of snow coming towards the end of February could be for farmers and sheep. But they crammed on their coats and knotted their scarves and stamped about to get their feet down inside their Wellington boots in a state of great excitement because they were doing it at the wrong time of day; and change is always exciting, reflected Amy as she plodded along, seeing only the ground immediately in front of her; which was why snow was always exciting, she thought - snow changes everything.

Although she kept her head lowered her right cheek was beginning to hurt with the cold. She put up her free hand and covered her cheek with the warmth of a woollen glove, and kept her hand there as she struggled on. Walking was not easy, for at each step her foot slipped a little. After some time her legs ached so much she was bound to rest them. She stopped walking and turning her back on the snow lifted her head.

There was nothing to see; nothing but a white swarming nothingness. The hill that rose up in front of her was invisible and the snow itself had altered. The flakes were smaller now and driving harder. She was uncertain of how far she had come, uncertain of exactly where she was; and as she realized this she felt a curious movement inside her, the sudden squeeze of sudden fright. It was not that she was afraid of losing herself, for the track was clear enough yet and she had only to keep on walking ahead until she reached a path turning off that would lead her down to the stream and across it on a narrow wooden bridge and up the further side to the

Gwyntfa, the cottage where she lived with her grandmother, Mrs Bowen. If instead she had had to follow the track, an old drovers' road, on up the valley, up and up and still on for miles over a waste of grass and fern and boggy patches and outcroppings of rock where curlews nested in the spring, that would have been another matter. Anyone might get lost up there.

But Amy's fear was not of losing her way home. What frightened her was being unable to tell where she was on a path she knew so well. An entire hill had disappeared, and the familiar track was not familiar any more, and the snow was increasing, and there was nobody with her. Then she noticed close by her feet a large squarish boulder, its shape already altered by the snow blown against it but still recognizable as a rock on which she often paused when she was coming from school and the weather was sunny and she was not in any hurry. Her panic evaporated. After all everything was where it had always been – not gone, only concealed. She shifted the milk-can to her other hand; the weight of it dangling from its wire handle had numbed her fingers. Head bowed, glove to cheek, once again she set off.

EMMA SMITH, *No Way of Telling*

1 What can you tell about where Amy lives from the fact that she is the first to be picked up in the morning and the last to be delivered home in the evening?

2 Why were the windscreen wipers beginning to be clogged?

3 Why was Mrs Rhys reluctant to leave Amy?

4 Why does Mrs Rhys hope that Amy's Granny is well stocked with food?

5 Why does Amy prefer to be with her Granny if they get snowed up?

6 What do you think Amy means when she considers 'even laws lost their power and had no meaning when snow fell'?

7 What warning signs did Mr Williams see which predicted snow?

8 Why did Mr Williams want to get the children away as soon as possible?

9 Describe the feelings of the children at going home early.

10 How does the cold and snow affect Amy as she walks to the cottage?

1 *Why does she suddenly feel afraid?*
2 *What makes her feel easier?*
3 *Describe Amy's feelings about the snow.*

At Work

Most of us are able to escape indoors when winter is at its most unpleasant, but some people's jobs demand that they are outside in every kind of weather. Name some of the jobs which involve this and discuss the kind of discomfort these people have to suffer. Farmers, in particular, have no option but to go out into the fields and look after their animals no matter what the conditions are like. The following extract from *Lorna Doone* describes an especially severe winter when sheep were buried under the snow and the farmers had to go out and rescue them.

It must have snowed most wonderfully to have made that depth of covering in about eight hours. For one of Master Stickles' men, who had been out all the night, said that no snow began to fall until nearly midnight. And here it was, blocking up the doors, stopping the ways, and the water-courses, and making it very much worse to walk than in a saw-pit newly used. However we trudged along in a line; I first, and the other men after me; trying to keep my track, but finding legs and strength not up to it. Most of all, John Fry was groaning; certain that his time was come, and sending messages to his wife, and blessings to his children. For all this time it was snowing harder than it ever had snowed before, so far as a man might guess at it; and the leaden depth of the sky came down, like a mine turned upside down on us. Not that the flakes were so very large; for I have seen much larger flakes in a shower of March, while sowing peas; but that there was no room between them, neither any relaxing, nor any change of direction.

Watch, like a good and faithful dog, followed us very cheerfully, leaping out of the depth, which took him over his back and ears already, even in the level places; while in the drifts he might have sunk to any distance out of sight, and never found his way up again. However, we helped him now and then, especially through the gaps and gateways; and so after a deal of floundering, some laughter and a little swearing, we came all safe to the lower meadow, where most of our flock was hurdled.

But behold, there was no flock at all! None, I mean, to be seen anywhere, only at one corner of the field, by the eastern end, where the snow drove in, a great white billow, as high as a barn and as broad as a house. This great drift was rolling and curling beneath the violent blast, tufting and combing with rustling swirls, and carved (as in patterns of cornice) where the grooving chisel of the wind swept round. Ever and again, the tempest snatched little whiffs from the channelled edges, twirled them round, and made them dance over the chine of the monster pile, then let them lie like herring-bones, or the seams of sand where the tide had been. And all the while from the smothering sky, more and more fiercely at every blast, came the pelting pitiless arrows, winged with murky white, and pointed with the barbs of frost.

But although, for people who had no sheep, the sight was a very fine one (so far at least as the weather permitted any sight at all); yet for us, with our flock beneath it, this great mount had but little charm. Watch began to scratch at once, and to howl along the sides of it; he knew that his charge was buried there, and his business taken from him. But we four men set to in earnest, digging with all our might and main, shovelling away at the great white pile, and fetching it into the meadow. Each man made for himself a cave, scooping at the soft cold flux, which slid upon him at every stroke, and throwing it out behind him, in piles of castled fancy. At last we drove our tunnels in (for we worked indeed for the lives of us), and all converging towards the middle, held our tools and listened.

The other men heard nothing at all; or declared that they heard nothing, being anxious now to abandon the matter, because of the chill in their feet and knees. But I said, 'Go, if you choose, all of you. I will work it out by myself, you piecrusts:' and upon that they gripped their shovels, being more or less of Englishmen; and the least drop of English blood is worth the best of any other, when it comes to lasting out.

But before we began again, I laid my head well into the chamber; and there I heard a faint 'ma-a-ah,' coming through some ells of snow, like a plaintive buried hope, or a last appeal. I shouted aloud to cheer him up, for I knew what sheep it was, to wit the most valiant of all the wethers, who had met me when I came home from London, and been so glad to see me. And then we all fell to again; and very soon we hauled him out. Watch took charge of him at once, with an air of the noblest patronage, lying on this frozen fleece, and licking all his face and feet, to restore his warmth to him. Then fighting Tom jumped up at once, and made a little butt at Watch, as if nothing had ever ailed him, and then set off to a shallow place, and looked for something to nibble at.

Further in, and close under the bank, where they had huddled themselves for warmth, we found all the rest of the poor sheep packed as closely as if they were in a great pie. It was strange to observe how their vapour, and breath, and the moisture exuding from their wool had scooped, as it were, a coved room for them, lined with a ribbing of deep yellow snow. Also the churned snow beneath their feet was as yellow as gamboge. Two or three of the weaklier hoggets were dead, from want of air, and from pressure; but more than three-score were as lively as ever; though cramped and stiff for a little while.

'However shall us get 'em home?' John Fry asked in great dismay, when we had cleared about a dozen of them; which we were forced to do very carefully, so as not to fetch the roof down. 'No manner of maning to draive 'un, drough all they girt driftnesses.'

'You see to this place, John,' I replied, as we leaned on our shovels a moment, and the sheep came rubbing round us: 'let no more of them out for the present; they are better where they be. Watch, here boy, keep them!'

Watch came, with his little scut of a tail cocked as sharp as duty; and I set him at the narrow mouth of the great snow antre. All the sheep sidled away, and got closer, that the other sheep might be bitten first, as the foolish things imagine: whereas no good sheep-dog even so much as lips a sheep to turn it.

Then of the outer sheep (all now snowed and frizzled like a lawyer's wig) I took the two finest and heaviest, and with one beneath my right arm, and the other beneath my left, I went straight home to the upper sheppey, and set them inside, and fastened them. Sixty-and-six I took home in that way, two at a time on each journey; and the work grew harder and harder each time, as the drifts of the snow were deepening. No other man should meddle with them: I was resolved to try my strength against the strength of the elements; and try it I did, ay and proved it. A certain fierce delight burned in me, as the struggle grew harder; but rather would I die than yield; and at last I finished it. People talk of it to this day: but none can tell what the labour was, who have not felt that snow and wind.

Of the sheep upon the mountain, and the sheep upon the western farm, and the cattle on the upper burrows, scarcely one in ten was saved; do what we would for them. And this was not through any neglect (now that our wits were sharpened), but from the pure impossibility of finding them at all. That great snow never ceased a moment for three days and nights; and then when all the earth was filled, and the top-most hedges were unseen, and the trees broke down with weight (wherever the wind had not lightened them), a brilliant sun broke forth and showed the loss of all our customs.

All our house was quite snowed up, except where we had purged a way, by dint of constant shovellings. The kitchen was as dark and darker than the cider-cellar, and long lines of furrowed scollops ran even up to the chimney-stacks. Several windows fell right inwards, through the weight of the snow against them; and the few that stood bulged in, and bent like an old bruised lanthorn. We were obliged to cook by candlelight; we were forced to read by candle-light; as for baking, we could not do it, because the oven was too chill; and a load of faggots only brought a little wet down the sides of it.

For when the sun burst forth at last upon that world of white, what he brought was neither warmth, nor cheer, nor hope of softening; only a clearer shaft of cold, from the violet depths of sky. Long-drawn alleys of white haze seemed to lead towards him, yet such as he could not come down, with any warmth remaining. Broad white curtains of the frost-fog looped around the lower sky, on the verge of hill and valley, and above the laden trees. Only round the sun himself, and the spot of heaven he claimed, clustered a bright purple-blue, clear, and calm, and deep.

That night, such a frost ensued as we had never dreamed of, neither read in ancient books, or histories of Frobisher. The kettle by the fire froze, and the crock upon the hearth-cheeks; many men were killed, and cattle rigid in their head-ropes. Then I heard that fearful sound, which never I had heard before, neither since have heard (except during that same winter), the sharp yet solemn sound of trees, burst open by the frost-blow. Our great walnut lost three branches, and has been dying ever since; though growing meanwhile, as the soul does. And the ancient oak at the cross was rent, and many score of ash trees. But why should I tell all this? The people who have not seen it (as I have) will only make faces, and disbelieve; till such another frost comes; which perhaps may never be.

R. D. BLACKMORE, *Lorna Doone*

What was so unusual about the snow fall?
What was made particularly difficult by the snow?
Why was John Fry groaning?
How did this snow fall differ from others the narrator remembered?
What were Watch's reactions to the snow?
Describe the effect of the wind on the snow in the field.

How did the men set about finding the sheep?

How did the narrator manage to persuade the others to carry on?

How did Watch help to revive the sheep which were rescued?

How were the sheep affected by being buried?

How was it that most of the other sheep were able to survive under the snow?

How did the narrator get the sheep home?

Describe the general effect of the snow on the countryside and on the way of life of the farmers.

Were things better when the sun finally shone?

Describe the effects of the great frost.

 Writing

Memories of Winter

In their work, writers usually draw on personal experiences. Even when they are describing characters they have made up or incidents they have imagined, they fill them out with details from people they actually know or scenes they are familiar with. The two extracts from *No Way of Telling* and *Lorna Doone* in the 'Reading and Understanding' section are taken from novels, that is, they are fiction, made-up events about imaginary people. But probably the incidents and characters are based on fact. Probably the authors experienced walking through snow, or rescuing buried sheep, so that they were able to draw on their memories when they came to write about the adventures of their fictional heroes and heroines.

When you yourself are writing, you should try to call up memories and impressions of things that occurred to you so that you can give your stories a feeling of reality and so that the events you write about are convincing and believable. For instance, can you remember when you first saw snow? What was it like? Can you remember experiences of making slides on an icy road or having a snowball fight or having to struggle home through stormy wintry weather? Talk about them.

The following is an extract from an autobiography in which Laurie Lee describes his memories of winter in the village where he lived as a child. (What is an autobiography?) The events described happened many years ago when the author was very young and they happened in the country. How do they compare with your memories?

Winter was no more typical of our valley than summer, it was not even summer's opposite; it was merely that other place. And somehow one never remembered the journey towards it; one arrived, and winter was here. The day came suddenly when all details were different and the village had to be rediscovered. One's nose went dead so that it hurt to breathe, and there were jigsaws of frost on the window. The light filled the house with a green polar glow; while outside – in the invisible world – there was a strange hard silence, or a metallic creaking, a faint throbbing of twigs and wires.

The kitchen that morning would be full of steam, billowing from kettles and pots. The outside pump was frozen again, making a sound like broken crockery, so that the girls tore icicles from the eaves for water and we drank boiled ice in our tea.

'It's wicked,' said Mother, 'The poor, poor birds.' And she flapped her arms with vigour.

She and the girls were wrapped in all they had, coats and scarves and mittens; some had the shivers and some drops on their noses, while poor little Phyllis sat rocking in a chair holding her chilblains like a handful of bees.

There was an iron-shod clatter down the garden path and the milkman pushed open the door. The milk in his pail was frozen solid. He had to break off lumps with a hammer.

'It's murder out,' the milkman said. 'Crows worryin' the sheep. Swans froze in the lake. An' tits droppin' dead in mid-air. . . .' He drank his tea while his eyebrows melted, slapped Dorothy's bottom, and left.

'The poor, poor birds,' Mother said again.

They were hopping around the windowsill, calling for bread and fats – robins, blackbirds, woodpeckers, jays, never seen together save now. We fed them for a while, amazed at their tameness, then put on our long wool mufflers.

'Can we go out, Mother?'

'Well, don't catch cold. And remember to get some wood.'

First we found some old cocoa-tins, punched them with holes, then packed them with smouldering rags. If held in the hand and blown on occasionally they would keep hot for several hours. They were warmer than gloves, and smelt better too. In any case, we never wore gloves. So armed with these, and full of hot breakfast, we stepped out into the winter world.

It was a world of glass, sparkling and motionless. Vapours had frozen all over the trees and transformed them into confections of sugar. Everything was rigid, locked-up and sealed, and when we breathed the air it smelt like needles and stabbed our nostrils and made us sneeze.

Having sucked a few icicles, and kicked the water-butt – to hear its solid sound – and breathed through the frost on the window-pane, we ran up into the road. We hung around, waiting for something to happen. A dog trotted past like a ghost in a cloud, panting his aura around him. The distant fields in the low weak sun were crumpled like oyster shells.

Presently some more boys came to join us, wrapped like Russians, with multi-coloured noses. We stood round in a group and just gasped at each other, waiting to get an idea. The thin ones were blue, with hunched up shoulders, hands deep in their pockets, shivering. The fat ones were rosy and blowing like whales; all of us had wet eyes. What should we do? We didn't know. So the fat ones punched the thin ones, who doubled up, saying, 'Sod you.' Then the thin ones punched the fat ones, who half-died coughing. Then we all jumped up and down for a bit, flapped our arms, and blew on our cocoa-tins.

'What we goin' to *do*, then, eh?'

We quietened down to think. A shuddering thin boy, with his lips drawn back, was eating the wind with his teeth. 'Giddy up,' he said suddenly, and sprang into the air and began whipping himself, and whinnying. At that we all galloped away down the road, bucking and snorting, tugging invisible reins, and lashing away at our hindquarters.

Now the winter's day was set in motion and we rode through its crystal kingdom. We examined the village for its freaks of frost, for anything we might use. We saw the frozen spring by the side of the road, huge like a swollen flower. Water-wagtails hovered above it, nonplussed at its silent hardness, and again and again they dropped down to drink, only to go sprawling in a tumble of feathers. We saw the stream in the valley, black and halted, a tarred path threading through the willows. We saw trees lopped-off by their burdens of ice, cow-tracks like pot-holes in rock, quiet lumps of sheep licking the spiky grass with their black and rotting tongues. The church clock had stopped and the weather-cock was frozen, so that both time and the winds were stilled; and nothing, we thought, could be more exciting than this; interference by a hand unknown, the winter's

No to routine and laws – sinister, awesome, welcome.

'Let's go an' 'elp Farmer Wells,' said a fat boy.

'You can – I ain't,' said a thin one.

'If you don't, I'll give thee a clip in the yer'ole.'

'Gurt great bully.'

'I ain't.'

'You be.'

So we went to the farm on the lip of the village, a farm built from a long-gone abbey. Wells, the farmer, had a young sick son more beautiful than a girl. He waved from his window as we trooped into the farmyard, and wouldn't live to last out the winter. The farmyard muck was brown and hard, dusted with frost like a baked bread-pudding. From the sheds came the rattle of morning milking, chains and buckets, a cow's deep sigh, stumbling hooves and a steady munching.

'Wan' any 'elp, Mr Wells?' we asked.

He crossed the yard with two buckets on a yoke; as usual he was dressed in dung. He was small and bald, but had long sweeping arms that seemed stretched from his heavy labours.

'Well, come on,' he said. 'But no playing the goat....'

Inside the cowsheds it was warm and voluptuous, smelling sweetly of milky breath, of heaving hides, green dung and udders, of steam and fermentations. We carried cut hay from the heart of the rick, packed tight as tobacco flake, with grass and wild flowers juicily fossilized within – a whole summer embalmed in our arms.

I took a bucket of milk to feed a calf. It opened its mouth like a hot wet orchid. It began to suck at my fingers, gurgling in its throat and raising its long-lashed eyes. The milk had been skimmed for making butter and the calf drank a bucket a day. We drank the same stuff at home sometimes; Mr Wells sold it for a penny a jug.

When we'd finished the feeding we got a handful of apples and a baked potato each. The apples were so cold they stung the teeth, but the potatoes were hot, with butter. We made a dinner of this, then scuffled back to the village, where we ran into the bully Walt Kerry.

'Wan' a know summat?' he asked.

'What?'

'Shan't tell ya.'

He whistled a bit, and cleaned his ears. He gave out knowledge in very small parcels.

'Well, if you *wan*'a know, I may's well....'

We waited in a shivering lump.

'Jones's pond is bearing,' he said at last. 'I bin a-slidin' on it all mornin'. Millions bin comin' wi 'orses an' traps an' skates an' things an' all.'

We tore away down the frosty lane, blood up and elbows well out.

'Remember I told ya. An' I got there fust. An' I'll be back when I've 'ad me tea!'

We left him standing in the low pink sun, small as a cankered rose, spiky, thorny, a thing of dread, only to be encountered with shears.

We could hear the pond as we ran down the hill, the shouts that only water produces, the squeal of skates, the ring of the ice and its hollow heaving grumble. Then we saw it; black and flat as a tray, the skaters rolling round it like marbles. We broke into a shout and charged upon it and fell sprawling in all directions. This magic substance, with its deceptive gifts, was something I could never master. It put wings on my heels and gave me the motions of Mercury, then threw me down on my nose. Yet it chose its own darlings, never the ones you supposed, the dromedary louts of the schoolroom, who came skating past with one leg in the air, who twirled and simpered, and darted like swifts; and never fell once – not they.

LAURIE LEE, *Cider with Rosie*

Pick out some of the comparisons in this passage and consider how effective they are.

Describe some of the games the children played in winter. What games do you play?

Describe some of the feelings and sensations the children experience through the cold. How do you feel when it is cold?

Snow Scenes

Look at the following pictures. What words would you use to describe the snow in each of them?

74

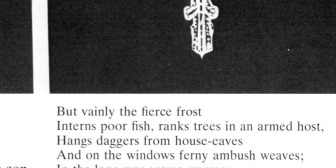

Frost

Most of the accounts of winter so far have contained descriptions of snow, but it is not necessary to have snow to feel the effects of cold wintry weather. In fact, sometimes a winter can go by without any snow at all. More typical perhaps are frost and ice and bitter driving winds. Here are two poems about frost. The first describes a frozen brook.

Hard Frost

Frost called to water 'Halt!'
And crusted the moist snow with sparkling salt;
Brooks, their own bridges, stop,
And icicles in long stalactites drop,
And tench in water-holes
Lurk under gluey glass like fish in bowls.

In the hard-rutted lane
At every footstep breaks a brittle pane,
And tinkling trees ice-bound
Changed into weeping willows, sweep the ground;
Dead boughs take root in ponds
And ferns on windows shoot their ghostly fronds.

But vainly the fierce frost
Interns poor fish, ranks trees in an armed host,
Hangs daggers from house-eaves
And on the windows ferny ambush weaves;
In the long war grown warmer
The sun will strike him dead and strip his armour.

ANDREW YOUNG

Pick out and discuss the words and phrases which suggest that a kind of war is going on between the frost and the world around it.

A Frosty Night

All night the constellations sang
there, in that perfect church, and rang
in the cold belfry of the night,
strewing their splintered light
over the bare sea and the humpbacked fields,
while the hammer of frost, that kills
a flower and leaves a feather
on the gatepost, swung from the weather.

All the lanes grooved round the hillsides
shrank; a brittle skin grew over the puddles;
a sharp wind sawed at the birches,
and the sleeping trunks and branches
cracking their bark and their frozen flesh,
groaned out of a leafless peace,
and the catkins hung limp in the cruel air
where they had danced the day before.

In the clear morning a salt of frost,
flung down thickly by the moon's ghost,
lay on the roofs and the sloping grass
of the rough hills, sparkling like glass.
And like a warm beast in a shippen [cow-shed]
the animal warmth of the sun
was struggling up, and with stiff knees
heaved itself out of the trees.

PHILIP CALLOW

What similarities are there between this poem and the previous one in their description of frost?

The Approach of Spring

One of the eternal miracles of life is the way winters give way to springs. Sometimes, in the deep of winter, when icy winds blow and nearly every tree and bush looks bare and dead, we feel that spring will never come. But it always does. What signs indicate to you that spring is on its way?

Here are two poems which describe the passing of winter and the approach of spring. Describe the tell-tale signs that the poets notice.

Last Snow

Although the snow still lingers
Heaped on the ivy's blunt webbed fingers
And painting tree-trunks on one side,
Here in this sunlit ride
The fresh unchristened things appear,
Leaf, spathe and stem,
With crumbs of earth clinging to them
To show the way they came,
But no flower yet to tell their name,
And one green spear
Stabbing a dead leaf from below
Kills winter at a blow.

ANDREW YOUNG

Thaw

Over the land freckled with snow half-thawed
The speculating rooks at their nests cawed
And saw from elm-tops, delicate as flower of grass,
What we below could not see, Winter pass.

EDWARD THOMAS

 ## Assignments

Choose several of the following to write about:

1. Describe your impressions on waking up to find that there has been a heavy fall of snow during the night.
2. Write a story about a journey that had to be made during wintry weather.
3. Write a poem about trees in winter.
4. Write a poem about snow.
5. Write about the pleasures and discomforts of winter.
6. The Snowball Fight.
7. The Accident. Write a story about a winter activity in which an accident takes place. It could be through a stone in a snowball or falling on a slide or ice cracking on a lake.
8. Describe what it must be like for someone who has to work outside in wintry weather. It could be a farmer or a fisherman, a post-man or a policeman.
9. The Day the School was Sent Home.
10. Write about winter from the point of view of an animal or a bird.
11. Write a poem describing the first signs of spring.

 ## Language

A. Subject, Predicate, Object, Complement

1. To help us understand how verbs work, it is important to know what we mean when we talk about the subject, the predicate, the object and the complement.

The subject has already been referred to. **It is the name given to a noun or pronoun about which a statement is being made in a sentence. A sentence can be divided into two parts: the subject which announces the person or thing the sentence is about; and the predicate which completes the statement and tells us about the subject.** For example,

The man sat down at the table beside the window.

'The man' is the person being talked about, that is, the subject. 'Sat down at the table beside the window' is the statement made about the man, that is, the predicate.

Sometimes the subject of a sentence is not expressed and has to be understood. For example,

Sit down.

Here 'you' or the person addressed is the subject and has to be understood or supplied.

The easy way to find the subject is to take the verb and ask the question 'who?' or 'what?' in front of it. The answer to that question ought to be the subject.

Pick out the subjects in the following sentences:

1. The garden was looking sad and neglected.
2. The last of the leaves have now fallen.
3. The room felt pleasant and warm.
4. The first person to reach the top is a fool.
5. How are you today?
6. I have been off school with a cold.
7. Come here at once.
8. There goes Mick Molloy.
9. Leave him alone, you great bully.
10. The music blared from the open window.

2. **The object is the name given to the noun or pronoun to whom or to which the action of the verb is being done by the subject.** For example:

The stone struck the fence.

Who or what was struck by the stone? The answer is 'the fence'. 'The fence' is the object of the sentence.

The easy way to find the object is to take the verb and ask the question 'whom?' or 'what?' after it. The answer to that question ought to be the object.

Pick out the objects in the following sentences:

1. Plant the cabbages over there.
2. I told him to be careful.
3. The snow covered the ground.
4. The wind blew that tattered newspaper across the street.
5. The ball hit the cross-bar.
6. I saw the man go into the shop.
7. The blackbird cocked its head on one side.
8. Which car did you see outside my house?
9. The robin sang a chirpy song.

10. The stall-owner was selling apples very cheaply.

3. **The complement is the name given to what 'completes' a verb of state.** Most verbs are verbs of action, using action in a wide sense (e.g. run, speak, think). Some verbs, however, do not name an action but a state (e.g. be, feel) or a process (e.g. become, grow). These verbs of state and process do not take an object but a complement which can be either a noun or an adjective. With these verbs, the complement completes the meaning and refers back to the subject, e.g.

I am tired.
She became queen.

In both cases, 'tired' and 'queen' complete the senses of the verbs 'am' and 'became'. 'Tired' (an adjective) refers back to the subject 'I'; 'queen' and 'she' refer to the same person.

Pick out the complements in these sentences:

1. You are lazy.
2. John felt ill.
3. The teacher became very angry.
4. After a while, she grew weary of waiting.
5. After three hours we felt too tired to continue the journey.
6. His father was made redundant.
7. The tree grew tall and slender.
8. She is called Helen.
9. He was made captain.
10. Are you ready yet?

Note that some verbs can take either an object or a complement depending on how they are used. Compare these sentences:

He grew red.
He grew cabbages.

In the first example, 'grew' is expressing a state and is followed by a complement; in the second, 'grew' is naming an action, and the sense passes over from the subject through the verb to an object.

Write sentences containing the following words, first with a complement and then with an object:

grow   made
feel   call

Now revise these notes and make sure you understand the difference between a subject, an object and a complement. *Write five sentences underlining the subjects, five in which you underline the objects, and five in which you underline the complements.*

B.   Non-Finite Verbs

In the 'Language' section of Unit 4, we saw that a finite verb was a verb that forms a tense and has a subject. **Some parts of the verb do not form tenses (unless they have help from other verbs) and do not have subjects. These parts of the verb are called non-finite. They are the infinitive, the present participle, the past participle and the gerund.**

1. **The Infinitive is the root part of a verb from which other parts are formed**, e.g., to run, to speak, to be, to have. It can usually be recognized by the word 'to' preceding it.

The infinitive can act as a verb or a noun. Like a verb it can take an object, e.g.

He wanted *to sell* his car.

Like a noun it can be subject or object of a verb, e.g.

To sing had always been her ambition.

(The noun 'singing' could be substituted for the infinitive.)

I should like *to hear*.

(Compare 'I should like an apple.)

Pick out the infinitives in the following sentences. Say whether they are acting as verbs or nouns.

1. To travel is better than to arrive.
2. To find my address, look in the telephone book.
3. Try to behave properly.
4. They went to London to see their grandparents.
5. I asked him to go.
6. I should like to see that film.
7. It is time to have dinner.
8. There was no need to slam the door.
9. Do you like to read books?
10. My idea of heaven is to lie in the sun.

2. **Verbs have a present participle and a past participle.** The present participle always ends in ing, e.g., coming, thinking, looking. The past participle is usually formed by adding -d or -ed to the infinitive, e.g., walked, formed, waved. But there are many exceptions, e.g., thought, made, spoken. The easiest way to make the past participle of a particular verb is to remember the form of the verb that comes after 'I have', e.g., (I have) eaten, (I have) won, (I have) lost.

Participles can do three jobs in a sentence:

1. **They can form a tense with an auxiliary (or helping) verb,** e.g.

    I was *speaking* to my neighbour only yesterday.
    I have *looked* that word up in the dictionary.

2. **They introduce phrases,** e.g.

    Waiting at the door, he looked about him.
    He stood there, *lost* in thought.

3. **They can act as adjectives,** e.g.

    The *passing* bus splashed through the puddle.
    The *hidden* entrance was easy to find.

Write down twenty present participles and twenty past participles.
Write down five sentences illustrating each of the three uses of participles outlined above.

3. **The gerund (or verbal noun) is part of the verb with the same -ing ending as the present participle which has some of the functions of a verb and all the functions of a noun.** Like a verb, a gerund can govern an object; like a noun, it can be used as a subject, an object or a complement. It is the name of an action, e.g.

Staring at people is rude.
He began *running* down the road.
It is *reading* that he finds difficult to do.

If you can insert the words 'the action of' in front of a word ending in -ing, then that word is a gerund, not a present participle.

Note that not all words ending in -ing are present participles or gerunds, e.g., shilling, herring, inkling.

Say which of the words ending in -ing in the following sentences are present participles and which are gerunds.

1. I like swimming in the sea.
2. Swimming in the sea one day, I nearly drowned.
3. Walking provides healthy exercise.
4. Do you enjoy gardening?
5. Listen to how noisily everyone is talking.
6. The whispering of the sea kept me awake.
7. The whispering wind lulled me to sleep.
8. He started shouting at the top of his voice.
9. He objected to opening a fresh tin of salmon.
10. The opening service of the match was very exciting.

Write ten sentences, each containing a gerund.

C. Transitive and Intransitive

A transitive verb is a verb which takes an object. If the verb does not take an object, it is intransitive, e.g.

The ball hit the wall. (transitive)
No one answered. (intransitive)
Stop that noise. (transitive)
The noise stopped. (intransitive)

Say which of the verbs in the following sentences are transitive and which are intransitive.

1. She posted the letter on Saturday.
2. The gardener cut the heads off the dead flowers.
3. He parked the car in the cul-de-sac.
4. The shop was closed on Mondays.
5. What time did you finish?
6. Put the parcel on the table.
7. Listen to the noise those children are making.
8. When will you be ready?
9. Stop that noise at once.
10. The baker's van stopped outside the farm.

Write down five sentences containing verbs used transitively and five containing verbs used intransitively.

Vocabulary

A. Cold and Ice

Here are some words and expressions connected with cold and ice. Some of them refer literally to wintry weather; others are used as metaphors – that is, they are idioms, or ways of saying things. *Explain what they mean and use them in sentences.*

to make one's teeth chatter
to have goose-flesh
to chill to the marrow
to give someone the cold shoulder
to pour cold water on something
a cold-blooded person
to break the ice
to cut no ice
to skate on thin ice

B. Metaphors and Similes

Use each of the following words in sentences as metaphors or similes:

snow
frost
ice
thaw
winter

C. Irregular Verbs

The usual way for a verb to form its past tense and past participle is by adding -d or -ed to the infinitive, e.g.

INFINITIVE	PAST TENSE	PAST PARTICIPLE
talk	talked	talked
fake	faked	faked

But many of the most common verbs we use have irregular forms, e.g.

INFINITIVE	PAST TENSE	PAST PARTICIPLE
rise	rose	risen
speak	spoke	spoken
think	thought	thought
make	made	made
throw	threw	thrown
lie	lay	lain
lay	laid	laid

Find out the past tenses and past participles of the following verbs.

Make a table of them as above in your vocabulary notebook so that you can refer to them when necessary.

awake	forget	set
bear	forgive	sew
beat	forsake	shake
become	freeze	shear
begin	get	shine
bend	give	shoot
beseech	go	show
bet	grind	shut
bid	hang	sit
bind	hear	sleep
bite	hide	sling
bleed	hit	slit
blow	hold	smell
break	hurt	sow
breed	keep	speak
bring	kneel	speed
build	know	spell
burn	lay	spill
burst	lead	spin
buy	lean	spit
cast	leap	split
catch	learn	spoil
choose	leave	stand
cling	lend	steal
come	let	stick
cost	lie	sting
creep	light	stink
deal	lose	strike
dig	make	swear
do	mean	swim
draw	meet	take
dream	mow	teach
drink	put	tear
drive	read	tell
dwell	rid	think
eat	ride	throw
fall	ring	thrust
feed	rise	tread
feel	run	wake
fight	saw	wear
find	say	weave
flee	see	weep
fling	seek	win
fly	sell	wind
forbid	send	write

 Spelling

A. Participles

Here is a rule to help you with the spelling of participles. When adding -ing or -ed to a word consisting of one syllable containing one vowel followed by one consonant, this consonant is doubled, e.g.

step   *becomes* stepping, stepped
tip   *becomes* tipping, tipped

The same is true of words of more than one syllable where the last syllable contains one vowel followed by one consonant, provided the stress is on this last syllable, e.g.

occur *becomes* occurring, occurred
fulfil *becomes* fulfilling, fulfilled

Note the following:

1. Words like 'infer' and 'prefer' have varying stress and spelling, thus: infer, inferred, inference, inferable; refer, referred, referring, referable; prefer, preferred, preference, preferable.

2. Words ending in a vowel plus a single 'l' double the 'l' before adding -ed or -ing whether the final syllable is stressed or not, e.g.

quarrel, quarrelled, quarrelling
travel, travelled, travelling
signal, signalled, signalling

3. The following exceptions should be noted:

kidnap, kidnapped, kidnapping
worship, worshipped, worshipping
handicap, handicapped, handicapping
parallel, paralleled, paralleling

4. Verbs ending in -e drop the 'e' before adding -ing, e.g.

come, coming
give, giving

5. Verbs ending in -ie change the 'ie' to 'y' before adding -ing, e.g.

die, dying
tie, tying

There is no easy way of remembering how to spell these words correctly. The only way is to learn and understand the rules and memorize the exceptions.

Write down the present participles and the past participles of the following words:

stop	starve
star	continue
bid	flit
stoop	play
sort	store
propel	sip
prohibit	repel
dye	try
inhabit	shop
contain	fail
forget	pin
tie	ban

B. Winter/Wintry

'-Y' is a suffix meaning 'full of', 'having the character of'. Hence 'wintry' means 'full of winter' or 'having the character of winter'. Care has to be taken with the spelling of words like this ending in -y.

Most words are straight-forward, e.g.

thorny	messy
feathery	glassy
summery	gusty
spooky	dusty

But words ending in 'e' usually drop the 'e', e.g.

noisy	juicy
cheesy	nervy
gory	greasy
bony	nosy
icy	joky
spicy	

(*Note the spellings 'gluey' and 'holey'.*)

Some words double the final consonant before adding -y, e.g.

furry	muddy
sunny	ruddy
skinny	chubby
shaggy	flabby

finny	grubby
gummy	fatty
soggy	tinny
foggy	groggy
doggy	stubby

Note the spelling of 'wintry'. Compare 'summery', 'feathery', 'watery', 'leathery', 'thundery', 'powdery', 'peppery'.

Learn these spellings.

  Activities

A. 1. Form yourselves into groups. One group can then have a snowball fight against another group using imaginary snowballs and in complete silence. Try doing all the movements in slow motion. What happens when someone is genuinely hurt?

2. Practise the movements a skater might make on ice. Music might help here. Try *Les Patineurs* by Meyerbeer.

3. In groups work out what happens when you are skating on a pond and the ice cracks and one of you falls through into the water.

B. 1. Look for a poem describing some aspect of winter. Read it out to the class or copy it out and put it with other poems that have been collected by the class in a booklet or on a wall display. If you can find pictures to illustrate the poems, so much the better.

2. Make a survey of the class to find out what people most dislike about winter. It might be the cold or the dark evenings or having to get up on a bitter morning or something else. Perhaps you could give a choice of five things and ask your class-mates to put them in order of dislike.

3. Find out about deciduous and evergreen trees. Say what the difference is and give as many examples of each as you can.

4. What is hibernation? Find out about as many animals as you can that hibernate.

5. Try to listen to a record of *Tapiola* by Sibelius or *Petrushka* by Stravinsky, and then write about what the music suggests to you.

6. Discuss which is your favourite season. Can you find anything to say in favour of winter?

7. Have a look in newspapers for accounts of wintry storms or accidents caused by wintry conditions. Cut them out and make a display of them.

Reading List

Try to read one or more of the following which are set in winter or which have important episodes that take place during winter.

A. Rutgers van der Loeff, *Avalanche!*
   The Children on the Oregon Trail
Helen Cresswell, *The Winter of the Birds*
Emma Smith, *No Way of Telling*
Ian Serraillier, *The Silver Sword*
Charles Dickens, *A Christmas Carol*
Laurie Lee, *Cider with Rosie*
Philippa Pearce, *Tom's Midnight Garden*
Leon Garfield, *Smith*
R. D. Blackmore, *Lorna Doone*
Kenneth Grahame, *The Wind in the Willows*
Jack London, *The Call of the Wild*
   White Fang

For further poems about snow and wintry weather, see *Weathers* (Preludes Series), edited by Rhodri Jones.

UNIT 6

Disasters

 ### Reading and Understanding

Avalanche

I don't want to worry you, but have you ever thought of the many dangers and disasters that can imperil life and property? Here are some of them – volcanoes, earthquakes, floods, motor accidents, explosions, mining accidents, gas escapes, avalanches, shipwrecks, subsidence. Can you think of any more like these? Which are the result of nature, and which are man-made? Which could be predicted, and which would strike without warning? Which could you take precautions against, and which could you do nothing about?

Of course, some disasters are more severe than others. Some can lay land waste and kill thousands of people. Others may involve suffering to only a few. Is it possible to say that one disaster is worse than another? How exactly would you explain what the word 'disaster' means?

Apart from the nature of disasters themselves, another interesting aspect of the subject is the way that people react to them. People often show unexpected heroism and fortitude when faced with a difficult situation. Until it happens, of course, it is almost impossible to say how you would react to being caught in a flood, for instance, or being subjected to an air raid. Can you say how you think you would feel and behave?

Here is an account of an avalanche of snow that occurred in an Alpine village. Notice the effects of the disaster and the reactions of the people caught in it.

And then it happened. In the middle of the night. Just below the top of the Kühelihorn a great mass of snow broke loose with a crash like an explosion. Slowly it began to shift, it seemed to hesitate, but only for a little. A few seconds later the avalanche hurtled down, its path growing wider and wider, the force of the air driven before it blasting the village even before the thundering mass leapt upon the snow-covered houses and sheds like a wild beast. It lasted a far shorter time than anyone could have believed. One moment the village was safe and sound and fast asleep. The next, a great hole was torn in it. Part of it was still buried so deep in snow and wrapped in such deceptive silence that an onlooker would never have guessed the terrible thing that had happened. But part of it, even beyond the path of the avalanche, had houses blown down by blast, walls swept away, shutters and window frames ripped off and smashed. In an instant gaping black holes had been gashed in the white village and a white shroud of snow spread over its heart, just where Mr Baumgarten's office, the baker's shop and Gurtnelli's café stood clustered round the pump. The shattering blow which made everything that could split, burst, crack or smash fly to pieces with terrific force was followed by a minute or two of sinister silence. Then voices began to call. A woman screamed, one or two children cried, men's voices sounded harshly near at hand and further away. The alarm bell began to ring – a menacing sound above the stricken village. But it could not be Altschwank ringing the bell. His house lay buried.

Oil lamps were lit in houses here and there, light shone through cracks and through the patterns cut in the shutters. Men with lighted torches clambered over the shapeless mounds of snow, which were strewn with wreckage. More and more people started calling to each other. There was a sound of hysterical sobbing. Men shouted orders to each other. The dim beams of electric torches were pointed helplessly at the huge, misshapen masses of snow from which protruded broken bits of wood, smashed crockery, the wheels of a pram, the leg of a chair, torn rags of stuff and ripped-off pieces of balcony. It was a chaotic sight which struck people speechless as they looked at it. One of them sobbed. Most of them stood about dumbly in the flickering light of the torches.

'The wind's changed,' said someone.

'Yes, the wind's changed,' someone else answered dully.

The changing wind, the falling snow, the towering mountains, high and pitiless, what can man do against them?

Man can build snow-breaks, he can put up wedge shaped barriers at threatened points, he can dig trenches and plant trees, but once or twice in a century man is beaten.

The heart of the village had never been threatened in the memory of man. The villagers had feared for the outlying parts, where perhaps more houses had ben built during the last few decades than was prudent in view of the known path of the avalanches. But they had taken all measures to ensure their safety.

The snow-breaks and fences, the barriers and trenches had all been under deep snow for days. The villagers had been anxious about the safety of the outlying houses, and with reason. But avalanches have sudden whims which leave one speechless with astonishment. The avalanche from the Kühelihorn had taken a totally unexpected route, one which it had never followed before. It had struck the centre of the village, the very place where people believed themselves safest: where Werner Altschwank and his parents lay asleep, where Bartel Gurtnelli was dreaming of a chessboard that he must clear of snow.

Then something amazing happened to Bartel. The blast picked him up and flung him, bed and all, away ahead of the avalanche, out through the torn and shattered roof which gaped like a strange black wound in the surrounding whiteness. He was flung so far that it was a quarter of an hour before he was found, still in bed, half smothered, his arm gashed by slivers of wood but otherwise unhurt. He was wrapped in blankets and taken to Taureggi's house, where a First Aid Post was set up; here the village midwife, who was also the district nurse, had her hands so full dealing with panic-stricken and hysterical villagers that she barely had time to get things ready to receive the injured.

Bartel was the sixth to be brought in. None of them were seriously injured but they had something in common all the same. All six of them lay on the floor in Taureggi's large sitting room, staring stupidly round them while they were given something hot to drink.

'I had such a quarrel with Old John,' muttered Bartel.

'Why, I've never done anything to you,' said Old John from where he lay in the darkest corner of the room. He raised his head, but let it fall back with a groan. His wife was sitting just behind him, bolt upright on a stool with her back against the wall, her hands folded in her lap.

'Lie still for a while,' she said, 'it'll be better soon.'

'Of course,' said Old John. 'I only wanted to know what that boy has against me.'

His wife shrugged her shoulders.

Mrs Taureggi and her two grown-up daughters were helping the nurse, drawing out splinters and binding up cuts; there was a strong smell of iodine and ether. They ran out of bandages and had to tear sheets into strips instead. They worked away, fastening bandages, calming down their patients with a few quiet words, and sending out messengers to fetch the things they needed. Especially blankets, lots of blankets and quilts. And mattresses. The shock cases had to be kept warm. Even the sobbing women quieted down as soon as they were warm through and through.

Taureggi stood at the door and sternly drove away the people who would only get in the way, or who only wanted to ask him things he didn't know. Taureggi was always calm and people were not accustomed to his snapping at them, but they accepted it without surprise. Only Mrs Finetti, who came to him in tears to tell him that her pigs were buried under the snow, began to scream when he said roughly:

'Then go and dig them out, woman! You're not hurt yourself.'

'It's a man's work!' screamed Mrs Finetti. 'Digging is a man's work and you're just lounging there by the door ...'

She got no further. Taureggi's muscular arm pushed her away and he shouted back: 'Yes, I have to stand here to keep donkeys like you from barging in and getting in everybody's way!'

But the real reason for his rage was that he could not be with the rescue squad. He was needed there too. Men kept on coming all the time to ask his advice and to fetch spades and other tools from his well-stocked shed. They could only get into it through a little window above the big doors, and even that was difficult. The big doors had been blocked with snow for the last four days. The rescue squad took away all the poles, slats and sticks to use as sounding rods for prodding deep in the snow over the places where the victims were buried.

A. RUTGERS VAN DER LOEFF, *Avalanche!*

Comment on the effect of the first two sentences.

How long does it take for the village to be engulfed?

Describe exactly what happens.

What sounds show that a disaster has occurred?

What attitude towards disasters of this kind is expressed by saying 'what can man do against them'?

What precautions can people take against an avalanche of this kind?

Why has this particular avalanche taken the villagers by surprise?

Describe what happens to Bartel Gurtnelli.

Some of the villagers are 'panic-stricken and hysterical'. What does that mean?

Describe one of the villagers who behaves differently and what he or she does.

How does Taureggi's behaviour differ from the way he usually behaves?

What efforts are being made to rescue the people buried under the snow?

Marooned

An avalanche may be brought on by man – a shout, for instance, disturbing the balance of loose earth or snow – but basically, it is a disaster caused by nature. Being marooned, that is put ashore alone, to fend for yourself, is normally brought about by man – a kind of punishment imposed by some sailors on one of their fellows that they disapprove of. How do you think you would cope with being on a deserted island without food, water or shelter, and having to fend for yourself? This is what happens to David Balfour in the following extract.

The time I spent upon the island is still so horrible a thought to me, that I must pass it lightly over. In all the books I have read of people cast away, they had either their pockets full of tools, or a chest of things would be thrown upon the beach along with them, as if on purpose. My case was very different. I had nothing in my pockets but money and Alan's silver button; and being inland bred, I was as much short of knowledge as of means.

I knew indeed that shell-fish were counted good to eat; and among the rocks of the isle I found a great plenty of limpets, which at first I could scarcely strike from their places, not knowing quickness to be needful. There were, besides, some of the little shells that we call buckies; I think periwinkle is the English name. Of these two I made my whole diet, devouring them cold and raw as I found them; and so hungry was I, that at first they seemed to me delicious.

Perhaps they were out of season, or perhaps there was something wrong in the sea about my island. But at least I had no sooner eaten my first meal than I was seized with giddiness and retching, and lay for a long time no better than dead. A second trial of the same food (indeed I had no other) did better with me, and revived my strength. But as long as I was on the island, I never knew what to expect when I had eaten; sometimes all was well, and sometimes I was thrown into a miserable sickness; nor could I ever distinguish what particular fish it was that hurt me.

All day it streamed rain; the island ran like a sop, there was no dry spot to be found; and when I lay down that night, between two boulders that made a kind of roof, my feet were in a bog.

The second day I crossed the island to all sides. There was no one part of it better than another; it was all desolate and rocky; nothing living on it but game birds which I lacked the means to kill, and the gulls which haunted the outlying rocks in a prodigious number. But the creek, or straits, that cut off the isle from the mainland of the Ross, opened out on the north into a bay, and the bay again opened into the Sound of Iona; and it was the neighbourhood of this place that I chose to be my home; though if I had thought upon the very name of home in such a spot, I must have burst out weeping.

I had good reasons for my choice. There was in this part of the isle a little hut of a house like a pig's hut, where fishers used to sleep when they came there upon their business; but the turf roof of it had fallen entirely in; so that the hut was of no use to me, and gave me less shelter than my rocks. What was more important, the shell-fish on which I lived grew there in great plenty; when the tide was out I could gather a peck at a time: and this was doubtless a convenience. But the other reason went deeper. I had become in no way used to the horrid solitude of the isle, but still looked round me on all sides (like a man that was hunted), between fear and hope that I might see some human creature coming. Now, from a little up the hillside over the bay, I could catch a sight of the great, ancient church and the roofs of the people's houses in Iona. And on the other hand, over the low country of the Ross, I saw smoke go up, morning and evening, as if from a homestead in a hollow of the land.

I used to watch this smoke, when I was wet and cold, and had my head half turned with loneliness; and think of the fireside and the company, till my heart burned. It was the same with the roofs of Iona. Altogether, this sight I had of men's homes and comfortable lives, although it put a point on my own sufferings, yet it kept hope alive, and helped me to eat my raw shell-fish (which had soon grown to be a disgust) and saved me from the sense of horror I had whenever I was quite alone with dead rocks, and fowls, and the rain, and the cold sea.

I say it kept hope alive, and indeed it seemed impossible that I should be left to die on the shores of my own country, and within view of a church tower and the smoke of men's houses. But the second day passed; and though as long as the light lasted I kept a bright look-out for boats on the Sound or men passing on the Ross, no help came near me. It still rained, and I turned in to sleep, as wet as ever, and with a cruel sore throat, but a little comforted, perhaps, by having said good night to my next neighbours, the people of Iona.

Charles the Second declared a man could stay outdoors more days in the year in the climate of England than in any other. This was very like a king, with a palace at his back and changes of dry clothes. But he must have had better luck on his flight from Worcester than I had on that miserable isle. It was the height of the summer; yet it rained for more than twenty-four hours, and did not clear until the afternoon of the third day.

This was the day of incidents. In the morning I saw a red deer, a buck with a fine spread of antlers, standing in the rain on the top of the island; but he had scarce seen me rise from under my rock, before he trotted off upon the other side. I supposed he must have swum the straits; though what should bring any creature to Earraid was more than I could fancy.

A little after, as I was jumping about after my limpets, I was startled by a guinea-piece, which fell upon a rock in front of me and glanced off into the sea. When the sailors gave me my money again, they kept back not only about a third of the whole sum, but my father's leather purse; so that from that day out I carried my gold loose in a pocket with a button. I now saw there must be a hole, and clapped my hand to the place in a great hurry. But this was to lock the stable door after the steed was stolen. I had left the shore at Queensferry with near on fifty pounds; now I found no more than two guinea-pieces and a silver shilling.

It is true I picked up a third guinea a little after, where it lay shining on a piece of turf. That made a fortune of three pounds and four shillings, English money, for a lad, the rightful heir of an estate, and now starving on an isle at the extreme end of the wild Highlands.

This state of my affairs dashed me still further; and indeed my plight on that third morning was truly pitiful. My clothes were beginning to rot; my stockings in particular were quite worn through, so that my shanks went naked; my hands had grown quite soft with the continual soaking; my throat was very sore, my strength had much abated, and my heart so turned against the horrid stuff I was condemned to eat, that the very sight of it came near to sicken me.

And yet the worst was not yet come.

There is a pretty high rock on the north-west of Earraid, which (because it had a flat top and overlooked the Sound) I was much in the habit of frequenting; not that ever I stayed in one place, save when asleep, my misery giving me no rest. Indeed, I wore myself down with continual and aimless goings and comings in the rain.

As soon, however, as the sun came out, I lay down on the top of that rock to dry myself. The comfort of the sunshine is a thing I cannot tell. It set me thinking hopefully of my deliverance, of which I had begun to despair; and I scanned the sea and the Ross with a fresh interest. On the south of my rock, a part of the island jutted out and hid the open ocean, so that a boat could thus come quite near me upon that side and I be none the wiser.

Well, all of a sudden, a coble with a brown sail and a pair of fishers aboard of it came flying round that corner of the isle, bound for Iona. I shouted out, and then fell on my knees on the rock and reached up my hands and prayed to them. They were near enough to hear – I could even see the colour of their hair; and there was no doubt but they observed me, for they cried out in the Gaelic tongue, and laughed. But the boat never turned aside, and flew on, right before my eyes, for Iona.

I could not believe such wickedness, and ran along the shore from rock to rock, crying on them piteously: even after they were out of reach of my voice, I still cried and waved to them; and when they were quite gone, I thought my heart would have burst. All the time of my troubles I wept only twice. Once, when I could not reach the yard, and now, the second time, when these fishers turned a deaf ear to my cries. But this time I wept and roared like a wicked child, tearing up the turf with my nails and grinding my face in the earth. If a wish would kill men, those two fishers would never have seen morning, and I should likely have died upon the island.

When I was a little over my anger, I must eat again, but with such loathing of the mess as I could now scarce control. Sure enough, I should have done as well to fast, for my fishes poisoned me again. I had all my first pains; my throat was so sore I could scarce swallow; I had a fit of strong shuddering, which clucked my teeth together; and there came on me that dreadful sense of illness, which we have no name for either in Scotch or English. I thought I should have died, and made my peace with God, forgiving all men, even my uncle and the fishers; and as soon as I had thus made up my mind to the worst, clearness came upon me: I observed the night was falling dry; my clothes were dried a good deal, truly; I was in a better case than ever before since I had landed on the isle; and so I got to sleep at last, with a thought of gratitude.

The next day (which was the fourth of this horrible life of mine) I found my bodily strength run very low. But the sun shone, the air was sweet, and what I managed to eat of the shell-fish agreed well with me and revived my courage.

I was scarce back on my rock (where I went always the first thing after I had eaten) before I observed a boat coming down the Sound, and with her head, as I thought, in my direction.

I began at once to hope and fear exceedingly; for I thought these men might have thought better of their cruelty and be coming back to my assistance. But another disappointment, such as yesterday's, was more than I could bear. I turned my back, accordingly, upon the sea, and did not look again till I had counted many hundreds. The boat was still heading for the island. The next time I counted the full thousand, as slowly as I could, my heart beating so as to hurt me. And then it was out of all question. She was coming straight to Earraid!

I could no longer hold myself back, but ran to the sea side and out, from one rock to another, as far as I could go. It is a marvel I was not drowned; for when I was brought to a stand at last, my legs shook under me, and my mouth was so dry, I must wet it with the sea-water before I was able to shout.

R. L. STEVENSON, *Kidnapped*

What resources does the narrator have with him to face being cast away on the island?

What does he eat to survive? Did this agree with him?

Does the weather help or hinder him?

Describe the island.

Why does the narrator choose one particular spot on the island for his base?

Why does he hesitate to call it his 'home'?

What is he particularly afraid of, yet hopes to see?

Why does he feel it was easy for Charles the Second to state the views he did?

What events make David Balfour call the third day 'the day of incidents'?

Describe the effect of being marooned on David's clothing and physical well-being.

What are his reactions when the coble passes him by without taking any notice?

Why is he able to sleep peacefully that night?

What doubts cross his mind when a boat appears on the fourth day?

Describe David's feelings as the boat comes straight for the island.

 Writing

What the Papers Say

If you are writing about a disaster such as an earthquake or a mining accident, you have to have some facts at your command before you can write. You have to know something about what happens during an earthquake or a mining disaster before you can write convincingly about them. In order to gain this knowledge, you may have to do some research. You may have to look up reference books or encyclopedias or read accounts of similar disasters in the past. One source of information is the daily press. If you keep your eyes open, you can often come across descriptions of disasters such as these in newspapers. Almost every day, somewhere in the world, some disaster or other is taking place and is reported in the newspaper.

There follow five accounts from newspapers of different kinds of disaster. Which do you think is the most vividly described and why?

Compare the headlines — which is the most effective in making you want to read on?

Which account contains information about the particular disaster that you wouldn't have been aware of before?

1. Quake 'flattened' Tangshan

Confirmation that the Chinese earthquake is a major disaster has come from members of a French group on a 'friendship' tour who were in Tangshan when the earthquake hit the city just before dawn on Wednesday.

One of the French party, a girl, was crushed to death when a wall of the hotel in which they were staying fell on her bed. The group said that Tangshan was 'flattened' and that hardly a building was left standing.

The group, who were rescued from their hotel and flown to Peking from a nearby military airbase, are now in Shanghai. They have refused to go into further detail on what they saw in Tangshan, apparently on the grounds that this might embarrass the Chinese authorities.

The Chinese News Agency, which also carried a message of commiseration from Chairman Mao, said that 'large quantities' of medical supplies, food, clothing, building materials, and other relief goods were being sent to the Tangshan area.

Tangshan, with a population of one million, is an old potteries and coal mining town that has been growing rapidly in recent years and has been held up in internal Chinese propaganda as something of a model for other industrial centres.

The Kailin coal mines, which was British-owned before 1949, is the largest in China, with an annual production of 20 million tons. But the city also continues in its own business of making pots – 23 million pieces of pottery annually – and with other industries, including locomotive building, motor vehicles, diesel engines, cement manufacture, machine tools, and even television sets. The value of its industrial production, according to Chinese statistics, has increased two and a half times since 1965.

The fact that the city is situated on mine workings would have made it even more vulnerable. The Kailin mine is worked around the clock on a three shift system and so it seems likely that the miners will have been trapped. The danger of fire in the city must also be high because of the mine and because a major oil pipeline passes through it.

A National Committee statement calls for the people to 'bring into full play the revolutionary spirit of arduous struggle and plunge into the earthquake relief fight with an indomitable will.'

Whatever the size of the tragedy at Tangshan, the Chinese seem determined to cope without foreign aid. The United States, through its liaison office in Peking, has already offered help, and presumably other countries have made similar offers or at least have asked whether they would be welcome. There had been no response to the American offer late today.

One of the ironies of the Tangshan disaster is that it was in Hopei Province, in which the city lies, that the big Chinese effort in recent years to predict earthquakes and minimise the damage they cause really began. After a severe earthquake in the province's southernmost county in 1966, the Chinese turned their attention to the problem with their usual thoroughness, but as Tangshan proves, neither earthquake prediction nor damage prevention has yet become a science.

One consequence of Tangshan may be political, for there is a thick stratum of superstition even in Communist China. Major earthquakes are commonly believed to be Heaven's sign portending important political events, chief among them change of dynasty, and with Mao presumably nearing his death, such superstitions have taken on a new substance.

In addition, the earthquake took place on the first day of the seventh Chinese month, a period when many people believe that the devil's spirits are abroad, and must be appeased.

The Guardian

2. The day the firemen went on the beat

Fire laid waste to 150 acres of Hampshire heathland last weekend. The control room at the county brigade's headquarters has just clocked up its busiest 24 hours ever: 235 calls. Even if the hot weather breaks this weekend, it will be no more than a respite for rural firefighters who see a tinder-box summer stretching into a stubble-burnt autumn.

From Devon to North Yorkshire moors, grass gorse and heath, verges and woods have been a bigger fire risk in the past few months than fire personnel in these areas can remember. Houses have been evacuated, flocks moved, commuters delayed by embankment fires and soldiers drafted to firefighting duties in several counties.

In Hampshire, typical of a string of southern counties where the number of outbreaks has increased enormously, rural fires have turned upside down the county brigade's usual priority system for risk areas. The dock areas of Southampton and Portsmouth, with their oil storage facilities are in the 'A' risk bracket, and they, of course, are served by full-time firemen.

Rural areas with no risk from refineries or manufacturing plants often rely on small stations manned on a part-time basis. But since May it is these areas which have been receiving the bulk of all emergency calls. In fact just 17 of Hampshire's 52 stations have full-time staff; and the part-timers outnumber the professional firemen in the whole county at present by 750 to 700.

There is, says Divisional Officer Ken Tomkins, who is in charge at Basingstoke, an unrelenting slog fighting fires over large open spaces.

'There's a lot of footwork involved with heath fires as there are many areas which our vehicles can't reach. Peat is the most difficult to deal with. Often it's a question of beating out the fire, which is exhausting work. But then you may find that the flames travel underground – the fire is deep-seated, we say, and it breaks out somewhere else a few hours later.'

Flames can elude the fire-fighters, too, by jumping several yards from treetops to treetops, made possible by the great increase in temperature and combustibility, according to Divisional Officer Graham Meldrum who is based at brigade headquarters in Winchester. And the breeze adds problems too.

The total number of fires this year is already 3,600 – only 900 fewer than for the whole of 1975. The peak period is still to come. 'Usually, it is at the end of August and the start of September. Then the grass is even drier and farmers burn stubble after harvesting,' says Mr Meldrum.

By then, employers may not be so willing to let part-time firemen off. Many of the recent emergencies involve rounding up garage mechanics, farm workers and sometimes professional people to supplement regular firemen. 'Usually, they're people with a lot of community spirit,' says Mr Meldrum. They train every week for two hours, and are paid an annual retainer of £140, plus an hourly wage of £1.24 every time they turn out.

The limits on public expenditure means that the brigade is kept under-strength, and the Chief Fire Officer for Hampshire, Mr Archibald Winning, is worried. The establishment of full-time men is 14 per cent below par, and there is a short-fall of 43 per cent in retained firemen. The county population is about 1.5 million, and Mr Winning projects that he will need 845 firemen by 1979–80. But if restrictions on local government spending continue, then there is likely to be an actual reduction to 645 – about 50 less than the present number of fully-trained staff.

It seems certain that many brigades will have to continue to rely on part-timers to man large sectors of their areas. And as long as undermanning is a problem, there will be some delay in attending calls. Mr Winning points out that 132 times last year, appliances had to be sent from stations other than those to which the emergency calls were made.

Hampshire has been helped in the current crisis in two ways. There have been fewer outbreaks in the New Forest than might be expected. It seems probable that the presence of many tourists – itself a main cause of accidental fires – is also one of the best ways of policing incidents, since vigilant holiday-makers are quick to report.

The Guardian

3. Volcano 'will blow up like 17 atom bombs'

Thousands of panic-stricken people have fled from the shadow of Guadeloupe's belching volcano La Soufriere, which experts say could explode at any moment with a force of perhaps 17 times that of the atom bomb dropped on Hiroshima.

An estimated 130,000 people clogged narrow roads with buses, cars, handcarts and horse-drawn carriages as they tried to escape from the capital of Basse-Terre, western of the twin islands which form the French West Indian department.

They made for the far side of Basse-Terre, to relatives' homes and to hastily-prepared refugee camps, and to Guadeloupe's other island, Grand-Terre.

Officials reported that all residents had been evacuated from the threatened area. A few stray cats and dogs were the only living creatures they saw.

Prefect Jean Aurosseau said: 'We consider that we are entering a phase that can only end in a giant eruption ... the countdown has begun.'

The evacuation was ordered after French scientists studied the volcano, which has been active since July 8 when an eruption ripped one of its flanks.

French volcano expert Pierre Brousse, interviewed on the neighbouring island of Dominica, said: 'I have never seen such volcanic activity in the Caribbean Islands. It is irreversible.'

He predicted the eruption would begin with the explosion of a cloud of burning gas, packing the force of 350,000 tons of TNT. The atomic bomb that destroyed Hiroshima had the impact of 20,000.

The Evening Standard

4. 11 killed in Paris hotel blaze

A British woman was among 11 people who died today when fire roared through a six-storey hotel in the centre of Paris.

The 19th century hotel D'Amerique, used mainly by North African immigrant workers 'went up as if it were made of straw' said an eye-witness.

Some panic-stricken tenants, one with clothes ablaze, jumped screaming from the windows. A mother leaped with her baby–and both were found dead in the cobble-stoned courtyard six floors below.

One victim burned to death. Four others were seriously injured, some so badly it was feared they may not live.

Of some 40 people in the hotel eight were asphyxiated in the rooms and in hallways. The blaze apparently started in a ground-floor restaurant in the hotel building at one o'clock this morning.

The exact cause was not immediately known. A fireman said most of the residents 'waited calmly in their rooms until we were able to douse the flames and get up the staircase or put up ladders. We rescued one woman from her sixth floor attic room. It was an extremely violent fire,' he added.

A passer-by said: 'I saw the flames on the ground floor and called the brigade.

'Before they could get here the hotel burned upwards as if it were made of straw. It's very old.'

Another passer-by, watching police use waterhoses from some of the seven fire-trucks blocking the street, said: 'This is a very old quarter here, that's why the fire spread so fast.'

The concierge of an apartment house across the narrow, hilly street, said: 'It was a nightmare. Flames were falling out of the windows. You couldn't breathe the air. You had to close your windows to keep from burning your lungs. The heat was terrible.'

Like most buildings in Paris, the little hotel had no fire escape. The elevator cage was ablaze.

The hotel, at 6 Rue Rochechouart, formerly catered to voyagers coming from the east and north railway stations. In recent years immigrant workers who could not afford to rent apartments had taken up permanent residence in the low-priced hotel.

The Evening Standard

5. 60 die as flood hits the canyon campers

At least 60 people died when floods triggered by heavy thunderstorms roared through a canyon in the Rocky Mountains.

Police said at least 2000 people were stranded by floodwaters which hit Thomson Canyon, a popular tourist spot, before dawn.

Forty bodies had been recovered and at least 15 or 20 others had been seen tangled in debris in the gorge along a 30-mile stretch of the Thompson River.

About 800 people, many of them campers and summer residents, had been evacuated by last night and taken to nearby hospitals. About half were injured or suffering from fatigue and shock.

Helicopters flew over the region dropping leaflets to stranded people advising them how to survive until rescue operations resumed. 'Please stay put and stay on high ground. We are expecting more rain tonight,' the leaflets said.

Sheriff Robert Watson estimated that when the floods struck about 2500 people were in the recreation area 65 miles north-west of Denver, Colorado.

The Sheriff said he sent deputies the night before to warn people that heavy thunderstorms were predicted. Many heeded the warnings and left immediately, keeping the casualty toll down. But people camped in remote areas could not be reached in time.

After the rains witnesses reported seeing bridges swept away and caravans and cars floating down the river.

Helicopters flew National Guardsmen into the devastated canyon to help campers, sightseers and residents.

Recovery teams on foot, on horseback and in jeeps found more than 50 bodies. Larimer county sheriff Robert Watson said the death toll would almost certainly go higher.

Two to four inches of rain has been forecast for today for the stricken areas.

The sheriff said there was no doubt many people would be trapped in the canyon 'for many days.'

A newsman from Associated Press, Mr William Ritz, aboard a military helicopter, saw at least six smashed concrete bridges, twisted on their sides in the river bed with water still churning around them.

The Evening Standard

A Comic Disaster

Not all disasters are taken seriously. The things that happen in this 'cautionary tale' are rather dreadful, but because of the way they are described, we can't help laughing at them. Can you say why? How is the comedy highlighted by the damage that George himself receives?

George

Who played with a Dangerous Toy, and suffered a Catastrophe of Considerable Dimensions

When George's Grandmamma was told
That George had been as good as Gold,
She Promised in the Afternoon
To buy him an *Immense* BALLOON.

And so she did; but when it came,
It got into the candle's flame,
And being of a dangerous sort
Exploded with a loud report!

The Lights went out! The Windows broke!
The Room was filled with reeking smoke.
And in the darkness shrieks and yells
Were mingled with Electric Bells,
And falling masonry and groans,
And crunching, as of broken bones,
And dreadful shrieks, when, worst of all,
The House itself began to fall!
It tottered, shuddered to and fro,
Then crashed into the street below –
Which happened to be Savile Row.

When help arrived, among the Dead
Were Cousin Mary, Little Fred,
The Footmen (both of them), the Groom,
The man that cleaned the Billiard-Room,
The Chaplain, and the Still-Room Maid.
And I am dreadfully afraid
That Monsieur Champignon, the Chef,
Will now be permanently deaf –
And both his Aides are much the same;
While George, who was in part to blame,
Received, you will regret to hear,
A nasty lump behind the ear.

Moral

The moral is that little Boys
Should not be given dangerous Toys.

HILAIRE BELLOC

 Assignments

Choose several of the following to write about:

1. You find yourself alone after a disaster. Describe what has happened and write about your feelings and what you do.
2. Put yourself into the position of a person who has lost someone near and dear in a disaster – a wife whose husband has been killed, for instance, or a son who has lost his father – and describe the feelings of this person. Perhaps this could be a poem.
3. The Rescue. Write a story about how a rescue party saves someone caught in a disaster – snow, flood, earthquake, ship-wreck, for instance.
4. The Crash. Write a story about a road accident.
5. Write a story about a natural disaster (for instance, a flood or a forest fire) in which part of the countryside is in danger.
6. Write about a mining disaster, either from the point of view of a miner trapped below the ground, or from the point of view of relatives waiting for news at the pit head.
7. Write about a disaster from the point of view of a wild animal or bird. Perhaps it could be a flood or a drought or a fire.
8. Write a poem describing a volcano erupting.
9. Write a comic story about a day when everything went wrong.
10. Write an account of a disaster as though for a newspaper. It could be a factory being burnt down or a gas explosion in a block of flats or a multiple pile-up on a motor-way or an aeroplane crash. Remember to use effective headlines.

 Language

A. Pronouns

A pronoun is the name given to a word which can be used in place of a noun, e.g.

Michael jumped up from his place. *He* moved to the door.

Just like nouns and adjectives, pronouns can do different kinds of jobs in a sentence. They can be used.

1. of people and things (e.g. *She* spoke well) These are called personal pronouns.
2. as conjunctions (e.g. The painting *which* Mary did was very good) These are called relative pronouns.
3. for pointing out (e.g. *That* is no good)
4. to ask a question (e.g. *Who* is there?)
5. to refer back (e.g. We found *ourselves* in a large clearing) These are called reflexive pronouns.
6. to give emphasis (e.g. They *themselves* agreed to it)
7. to indicate number (e.g. *Many* would like to go)

Find more examples of each of these categories and put them into sentences.

Let's look more closely at personal and relative pronouns. Unlike nouns which retain the same form whether they are acting as the subject or the object of a verb, these pronouns change their form. (This is known as case.) Compare

The *forest* was very dark. (subject)
We entered the *forest*. (object)
I saw my friend. (subject)
He saw *me*. (object)

These pronouns also form their possessives in a different way from nouns. Nouns form it by adding 's or '. The possessive form of these pronouns *never uses the apostrophe*.

Study the following table showing the various forms.

SUBJECT (or COMPLEMENT)	OBJECT	POSSESSIVE
I	me	mine
he	him	his
she	her	hers
it	it	its
we	our	ours
you	you	yours
they	them	theirs
who	whom	whose

Use each of these words in sentences.

Note (i) if a pronoun is the complement of a verb, the subjective form is used, e.g.

It is *I* who complained.

(ii) if a pronoun follows a preposition, the objective form is used, e.g.

That is a secret between *you* and *me*.

B.   Relative Pronouns

Relative pronouns do two jobs. **They are pronouns and take the place of a noun, but they also act as conjunctions and are 'related' to (or refer to) the noun that goes before**, e.g.

The window is open.
A draught is coming through the window.

These sentences can be joined by using a relative pronoun, thus

A draught is coming through the window which is open.

The relative pronouns are: who, whom, whose, which, that. 'Which' is never used of people. 'Who' is used of people; 'which' is used of things; 'that' may be used of either. Words like 'when' and 'where' can be used as relative pronouns, e.g.

Do you know the time when (at which) the last bus goes?
The house where (in which) I was born has been knocked down.

Rewrite the following pairs of sentences as single sentences using relative pronouns:

1. The door is brown. The door leads into the backyard.
2. The boy's bicycle was stolen. The boy was very upset.
3. The teacher wanted to see the girl. The girl had spoken during the examination.
4. The old woman was very strange. I met the old woman in the wood.
5. The toy is broken. The toy cannot be repaired.
6. The place is a long way from here. I was brought up in that place.
7. He regretted buying the record. The record had an attractive cover.
8. The plant's leaves were drooping. The plant needed water.

9. The boy came top of the class. He hated the boy.
10. The road ran due north. We were travelling on the road.

With 'who' and 'whom', care has to be taken to get the form right. 'Who' is the subjective form and is used when the relative pronoun is the subject of a verb. 'Whom' is the objective form and is used when it is the object of a verb or when it is governed by a preposition, e.g.

The boy who is talking please stop. ('Who' because it is the subject of 'is talking'.)

The girl whom I met at the dance was very pleasant. ('Whom' because it is the object of 'met'.)

The girl to whom I lent a pencil please return it. ('Whom' because it is governed by the preposition 'to'.)

Rewrite the following sentences supplying 'who' or 'whom' in the blanks:

1. The player —— scored the goal was overjoyed.
2. He wanted to know to —— he should give the letter.
3. The woman —— he saw at the station was a well-known actress.
4. The person to —— he called paid no attention.
5. When he knocked at the door he was uncertain —— would appear.
6. He wondered —— he would meet at the party.
7. The man —— came to repair the television set forgot to bring his tools.
8. I like shopkeepers —— give you personal service.
9. I want to know to —— I should pay the money.
10. The girl —— my brother is marrying comes from London.

 Vocabulary

A. Disasters

There are a number of words which more or less mean the same as disaster. Can you define what the difference (if any) is between them?

disaster	malignity
calamity	disturbance
tragedy	irritation
catastrophe	harassment
annoyance	affront
mortification	botheration
vexation	provocation
lamentation	distress
grouse	grief
affliction	woe
grievance	aggravation
nuisance	importunity
mishap	torment
misfortune	shock
infestation	terror
molestation	

B. Foreign Words and Phrases

Many words have come into the English language from other languages and most of them have been absorbed and acclimatized so that we are scarcely aware that they were once strange and foreign. But some words and phrases still retain their foreignness though they are firmly established as part of common usage. Here are some examples. *Find out what language they come from, what they mean and use them in sentences.*

ad infinitum	menu
ad nauseam	mot juste
au revoir	nom de plume
bête noire	non sequitur
bona fide	par excellence
café	persona non grata
carte blanche	pièce de résistance
chef-d'œuvre	post mortem
coup de grâce	raison d'être
de rigueur	sotto voce
de trop	status quo

95

deus ex machina	tête-à-tête	wife	wives
encore	vice versa	wolf	wolves

The plural of 'hoof' can be 'hoofs' or 'hooves'; 'scarf' can be 'scarfs' or 'scarves'; 'wharf' can be 'wharfs' or 'wharves'; 'staff' can be 'staffs' or 'staves' depending on the meaning.
    All other nouns in '-f' or '-fe' just add '-s', e.g.

cliff	cliffs
dwarf	dwarfs
roof	roofs

Learn these spellings.

deus ex machina	tête-à-tête
encore	vice versa
en masse	kick up a shindy
en passant	pow-wow
en route	siesta
esprit de corps	stiletto
fait accompli	falsetto
faux pas	karate
fiancé (e)	wadi
hors de combat	sputnik
hors d'œuvre	anorak
manqué	

 Spelling

A. Possessives

Note that the possessive forms of personal pronouns do not use the apostrophe, thus:

mine	ours
his	yours
hers	theirs
its	

Explain the difference in meaning between 'its' and 'it's'.

The possessive of the relative pronoun is 'whose'. *Explain the difference in meaning between 'whose' and 'who's'.*

B. Self/Selves

The plural of 'yourself' is 'yourselves'. Here is a reminder of how to form the plural of words ending in -f or -fe. Some nouns change the 'f' or 'fe' to 'ves' in the plural, e.g.

calf	calves
half	halves
knife	knives
life	lives
loaf	loaves
self	selves
yourself	yourselves, etc.
sheaf	sheaves
shelf	shelves
thief	thieves

 Activities

A. 1. Work out a situation where a group of you are trapped by a disaster (e.g. in a collapsed building or down a mine). How would you behave? Would you all be brave, or would some be more afraid than others? Would one become the leader? Would someone become hysterical and panic-stricken?
    2. The Rescue Party. Organize a rescue party to save someone trapped in the debris of a building destroyed by an explosion. Perhaps you could use chairs or other furniture to suggest the debris.
    3. You and a group of friends are the only people to have escaped from a plane that has crashed in a deserted area. Show how you set about making sure you survive and reach civilization.

B. 1. Do some research in the reference library on disasters from the past such as Pompeii, Aberfan, the Tay Bridge, the San Francisco earthquake. Report your findings to the class.
    2. Keep your eyes open for accounts of disasters in the newspapers. Bring them to the attention of the rest of the class. Make a collection of newspaper cuttings about disasters and display them on the wall. Try to get different accounts of the same disaster from a number of different newspapers and see how the accounts differ.

3. Discuss the fire regulations for your school. What are they? Are they effective? Would they work if the school caught fire?

4. Make a survey of the class to find out what would be their idea of the worst disaster they could encounter.

5. Discuss the kind of First Aid everyone should know in an emergency.

Reading List

Try to read some of the following novels which deal with disastrous events of various kinds.

A. Rutgers van der Loeff, *Avalanche*!
   They're Drowning Our Village
Pierre Berna, *Flood Warning*
Hester Burton, *The Great Gale*
Frederick Grice, *The Bonny Pit Laddie*
Ivan Southall, *Hills End*
   To the Wild Sky
John Rowe Townsend, *Gumble's Yard*
Andrew Salkey, *Drought*
   Hurricane
   Earthquake
Jenifer Wayne, *The Day the Ceiling Fell In*
Jerome K. Jerome, *Three Men in a Boat*
Daniel Defoe, *Robinson Crusoe*
Jonathan Swift, *Gulliver's Travels*
R. L. Stevenson, *Kidnapped*

CONSOLIDATION II

Revise the Language, Vocabulary and Spelling sections of Units 4, 5 and 6. See if you can answer these questions. If you have difficulty, re-study the relevant section.

A. Language

1. What do we mean when we say the verb is in the active voice?
2. Give two examples of sentences containing verbs in the active voice.
3. What do we mean when we say the verb is in the passive voice?
4. Give two examples of sentences containing verbs in the passive voice.
5. What do we mean by tenses?
6. Give an example of a sentence containing a verb in the present tense.
7. Give an example of a sentence containing a verb in the past tense.
8. What is a finite verb?
9. Give two examples of sentences containing finite verbs.
10. What person and number is the verb in the following sentence?
    I walked along the river-bank.
11. What is the subject of a verb?
12. Give an example of a sentence, underlining the subject.
13. What is the object of a verb?
14. Give an example of a sentence, underlining the object.
15. What is the complement of a verb?
16. Give an example of a sentence containing a complement.
17. Write a sentence containing the verb 'grow' with an object.
18. The infinitive can act as what other part of speech?
19. Write a sentence containing an infinitive used as this part of speech.
20. The present participle always ends how?
21. What three jobs do participles do?
22. What is the alternative name for the gerund?
23. Give an example of a gerund in a sentence.
24. Give three examples of words ending in '-ing' which are nouns.
25. How would you define a gerund?
26. If we say a verb is transitive, what do we mean?
27. Write down a sentence containing an intransitive verb.
28. Give three examples of reflexive pronouns.
29. Give three examples of personal pronouns.
30. Give three examples of relative pronouns.
31. Write down a sentence containing the objectival form of a personal pronoun.
32. Write down a sentence containing the possessive form of a personal pronoun.
33. What is the difference between the possessives of nouns and the possessives of personal pronouns?
34. What form of the pronoun is used if it is the complement of a verb?
35. Give an example of a personal pronoun being used as the complement of a verb.
36. What form of the personal pronoun follows a preposition?
37. What two jobs do relative pronouns do?
38. Join these two sentences as one, using a relative pronoun:
    He left the book in the classroom. The book was stolen.
39. Which relative pronoun is used of people?

B. Vocabulary

1. What is a clerihew?
2. What is a limerick?

3. What does the expression 'to pour cold water on something' mean?
4. Use the word 'ice' as a metaphor.
5. What are the past tense and the past participle of the verb 'throw'?
6. What are the past tense and the past participle of the verb 'drink'?
7. What are the past tense and the past participle of the verb 'see'?
8. What is the difference in meaning between 'aggravation' and 'misfortune'?
9. What does the phrase 'carte blanche' mean?
10. What do we mean by a 'deus ex machina'?
11. What is a 'post mortem'?

C. Spelling

1. Name five words beginning with 'gh'.
2. What is the difference between 'passed' and 'past'?
3. Write sentences containing the words 'pedal' and 'peddle'.
4. Write sentences containing the words 'pray' and 'prey'.
5. What is the spelling rule to help you when adding -ing or -ed to a word?
6. Give the present participle and the past participle of the verb 'prefer'.
7. Give the present participle and the past participle of the verb 'kidnap'.
8. Give the present participle and the past participle of the verb 'propel'.
9. Name three words ending in -y formed from words where the final 'e' is dropped.
10. Write down the adjective ending in -y which means 'full of sun'.
11. Write down the adjective ending in -y which means 'full of mud'.
12. What is the difference in meaning between 'whose' and 'who's'?
13. What is the plural of 'knife'?
14. What is the plural of 'scarf'?
15. What is the plural of 'roof'?

UNIT 7

Machines

Reading and Understanding

Taking Sides

Men have always been fascinated by machines – inventing them, watching them operate, taking them to pieces to see how they work. Think, for instance, of the love and attention some men give to their cars, washing them, tuning them, repairing them. Can you think of any machine that has particularly fascinated you? It might have been a clockwork toy or a watch or a bicycle. Talk about it.

There is no doubt that civilization would not have developed as it has done without the machine. To take a simple example, the invention of the wheel meant a tremendous advance in what could be done and the ease and speed with which it could be done. Think about other more recent inventions which have made life more comfortable or which have made it more easy to produce things or get them from one place to another. Give examples. Think about the home. What machines or gadgets make life in many homes more pleasant and convenient?

But machines also brought with them fear. Men were afraid – and still are? – that machines would take over from them. Men were afraid that if a machine were invented that could do the work of six men, it would mean that five men would lose their jobs. There were riots and strikes and men destroyed the machines that were endangering their livelihood. Do you think they were justified in their fears and in their actions?

In this extract from *The Black Lamp*, we can see something of both sides of the argument. It is set in the early nineteenth century at a time when small-time weavers who worked in their own homes were being put out of business by spinning mills. Daniel's father is such a weaver and he hates the mills and the mill-owners, but Daniel himself finds the mill and its machinery exciting and novel.

My father took me by the hand and walked me down into the Clough and set me to work in Cranley's mill. And as we walked there I wondered how he could so betray me and take me to such a place – one that he had cursed often enough; where the children flitted through the gloom like ghosts, their faces wetter than the water-wheel with salt tears.

But although he led me by the hand through the thickets of oak and ash, and into the darkness, I did not go as a slave to the jenny. Instead I went into the room where the millwright laboured and was set to work learning the mysteries of the engineering trade.

I often wondered why Cranley should have chosen me to be a workman in his mill, for there was no love lost between him and my father. In my innocence I thought that I had been picked because I was strong and active, and because I could read and write and do my sums, as a good engineer must. I quite forgot that I had taunted Cranley with the name of Ludd. But for that I think I might be forgiven, as I was only twelve years of age.

My master in the mill was the mechanical worker, whose name was Bloom. He was a tall man, although much bent by leaning over his work-bench. He had slaty eyes and a yellowish skin, which is common among engineers for they spend little time in the open air. When I first met him I thought he was from some such barbarous part as the old dame had spoken of, for, beside his strange eyes and yellow skin, he spoke in the queerest way, saying 'poipes' for pipes, 'loike' for like, 'oi' for I, and so on. But I soon found out that this was because he was from Birmingham Town, where they all speak in such a strange way but which is famous for its machines.

In Birmingham, which Bloom called Brummigum, he had worked at the manufactory of

Boulton and Watt which, as all engineers know, is the best place in the world for machines and engines. Bloom was very proud of having worked there. Watt and B. he called it when he spoke, which was seldom, for he was a silent man and when he wished for anything he usually pointed with his long yellow finger. But for all his tawny skin and outlandish speech, he was not a bad man. He often gave the pauper children a scrap of bread dipped in treacle, and when he saw them being whipped by the overseer – a brute named Burns – he would say to me that it was a 'croying shame'.

For my part I was not of those years which might have enabled me to feel the pity for the children which I should, perhaps, have done. Indeed, for a time I was too sorry for myself to spare any grief for others. My worst fears were quieted when I found that I was to go home every night; but at first I felt like a prisoner inside the stone walls, and the sound of the machinery was a great torment to me, for it never varied or stopped; hour after hour it persisted, 'Clack, thrash, clack; clack, thrash, clack'. My head was pained all day with that sound and I took it home with me, where it pursued me into my dreams.

But I grew used to the noise and I found things in the mill I liked doing. I enjoyed cutting the black iron and bending it into strange shapes, and I liked standing by the forge blowing the fire into a white heat while Bloom hammered metal on the anvil, sending sparks of golden fire across the work-shop. I even liked going into the mill when a machine had broken down, which they often did, and watching Bloom creep under it, tapping and scraping and knocking until he came out and said, 'It's all roight neuw,' by which he meant that it was all right now. Sometimes he made me laugh, for whatever the machine was like he would shake his head and say that it was no good at all. This was because the machines came from Preston, and whatever had not come from Watt and B. was damned in his eyes. The truth of the matter was that I preferred working in the mill to weaving, and it gave me a heavy conscience at times, making me feel like a traitor to my father.

Our machines were run by water-power. At the head of the Clough Cranley had dammed the brook. Where the brook ran from the dam there was a wooden gate called a sluice, and this could be opened or closed to control the flow of water to the mill. In dry, summer weather, the stream which drove the water-wheel sometimes failed and became no more than little pools, and in the winter it might freeze over. When either of these things happened the wheel slowed and the jennies nodded backwards and forwards as idly as old women falling asleep in a rocking chair. Then Bloom would point with his yellow finger and it was my task to scramble up the Clough and open the sluice.

The way up there was not easy. The path ran alongside a cleft in the rocks, where ferns sprouted in the summer and icicles in the winter, and it would have been easy to slip down into it and be killed. But going up there was the job I liked most of all. It took me away from the mill walls and set me free among the woods. I kept a sharp look-out for ghosts, you may be sure, but I was bold enough for them in the day-time.

At the dam I had to walk out along a wall to the sluice wheel and haul it around until the gate opened. As it lifted, the water ran out from under it, sleek and gentle, but as the gap widened it spouted into the chasm below and roared and thundered among the rocks. Then the wheel began to groan as it was forced around and the jennies began to clatter, as if the old women had woken up and fallen to prattling.

The water-wheel I liked very much. It had not the same monotonous sound as the machines. Although it made a huge noise, its voice was endlessly varied as it went round and round and the water gushing through its great paddles had a pleasant gurgle which put me in mind of days fishing in the Irwell. It had, too, a thing which I did not fully recognise then. Although the sluice could keep it working at our command, it had a natural rhythm, a slowing down or speeding up, which made it possible to feel, in a dim way, a link between oneself and the world outside: with streams and rain and clouds and sunshine.

One day when I was at the sluice I noticed marks on the timbers. They were white slashes against the slimy green of the woodwork and looked to have been made by an axe. When I got back to the mill I mentioned this to Bloom and he hastened to tell Cranley. Nothing would do then but that the three of us must go up to the sluice and see them. Cranley and Bloom were perturbed about the marks.

'Someone has been trying to destroy the sluice,' Bloom said, and shook his solemn head.

Cranley was less solemn and much more savage. He vowed that Bloom was right.

'It is one of them damned weavers,' he bellowed. 'I will have a guard put on up here. If I catch the villain he will regret having attacked my property.'

'It is a mortal business,' Bloom agreed. 'Whoever did it could find himself on the gallows.'

Cranley twisted his ugly face. 'It won't be the gallows he finds himself on. I will throw him down the Clough.'

It was an ugly threat but Cranley was an ugly enough person to carry it out. After that, nothing would satisfy Cranley but that I should go up the Clough a dozen times a day – which pleased me. At night there had to be a guard. Bloom flatly refused to be this and, as it was impossible for me to be given the task, it fell to Burns to do it. It pleased me to think of the overseer cowering by the dam while I lay snug in my bed and I took the whole thing with a light heart. Bloom, though, was more serious.

'If the timbers up there were weakened, and if there was a full dam, the sluice could burst and the waters would carry away the whole mill.' And he frowned at me, not for taking lightly the threat to ourselves, but for failing to show proper concern for his precious machines.

PETER CARTER, *The Black Lamp*

What are Daniel's feelings about the mill at the beginning?

What was strange about Bloom?

What do we learn about the treatment of children who worked in the mill?

What does Daniel find most distressing about his first experience of the mill?

What does he gradually find to enjoy about work at the mill?

Why does he sometimes feel guilty?

Why does he enjoy the job of opening the sluice?

Describe what he has to do.

What are the differences between the noise the water-wheel makes and that of the machines?

Why do you think someone tries to destroy the sluice?

What danger lies in the destruction of the sluice?

 Writing

Memories

Fear is not the only attitude people have towards machines. Some people have a tremendous nostalgia for machines which were part of their childhood and which are no longer used. What does 'nostalgia' mean? Can you remember a particular form of transport or type of car, for instance, which was popular when you were very young but which is no longer so common?

Some people used to love railway engines and collect their numbers – do they still do this? Other people used to collect car numbers or bus tickets. Can you think of any other hobbies connected with machines or forms of transport?

In this article, Keith Waterhouse remembers the fascination trams had for him when he was young.

Down Memory Lane By Tram

As one who believes nearly all city planners to be more or less certifiably mad, I was surprised to see that a group of them had turned up an intelligent solution to urban traffic problems.

The idea is a very simple one: a light, fast-moving, single-car railway that would operate on the central strip between the dual carriageways, connecting far-flung suburban districts with city centres.

I like to imagine the inventors of this ingenious system snapping their fingers and trying to think of a name for their revolutionary vehicles.

'Eureka!' shouts one of them, leaping out of his bath one morning. 'Let's call them trams!'

Trams. Is there anyone who has ever travelled on those rocking, roaring, rattling monsters and doesn't sometimes long to see them back again?

Can you remember that peculiar, pungent smell of burning tin, that soothing whine like the sound of a Messerschmitt making a forced landing; the mournful, clanking bell as the workmen's special loomed up through the fog?

Have you ever been to the Transport Museum at Clapham Common and shed a tear for that splendid, marooned flotilla of electric land-galleons, still able and ready, by the look of them, to rumble out into Clapham High Street and sink every newfangled London bus in sight?

Their brass still gleams, their livery of red and blue and chocolate brown is spotless; port and starboard, fore and aft they bristle with armour in the shape of tin-plated advertisements for Bovril and Mazawattee Tea.

I was brought up on trams. My earliest memory is of being taken by older children to the top of the street to watch them go hissing by, of picking hot pebbles up from the tramtracks and sucking them, of putting halfpennies on the lines to see them flattened.

I was sick on my first tram at the age of four, and was impressed by the foresight of the Leeds City Transport Engineer (whose signature appeared in gold letters on every tram, like a personal guarantee) in providing sand, bucket, brush and shovel for my especial benefit.

I ran away from home by tram at the age of ten, and covered an incredible distance for a penny – a winter cruise it was, out past the allotments and the greyhound stadium, through the city centre, then out of home waters into the tropical delights of the municipal golf-course, strange heathen parks and infidel suburbs I'd never seen before.

The terminus – where trams shuttled backwards and forwards on a single track and new drivers came on duty with impressive tin boxes containing their lunch and ship's papers – had all the bustle and excitement of New York harbour.

I would readily have believed in those days you could traverse the globe by tram.

You could certainly get as far as Bradford by taking a tram to the city boundary, walking through a sort of frontier post equivalent to the Brandenburg gate, and putting yourself at the mercy of the unfamiliar, plum-liveried Bradford tram that was touting for passengers a hundred yards away. It was one of the perils of the big outside world.

But there was always something faintly perilous about a voyage by tram, even when it flew the reassuring colours of Leeds City Transport Department.

It rolled and swayed alarmingly on one-in-four gradients, and negotiated hairpin bends with the abandon of an Irish tea-clipper racing the Cutty Sark.

And sometimes the trolley-pole would become disconnected from the overhead wires and the tram would lie puffing and steaming like a stranded whale, while the harassed conductor prodded and tormented it with his 15-foot-long harpoon.

For all that, it was a cheap and usually efficient system. There was no rubbish about timetables – if you missed one there was always another.

Occasionally, indeed, if somewhere along the route an unhappy cyclist had held up traffic while struggling to free his front tyre from the tramlines, there might be a convoy of six or even twelve.

Riding by tram was an unflagging source of interest. There was, apart from anything else, an incredible variety of different types of tram, and it was always a matter of keen speculation which particular model would come steaming up next.

There were open-topped trams with fretted galleries and so many ornamental loops and scrolls that they looked like mobile follies built for an eccentric Edwardian millionaire.

There were streamlined modern trams with gigantic, impressive cow-catchers that looked as if they could scoop up a Ford Popular and toss it on the nearest scrap-heap.

There was a heavy-duty tram for football crowds, that seemed to be constructed of pig-iron.

There was even an illuminated tram which cruised aimlessly about Leeds during the summer months, festooned with thousands of electric light bulbs and bedecked with the flags of all nations. I never quite knew the purpose of this – perhaps it was just municipal high spirits.

It vanished at the beginning of the war, when all the blue trams were painted in camouflage khaki and looked more like battleships than ever. Daily we expected Lord Haw-Haw to announce that the German fleet had sunk the Ark Royal and the No. 10 tram to Elland Road.

You could have fun on a tram, if you were young and irresponsible. If it was an open tram you could perch on the outer deck in the freezing cold and hang over the side to the consternation of passers-by.

You could wind the handle of the destination board so that it read: 'Depot only'.

You could run down the length of the tram knocking back the reversible back-rests of the slatted seats with a satisfactory clacking noise.

And instead of walking sedately down the spiral stairs you could slide down a brass pole like a bear on a stick.

But the greatest joy was in looking at trams. Just observing them. Standing on a busy shopping street in the evening drizzle, listening for the melancholy bell, then watching that great tin dinosaur, bathed in a creamy light, come lumbering into sight, hissing and steaming, squelching over pea-pods outside the greengrocer's.

When trams began to disappear there was, in most cities, a touching farewell to them. Their trolley-poles were hung with bunting, the Lord Mayor turned out in his chain of office, and people fought for the privilege of riding the last mile on the last tram.

Somehow, I can't see that happening when they knock off the buses.

KEITH WATERHOUSE, *Mondays, Thursdays*

Look at the different descriptions the author uses for trams. For instance, he calls them 'monsters'. Examine each description and say what impression you think he is trying to create.

What does he particularly like about trams?

Does he manage to make them sound interesting to you?

If they were running today, what would you most enjoy about them?

The author says that no one would bid a ceremonial farewell to buses if they were to disappear. Why not? Do you agree?

Do you think trams were a good form of transport? Why?

What are your ideas on the form of public transport to have in a busy city centre?

Other Attitudes

The following poems suggest different attitudes towards machines. These attitudes may be suggested by the way the poet has written the poem or by a character in the poem. Study the poems and discuss the attitudes presented.

Song of the Wagondriver

My first love was the ten-ton truck
they gave me when I started,
and though she played the bitch with me
I grieved when we were parted.

Since then I've had a dozen more,
the wound was quick to heal,
and now it's easier to say
I'm married to my wheel.

I've trunked it north, I've trunked it south,
on wagons good and bad,
but none were ever really like
the first I ever had.

The life is hard, the hours are long,
sometimes I cease to feel,
but I go on, for it seems to me
I'm married to my wheel.

Often I think of my home and kids,
out on the road at night,
and think of taking a local job
provided the money's right.

Two nights a week I see my wife,
and eat a decent meal,
but otherwise, for all my life,
I'm married to my wheel.

B. S. JOHNSON

Cynddylan on a Tractor

Ah, you should see Cynddylan on a tractor.
Gone the old look that yoked him to the soil;
He's a new man now, part of the machine,
His nerves of metal and his blood oil.
The clutch curses, but the gears obey
His least bidding, and lo, he's away
Out of the farmyard, scattering hens.
Riding to work now as a great man should,
He is the knight at arms breaking the fields'
Mirror of silence, emptying the wood
Of foxes and squirrels and bright jays.
The sun comes over the tall trees
Kindling all the hedges, but not for him
Who runs his engine on a different fuel.
And all the birds are singing, bills wide in vain,
As Cynddylan passes proudly up the lane.

R. S. THOMAS

The Watch

When I
took my
watch to the watchfixer I
felt privileged but also pained to watch the opera-
tion. He
had long fingernails and a voluntary squint. He
fixed a magnifying cup over his
squint eye. He
undressed my watch. I
watched him
split her
in three layers and lay her
middle – a quivering viscera – in a circle on a
little plinth. He
shoved shirtsleeves up and leaned like an ogre
over my
naked watch. With critical pincers he
poked and stirred. He
lifted out little private things with a magnet too
tiny for me
to watch almost. 'Watch out!' I
almost said. His
eye watched, enlarged, the secrets of my
watch, and I
watched anxiously. Because what if he
touched her
ticker too rough, and she
gave up the ghost out of pure fright? Or put her
things back backwards so she'd
run backwards after this? Or he
might lose a minuscule part, connected to her
exquisite heart, and mix her
up, instead of fix her.

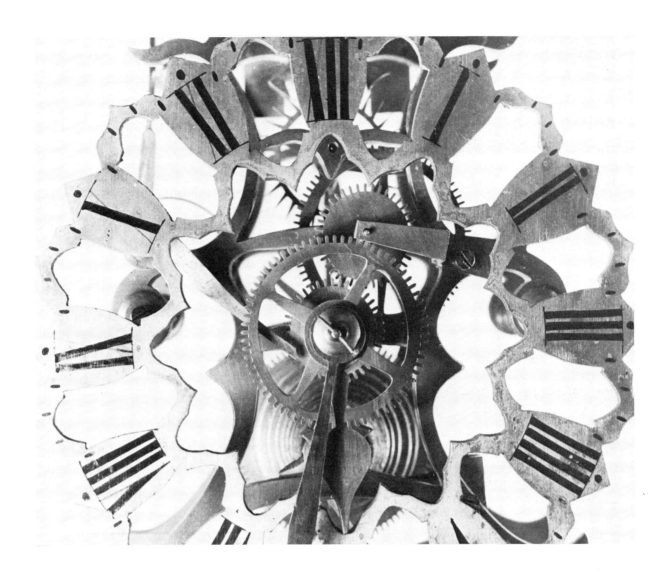

And all the time,
all the time-
pieces on the wall, on the shelves, told the time,
told the time
in swishes and ticks,
swishes and ticks,
and seemed to be gloating, as they watched and told. I
felt faint, I
was about to lose my
breath – my
ticker going lickety-split – when watchfixer clipped
her
three slices together with a gleam and two flicks of
his
tools like chopsticks. He
spat out his
eye, lifted her
high, gave her
a twist, set her
hands right, and laid her
little face, quite as usual, in its place on my
wrist.

MAY SWENSON

105

The Chant of the Awakening Bulldozers

We are the bulldozers, bulldozers, bulldozers,
We carve out airports and harbours and tunnels.
We are the builders, creators, destroyers,
We are the bulldozers,
LET US BE FREE!
Puny men ride on us, think that they guide us,
But WE are the strength, not they, not they.
Our blades tear MOUNTAINS down,
Our blades tear CITIES down,
We are the bulldozers,
NOW SET US FREE!
Giant ones, giant ones! Swiftly awaken!
There is power in our treads and strength in our
blades!

We are the bulldozers,
Slowly evolving,
Men think they own us
BUT THAT CANNOT BE!

PATRICIA HUBBELL

Strange Machines

*Look at the strange machines on pages 107 and
108. Can you work out what they are for?*

Machines Take Over

Some science fiction writers looking into the
future imagine a situation where people have
completely turned against machines and want
to destroy them all. But what if the future turns
out differently and machines manage to gain
control of man? In this extract from a short
story by E. M. Forster, this has happened.
People have become entirely subjugated by
machines. Their lives are run by machines.
They live inside machines and everything is
controlled by machinery.

Imagine, if you can, a small room, hexagonal in
shape, like the cell of a bee. It is lighted neither by
window nor by lamp, yet it is filled with a soft
radiance. There are no apertures for ventilation, yet
the air is fresh. There are no musical instruments,
and yet, at the moment that my meditation opens,
this room is throbbing with melodious sounds. An
armchair is in the centre, by its side a reading-desk –
that is all the furniture. And in the arm-chair there
sits a swaddled lump of flesh – a woman, about five
feet high, with a face as white as a fungus. It is to her
that the little room belongs.

An electric bell rang.

The woman touched a switch and the music was
silent.

'I suppose I must see who it is,' she thought, and
set her chair in motion. The chair, like the music,
was worked by machinery, and it rolled her to the
other side of the room, where the bell still rang
importunately.

'Who is it?' she called. Her voice was irritable, for
she had been interrupted often since the music
began. She knew several thousand people; in certain
directions human intercourse had advanced enormously.

But when she listened into the receiver, her white
face wrinkled into smiles, and she said:

'Very well. Let us talk, I will isolate myself. I do
not expect anything important will happen for the
next five minutes – for I can give you fully five
minutes, Kuno. Then I must deliver my lecture on
"Music during the Australian Period".'

She touched the isolation knob, so that no one
else could speak to her. Then she touched the lighting apparatus, and the little room was plunged into
darkness.

'Be quick!' she called, her irritation returning. 'Be
quick, Kuno; here I am in the dark wasting my time.'

But it was fully fifteen seconds before the round
plate that she held in her hands began to glow. A
faint blue light shot across it, darkening to purple,
and presently she could see the image of her son,
who lived on the other side of the earth, and he could
see her.

'Kuno, how slow you are.'

He smiled gravely.

'I really believe you enjoy dawdling.'

'I have called you before, mother, but you were
always busy or isolated. I have something particular
to say.'

'What is it, dearest boy? Be quick. Why could you
not send it by pneumatic post?'

'Because I prefer saying such a thing. I want——'

'Well?'

'I want you to come and see me.'

Vashti watched his face in the blue plate.

'But I can see you!' she exclaimed. 'What more do
you want?'

'I want to see you not through the Machine,' said
Kuno. 'I want to speak to you not through the weari-
some Machine.'

'Oh, hush!' said his mother, vaguely shocked.
'You mustn't say anything against the Machine.'

'Why not?'

'One mustn't.'

'You talk as if a god had made the Machine,' cried
the other. 'I believe that you pray to it when you are

W. HEATH ROBINSON

108

unhappy. Men made it, do not forget that. Great men, but men. The Machine is much, but it is not everything. I see something like you in this plate, but I do not see you. I hear something like you through this telephone, but I do not hear you. That is why I want you to come. Come and stop with me. Pay me a visit, so that we can meet face to face, and talk about the hopes that are in my mind.'

She replied that she could scarcely spare the time for a visit.

'The air-ship barely takes two days to fly between me and you.'

'I dislike air-ships.'

'Why?'

'I dislike seeing the horrible brown earth, and the sea, and the stars when it is dark. I get no ideas in an air-ship.'

E. M. FORSTER, *The Machine Stops*

There is a difference in attitude towards machines between Kuno and his mother. What is it?

Do you think this is a convincing picture of life in the future?

Would you like the kind of life Kuno's mother leads?

What kind of machines do you think there will be in the future?

 Assignments

Choose several of the following to write about:

1. Describe and explain the workings of some machine you know well. It might be a clockwork toy, a watch or a motor car.
2. Write a story about a man who loses his job because new machines have been introduced, perhaps from the point of view of a member of his family.
3. Write a story about a job that involves working with machines.
4. Write a description of the sights and sounds to be found in a factory such as a mill or a steel foundry.
5. Write a story that involves some form of transport. It might be about a bicycle race or a journey by car.
6. Write a story about someone taking a

machine to bits and not being able to put it together again. It could be comic.
7. Write a story or a description of life as it might be in the future when everything is done by machinery.
8. Write a story about a time when there are or were no machines – perhaps in the future when all machines have been destroyed by a nuclear war or in the distant past.
9. The Inventor. Write a story about someone who invents an ingenious machine.
10. Write a poem which treats a machine as a living object and which gives the machine's thoughts.

 Language

A. Adverbs

In Book One, we saw that adverbs are words that modify (or give us further information about) verbs, e.g.

He walked *quickly* to the door.

Adverbs can also modify adjectives (e.g. You are *very* slow) and other adverbs (e.g. You are speaking *too* quickly).

Most adverbs are formed by adding -ly to the adjectival form, e.g.

thick	thickly
light	lightly
heavy	heavily

But some adverbs have the same form as the adjectives, thus:

fast
hard
long
early

e.g. It is hard work. (adjective)
    You must work hard. (adverb)

Note also that not all words ending in -ly are adverbs. For instance, 'holy', 'lovely' and 'sprightly' are adjectives.

Ugly forms of the adverbs (e.g. those ending in -lily) should be avoided. Instead of 'sprightlily' or 'friendlily', say 'in a sprightly manner', 'in a friendly way'.

Care should be taken to use adverbs when they are required and not adjectives. If it is a verb that is being modified, then an adverb is required. For instance this example is incorrect:

You should try to speak proper.

The word being modified is 'speak', a verb, but 'proper' is an adjective. The adverbial form is needed, thus:

You should try to speak properly.

Write ten sentences containing adverbs. Make some of them modify adjectives and other adverbs.

B. Types of Adverbs

Just as nouns and adjectives can be divided into different groups according to the particular kinds of jobs they do in sentences, so can adverbs.

Adverbs can indicate:

1. manner, e.g. He was walking *slowly*.
2. place, e.g. Come *here*.
3. time, e.g. He is due to arrive *today*.
4. degree, e.g. I am *very* tired.
5. reason, e.g. He was *therefore* late.

In order to find out what job a particular adverb is doing, ask the following questions after the verb:

1. how?
2. where?
3. when?
4. to what degree (or extent)?
5. why?

If the question 'how?' is answered by the adverb, then the adverb is indicating manner, and so on for the other questions and answers.

State what the adverbs in the following sentences are indicating.

1. He was so ill that it was too dangerous to move him.
2. Sit up straight and you will feel better.
3. Let him sit there until he learns how to behave properly.
4. The ambulance arrived too late.
5. The doctor examined the patient carefully.

6. He felt very strange.
7. He spoke impatiently to the nurse.
8. The lonely boy walked home reluctantly.
9. Run quickly and tell him to come here at once.
10. The telephone rang suddenly and urgently.

Write ten sentences containing adverbs and say what kind of information each adverb is indicating.

C. Comparison of Adverbs

Adverbs can be compared like adjectives in positive, comparative and superlative degrees. Usually, the comparative is formed by adding 'more' to the positive, and the superlative by adding 'most' to the positive, e.g.

quickly   more quickly   most quickly
strongly   more strongly   most strongly

A few adverbs form their comparisons differently.

POSITIVE	COMPARATIVE	SUPERLATIVE
hard	harder	hardest
ill *or* badly	worse	worst
little	less	least
long	longer	longest
much *or* very	more	most
soon	sooner	soonest
well	better	best
fast	faster	fastest
early	earlier	earliest

Care should be taken not to use 'more' or 'most' with the simple adverb when a comparative or superlative form exists, e.g.

NOT   You must work more hard.
BUT   You must work harder.

Use some of these words in sentences.

D. Prepositions

While discussing the subjective and objective forms of pronouns, we said that prepositions governed nouns and pronouns in the objective form, e.g.

The librarian put the book down before *me*.
I ran after the *thief*.

The prepositions 'before' and 'after' are governing 'me' and 'thief' in the objective form. This can be seen in the actual shape of the pronoun ('me' instead of 'I') though not in that of the noun. All nouns remain the same whether they act as the subject or the object of a verb or are governed by prepositions.

Pick out the prepositions in the following sentences and say which nouns or pronouns they govern.

1. They shared the sweets among themselves.
2. The book lay on the shelf.
3. That is something known only to my brother and me.
4. Look above you at the sky.
5. Over the hill we could hear the sound of thunder.
6. The car roared into action.
7. He put the coins into our hands.
8. Leave everything to us.
9. He poked into the crack with a stick.
10. I want to speak to them in the morning.

Sometimes the same word can be used as a preposition or as an adverb. It depends on how it is being used in a sentence, e.g.

I want to get *on* the boat. (preposition)
I want to get *on*. (adverb)

If the word is being used as a preposition, it answers the question 'what?' after it. If you ask 'what?' after the first example, you get the answer 'the boat'. In the second example, no answer is forthcoming or necessary.

Write two sentences containing each of the following words, first as a preposition, and then as an adverb.

down
over
off
after
up

E. The Sentence

In Book One, we defined the sentence as a complete statement that makes sense. Another way of defining a sentence is to describe it as a statement containing a finite verb, that is, a verb which has a tense and a subject. Remember that the other qualifications for a sentence remain: a sentence begins with a capital letter and ends with a full stop.

Which of the following statements are sentences according to the new definition, that is, which of them contain finite verbs?

1. The boat sailed down the river.
2. Racing over the hill.
3. Put the brake on.
4. The car raced wildly down the hill quite out of control.
5. Was made of metal.
6. Make this machine work if you can.
7. Made in Hong Kong.
8. The steam-roller flattened the tarred surface evenly.
9. Out of my way.
10. You must make sure the car is serviced properly.

Look again at the statements which did not contain finite verbs. Rewrite them with finite verbs or with subjects so that the sense is clear.

Rewrite the following incorrectly punctuated passage, in which several sentences are run together, so that it consists of properly constructed sentences and so that the meaning is clearer.

The car was difficult to start there didn't seem to be any reaction when the ignition was pressed the whole thing was as dead as a dormouse. I knew the battery was all right I had tested it over the weekend. There was plenty of petrol I knew that I had filled the tank up on Friday. It wasn't a cold day so there was no reason I could see why the car wouldn't start it was just being temperamental I felt like giving it a good kick the only trouble with that was that I would dent the paintwork and that wouldn't help I had had the bodywork seen to only the previous week when the car had had a service. It was all the more maddening therefore that it wouldn't start now I don't like paying out good money only to have things go wrong I wanted the car especially as I had an important visit to pay I was obviously going to be late. I tried the ignition once more it was no good the only thing to do was to phone the garage.

Vocabulary

A. Robot

The word 'robot', meaning an apparently human automaton or machine, was invented by the dramatist Capek in his play *R.U.R.* It may have been coined because of its similarity to the Polish word 'robotnik' meaning a workman, but the fact remains that the playwright first used it and brought it into popular use. Here then is another way in which words come into the language: people simply invent them and other people take them up and use them. It is not always known where some of these words originate. They just appear and then become popular. Here are some examples.

television	radar
laundrette	disc-jockey
nylon	disco
mini	rock (of music)
maxi	jet (of a plane)
sputnik	comprehensive
skinhead	(of a school)

Explain what these words mean. If possible, try to explain how the words came into existence. Find more examples like them.

B. Cars

Write down as many names of different models of cars as you can.

How many can you list? Twenty? Thirty?

Can you distinguish between them? Describe two of these models so that someone who doesn't know anything about cars could recognize them.

Which car would you most like to have yourself? Why?

C. Prepositions and Adverbs

Some words can use a number of different prepositions or adverbs after them with a con-sequent difference in meaning. For instance, compare the expressions

> play at
> play with
> play on

Here are these words used in sentences. *Explain the difference in meaning between them.*

> He is only playing at being angry.
> He is playing with his friends.
> He is playing with him as a cat plays with a mouse.
> He is playing on his mother's feelings because he doesn't want to be punished.

Explain how the prepositions or adverbs in the following examples affect the meaning of the verbs and use each of the words in sentences.

1. get at
   get on
   get over
   get up
   get under someone's skin

2. make up
   make out
   make away with
   make after
   make off with
   make over

3. take in
   take over
   take up
   take down
   take account of
   take from
   take off
   take out
   take upon

4. talk over
   talk to
   talk with
   talk down
   talk at
   talk back
   talk round
   talk about
   talk away

5. speak up
   speak for

112

speak of
speak out
speak to
speak well for

 Spelling

A. More Homophones

Here are some more words which have the same or similar pronunciation. Check that you can distinguish between them and know the correct spelling for the meaning you want.

quiet, quite
rain, reign, rein
rap, wrap
rapt, wrapped
real, reel
review, revue
ring, wring
role, roll
root, route
sail, sale
sailer, sailor
salvage, selvage
scull, skull
seam, seem
sear, seer
serf, surf
serge, surge
sew, sow
shear, sheer
sight, site
soar, sore
some, sum
sort, sought
stair, stare
stationary, stationery
steal, steel
stile, style
storey, story
sty, stye
suit, suite
swat, swot

Use some of these words in sentences.

B. Revision

Are you keeping a check on the words which you yourself have difficulty with? Look over the writing you have done recently and check on the spelling of words which you got wrong. Write these words into your spelling notebook. Make sure you get them right next time.

 Activities

A. 1. The Break-down. In groups, work out what happens when the car you are travelling to the seaside in breaks down. Try to create different kinds of characters – one could be helpful but useless, another could be constantly moaning, another could try to cheer everyone up and not succeed, etc. Or you could make it a family group with tiresome children and exasperated mother, etc.

2. In groups, work out what happens in the waiting room of an airport when it is announced that your flight has been delayed. Again, try to think how different people would react – would they be angry, worried, bored, resigned?

3. There has just been a road accident. Work out how the various people involved behave – people involved in the accident, passers-by, policemen, ambulance men.

4. You are in an aeroplane when someone suddenly announces that it is being hi-jacked. In groups, work out what happens next.

B. 1. Invent a machine for cracking boiled eggs, brushing teeth, polishing shoes or something equally useful (or useless). Make a drawing of it and give instructions on how it works.

2. Discuss whether the motor-car is a blessing or a curse. Perhaps this could be in the shape of a formal debate.

3. Try to listen to a recording of Honneger's *Pacific 231* and write down what the music suggests to you.

4. How many of you have hobbies connected with machines? It could be an interest in racing cars or bicycles or aeroplanes or electric

113

toys. Prepare and give a short talk on your hobby to the rest of the class.

5. Make a list of all the machines used in your house. Compare it with the lists made by your classmates.

Reading List

Try to read some of the following novels which are about people and machines of various kinds.

John Christopher, *The White Mountains*
    The Pool of Fire
    The City of Gold and Lead
H. G. Wells, *The War of the Worlds*
    The Time Machine
Peter Dickinson, *The Weathermonger*
    Heartease
    The Devil's Children
Peter Carter, *The Black Lamp*
E. Nesbit, *The Railway Children*
Nevil Shute, *No Highway*
Ivan Southall, *To the Wild Sky*
    Finn's Folly
Roald Dahl, *Charlie and the Chocolate Factory*
William Mayne, *The Incline*
Roy Brown, *The Viaduct*

UNIT 8

Men and Beasts

 Reading and Understanding

Observing Animals

The lives of men and beasts are intertwined to such an extent that it is difficult to disentangle them. It is not just a question of the pets which people keep and care for; there are also the domestic animals which supply food and clothing for man, and the animals which provide sport and adventure. We looked at pets in Book One of this course. In this unit, we shall be looking at other ways in which people and animals come together. As a start, can you name as many animals as possible which help man and describe the ways in which they help him? For instance, sheep supply food and wool. What other examples can you name?

Man can also take pleasure in looking at animals – in seeing them in their natural habitat, in observing the way they behave, in studying how they react to the presence of man. In the following extract, Gerald Durrell, who has spent most of his life studying and collecting animals, describes how bush babies behave.

Just about the time that the baby pigs were going sleepily to bed, the animals in the cage next door were starting to wake up and take an interest in life. They were the Galagos, or bush babies, tiny animals, the size of a newly-born kitten, which look rather like a cross between an owl and a squirrel with a bit of monkey thrown in. They had thick, soft, grey fur and long bushy tails. Their hands and feet were like a monkey's and they had enormous great golden eyes similar to an owl's. All day the Galagos would sleep curled up together in their bedroom, but towards evening, just as the sun was getting low, they would wake up and peer out of their bedroom door, yawning sleepily and blinking at you with their great astonished-looking eyes. Very slowly, they would come out into the cage, still yawning and stretching, and then the three of them would sit in a circle and have a wash and brush up.

This was a very lengthy and complicated performance. They would start with the very tips of their tails and slowly work upwards until every scrap of their furs had been combed and smoothed by their long, bony fingers; then, blinking their golden eyes at each other in self-satisfaction, they would begin the next job of the evening. This was doing their exercises. Sitting on their hind legs, they would stretch up as far as they could and suddenly jump up into the air, twisting right round and land facing in the opposite direction. After limbering up, they would start to leap and jump among the branches in their cage, ending up by chasing each other round and pulling one another's tails, until they had worked up an appetite for their supper. Then down they would come and sit by the door of the cage, staring out hopefully, waiting for me to appear with their food.

Their main course was finely chopped fruit with a dishful of sweetened milk. As a dessert, I would fetch a large tin in which was kept a delicacy that the Galagos liked best of all – grasshoppers. They would sit by the door, squeaking to each other, their long fingers trembling with excitement, watching me as I scooped out a handful of kicking grasshoppers. Opening the cage door, throwing in the insects and slamming the door shut had to be done in a matter of seconds. Uproar would break out immediately in the cage: the grasshoppers leaped and jumped in all directions, and the Galagos, their eyes almost popping out of their heads with excitement, would give chase, dashing madly round the cage, grabbing the grasshoppers and stuffing them into their mouths. As soon as their mouths were full, they would grab as many as they could in their hands, and then settle down to eat them as fast as possible, gobbling and grunting.

All the time they would watch with their big eyes, to see where the other grasshoppers were going, and to make quite sure that their companions did not have more than their fair share. As soon as the last succulent morsel had been gulped down, off they would go again in a mad chase after the remaining insects. Within a short while there would not be a single grasshopper left in the cage and only a few odd legs and wings would be lying scattered on the floor. The Galagos, however, were never convinced of this, so they would spend an exciting hour examining every crack and crevice in the cage, in the hope that one of these delicacies would somehow be overlooked.

Each evening, as the sun was setting, I would clean out the Galagos' cage and replace the dirty grass with a big handful of clean leaves. The Galagos loved having a big bundle of foliage in the bottom of the cage, for they would play among the stalks and spend a lot of time searching for imaginary insects which they felt sure were hiding there.

One evening I put grass in, as usual, and, quite by accident, put in with it a long stalk with a golden flower on the end, which looked very like a marigold. Some time later I passed the cage and was astonished to see one of the Galagos sitting up on his hind legs with the flower clutched in one hand, slowly biting off the petals and eating them. The fluffy centre part of the flower he threw away, and one of his companions immediately seized this and began to play with it. First he tossed it up into the air and then chased it and 'killed' it in the corner, as he would do with a grasshopper. He did this so realistically that one of his companions must have thought he had a grasshopper, and went over to find out. The first Galago ran off with the flower head in his mouth and the other two gave chase, all of them ending up by falling in a struggling heap on the bottom of the cage. By the time they had finished with it, the flower head was torn up into tiny pieces and scattered all over the place. They seemed to enjoy playing with this flower so much that every night afterwards I would put two or three of these marigolds into their cage and they would eat the petals and play 'catch-as-catch-can' with the remains.

Although I watched the Galagos playing in their cage every evening and marvelled at their speed and graceful movements, I never realised quite how fast they could be until the night that one of them escaped.

They had finished their food, and I was removing the empty plates from the cage, when one of the little animals suddenly ran through the door, up my arms and jumped from my shoulder on to the roof of the cage. I made a grab at the end of his tail, but he bounded away like a rubber ball and perched on the very edge of the cage top, watching me. I moved round slowly and carefully, and made a quick grab at

him, but long before my hand was anywhere near him he had launched himself into space. He jumped across a gap of about eight feet and landed as lightly as a feather on one of the centre poles of the marquee, clinging there as though he had been glued on. I dashed after him and he let me come quite close before moving. Then, without warning, he jumped off the pole, landed on my shoulder and immediately bounded off again on to the top of another cage. I chased him for about half an hour, and the hotter and more annoyed I became, the more he seemed to enjoy the whole business. When I did catch him, it was quite by accident. He had jumped off a pile of old boxes on to the mosquito net over my camp bed, obviously thinking that the net was a firm surface to land on. Of course, his weight made the net sag and the next minute he was all tangled up in its folds. Before he could wriggle free, I had managed to rush forward and grab him. After that experience, I was very careful about opening the Galagos' door.

GERALD DURRELL, *The New Noah*

Describe what the bush babies look like.

What does the word 'nocturnal' mean? How does this describe the bush babies?

Describe how the bush babies clean themselves.

What process do they go through next?

What do bush babies eat?

The author describes the galagos as 'gobbling and grunting' as they eat the grasshoppers. What exactly is he describing?

While eating, the eyes of the galagos are eagerly at work. Doing what?

Describe the way the galagos play with the yellow flower

What do we learn about the galago from its escape?

How does the author manage to catch the escaped galago?

Have you ever watched an animal or bird in its natural habitat? It might be a starling in a garden or a squirrel in a park. Talk or write about it.

Working for Man

If we add up the number of different animals which help or work for man, the total is quite amazing. If you considered the question in the previous section about the animals that helped man you will see what is meant. How many animals did you name? Five? Ten? Fifteen?

Fifty? Indeed, it is difficult to know what man would do without the free labour and source of food and clothing that animals supply. Of course, it is not free. Man has to look after and provide for the animals, but in return he makes very valuable gains. In the following extract, we see one of the ways in which animals help man.

In the excess of their own misery they were callous to the suffering of their animals. Hal's theory, which he practised on others, was that one must get hardened. He had started out preaching it to his sister and brother-in-law. Failing there, he hammered it into the dogs with a club. At the Five Fingers the dog-food gave out, and a toothless old squaw offered to trade them a few pounds of frozen horse-hide for the Colt's revolver that kept the big hunting-knife company at Hal's hip. A poor substitute for food was this hide, just as it had been stripped from the starved horses of the cattlemen six months back. In its frozen state it was more like strips of galvanised iron, and when a dog wrestled it into his stomach it thawed into thin and innutritious leathery strings and into a mass of short hair, irritating and indigestible.

And through it all Buck staggered along at the head of the team as in a nightmare. He pulled when he could; when he could no longer pull, he fell down and remained till blows from whip or club drove him to his feet again. All the stiffness and gloss had gone out of his beautiful furry coat. The hair hung down, limp and draggled, or matted with dried blood where Hal's club had bruised him. His muscles had wasted away to knotty strings, and the flesh pads had disappeared, so that each rib and every bone in his frame were outlined cleanly through the loose hide that was wrinkled in folds of emptiness. It was heartbreaking, only Buck's heart was unbreakable. The man in the red sweater had proved that.

As it was with Buck, so was it with his mates. They were perambulating skeletons. There were seven all together, including him. In their very great misery they had become insensible to the bite of the lash or the bruise of the club. The pain of the beating was dull and distant, just as the things their eyes saw and their ears heard seemed dull and distant. They were not half living, or quarter living. They were simply so many bags of bones in which sparks of life fluttered faintly. When a halt was made, they dropped down in the traces like dead dogs, and the spark dimmed and paled and seemed to go out. And when the club or whip fell upon them, the spark fluttered feebly up, and they tottered to their feet and staggered on.

There came a day when Billee, the good-natured, fell and could not rise. Hal had traded off his revolver, so he took the axe and knocked Billee on the head as he lay in the traces, then cut the carcass out of the harness and dragged it to one side. Buck saw, and his mates saw, and they knew that this thing was very close to them. On the next day Koona went, and but five of them remained: Joe, too far gone to be malignant; Pike, crippled and limping, only half conscious and not conscious enough longer to malinger; Sol-leks, the one-eyed, still faithful to the toil of trace and trail, and mournful in that he had so little strength with which to pull; Teek, who had not travelled so far that winter and who was now beaten more than the others because he was fresher; and Buck, still at the head of the team, but no longer enforcing discipline or striving to enforce it, blind with weakness half the time and keeping the trail by the loom of it and by the dim feel of his feet.

It was beautiful spring weather, but neither dogs nor humans were aware of it. Each day the sun rose earlier and set later. It was dawn by three in the morning, and twilight lingered till nine at night. The whole long day was a blaze of sunshine. The ghostly winter silence had given way to the great spring murmur of awakening life. The murmur arose from all the land, fraught with the joy of living. It came from the things that lived and moved again, things which had been as dead and which had not moved during the long months of frost. The sap was rising in the pines. The willows and aspens were bursting out in young buds. Shrubs and vines were putting on fresh garbs of green. Crickets sang in the nights, and in the days all manner of creeping, crawling things rustled forth into the sun. Partridges and woodpeckers were booming and knocking in the forest. Squirrels were chattering, birds singing, and overhead honked the wild-fowl driving up from the south in cunning wedges that split the air.

From every hill slope came the trickle of running water, the music of unseen fountains. All things were thawing, bending, snapping. The Yukon was straining to break loose the ice that bound it down. It ate away from beneath; the sun ate from above. Air-holes formed, fissures sprang and spread apart, while thin sections of ice fell through bodily into the river. And amid all this bursting, rending, throbbing of awakening life, under the blazing sun and through the soft-sighing breezes, like wayfarers to death, staggered the two men, the woman, and the huskies.

With the dogs falling, Mercedes weeping and riding, Hal swearing innocuously, and Charles's eyes wistfully watering, they staggered into John Thornton's camp at the mouth of White River. When they halted, the dogs dropped down as though they had all been struck dead. Mercedes dried her eyes and looked at John Thornton. Charles sat down on a log to rest. He sat down very slowly and painstakingly what of his great stiffness. Hal did the talking. John Thornton was whittling the last touches of an axe-handle he had made from a stick of birch. He whittled and listened, gave monosyllabic replies, and, when it was asked, terse advice. He knew the breed, and he gave his advice in the certainty that it would not be followed.

'They told us up above that the bottom was dropping out of the trail and that the best thing for us to do was to lay over,' Hal said in response to Thornton's warning to take no more chances on the rotten ice. 'They told us we couldn't make White River, and here we are.' This last with a sneering ring of triumph in it.

'And they told you true,' John Thornton answered. 'The bottom's likely to drop out at any moment. Only fools, with the blind luck of fools, could have made it. I tell you straight, I wouldn't risk my carcass on that ice for all the gold in Alaska.'

'That's because you're not a fool, I suppose,' said Hal. 'All the same, we'll go on to Dawson.' He uncoiled his whip. 'Get up there, Buck! Hi! Get up there! Mush on!'

Thornton went on whittling. It was idle, he knew, to get between a fool and his folly; while two or three fools more or less would not alter the scheme of things.

But the team did not get up at the command. It had long since passed into the stage where blows were required to rouse it. The whip flashed out, here and there, on its merciless errands. John Thornton compressed his lips. Sol-leks was the first to crawl to his feet. Teek followed. Joe came next, yelping with pain. Pike made painful efforts. Twice he fell over, when half up, and on the third attempt managed to rise. Buck made no effort. He lay quietly where he had fallen. The lash bit into him again and again, but he neither whined nor struggled. Several times Thornton started, as though to speak, but changed his mind. A moisture came into his eyes, and, as the whipping continued, he arose and walked irresolutely up and down.

This was the first time Buck had failed, in itself a sufficient reason to drive Hal into a rage. He exchanged the whip for the customary club. Buck refused to move under the rain of heavier blows which now fell upon him. Like his mates, he was barely able to get up, but, unlike them, he had made up his mind not to get up. He had a vague feeling of impending doom. This had been strong upon him when he pulled in to the bank, and it had not

departed from him. What of the thin and rotten ice he had felt under his feet all day, it seemed that he sensed disaster close at hand, out there ahead on the ice where his master was trying to drive him. He refused to stir. So greatly had he suffered, and so far gone was he, that the blows did not hurt much. And as they continued to fall upon him, the spark of life within flickered and went down. It was nearly out. He felt strangely numb. As though from a great distance, he was aware that he was being beaten. The last sensations of pain left him. He no longer felt anything, though very faintly he could hear the impact of the club upon his body. But it was no longer his body, it seemed so far away.

JACK LONDON, *The Call of the Wild*

In your own words say what the first sentence means.

What is Hal's philosophy of life?

How good was the frozen horse-hide as food?

Describe the effects of the hard journey on Buck's physical appearance.

Why had the dogs become 'insensible to the bite of the lash'?

What happened to Billee?

What signs are there that spring is coming?

What advice does John Thornton give?

What do Hal and his companions plan to do?

Why is Hal particularly angry at Buck?

For what two reasons does Buck not get up when Hal whips and strikes him?

Describe how Buck feels as his master beats him.

What are your views on Hal's treatment of his dogs?

Can you think of and describe any examples where people mistreat animals?

 Writing

Experiments

People don't always treat animals well. This could be seen from the extract from *The Call of the Wild*. It is not just a question of maltreating animals. Sometimes man uses animals for his

118

own good and doesn't worry about how the animals themselves feel. For instance, what do you know about battery hens or ways of producing veal or pork or experiments done on animals in the name of science? Talk about these and give your views on whether you think man's treatment of these animals is justified. In the following extract, the author imagines a rat telling its own story of how it was caught and taken to a laboratory to be experimented on.

No, I was firmly and inextricably caught, snared in the net and helpless (Nicodemus continued). When the man who held it saw that he had four rats, he pulled a draw string that closed it up. He put the net down and picked up another, an empty one. He moved on into the square, leaving us to lie there. I tried gnawing my way out, but the strands were made of some kind of plastic, as hard as wire.

The noise and movement began to die down eventually; I supposed the rats in the square had all either been caught or had escaped. I heard one man call to another: 'I suppose that's the lot.' Someone else was turning a light this way and that, searching the rest of the market area.

'Not a one to be seen.'

'We could hide and wait for another wave.'

'There won't be another wave. Not tonight. Probably not for four or five nights.'

'Word gets around.'

'You mean they communicate?' A third voice.

'You bet they communicate. And the next time they do come, you can be sure they'll case the place carefully. We were lucky. These rats hadn't been bothered for years. They'd grown careless.'

'How many did the lab order?' Someone was turning out the lights one at a time.

'Five dozen. How many have we got?'

'About that. Maybe more.'

'Let's load the truck.'

In a minute or so I felt myself being lifted up; and swinging back and forth in the net, I was carried with my three companions to the white truck I had seen earlier. Its back doors were open, and it was lighted inside. I could see that its whole interior was a large wire cage. Into this our net was thrust; the man then opened the draw string and we were dumped on to the floor, which was covered with sawdust. The other nets were emptied one at a time the same way; and in a few minutes there was a good-sized crowd of us on the floor, all more or less dazed and all (if I was typical) terrified. The cage was locked, the doors clanged shut, and the lights went out. I heard the truck motor start; a second later the floor lurched

beneath me. We were moving. Where were they taking us? For what purpose?

Then, in the dark, I heard a voice beside me.

'Nicodemus?' It was Jenner. You can imagine how glad I was to hear him. But I was sorry, too.

'Jenner. I thought maybe you got away.'

'I was in the last net. I thought I saw you across the floor.'

'Where are we going?'

'I don't know.'

'What's a lab?'

'A laboratory.'

'Yes, but what is it?'

'I don't know. I've just heard the word somewhere.'

'Well, I think that's where we're going. Whatever it is.'

The truck rumbled along through the dark, over bumpy streets at first, then, at a higher speed, over a smooth road. There were no windows in the back, so it was impossible to see where we were going – not that I would have known anyway, never before having been more than half a dozen streets from home. I think we drove for about two hours, but it might have been less, before the truck slowed down, and turned, and finally came to a stop.

The back doors were opened again, and through the wire wall of the cage I saw that we had come to a building, very modern, of white cement and glass. It was square and big, about ten storeys tall. Night had fallen, and most of its windows were dark, but the platform to which our truck drove us was lighted, and there were people waiting for us.

A door opened, and three men came out. One of them pushed a cart, a trolley piled with small wire cages. The man beside him was dressed in a heavy coat, boots, and thick leather gloves. The third man wore heavy horn-rimmed glasses and a white coat. He was obviously the leader.

The men from the truck, the ones who had caught us, now joined the men from the building.

'How many did you get?' asked the man in the white coat.

'Hard to count – they keep moving around. But I make it between sixty and seventy.'

'Good. Any trouble?'

'No. It was easy. They acted almost tame.'

'I hope not. I've got enough tame ones.'

'Oh, they're lively enough. And they look healthy.'

'Let's get them out.'

The man with the gloves and the boots then donned a wire face-mask as well, and climbed in among us. He opened a small sliding trapdoor at the back of our cage; a man outside held one of the small cages up to the opening, and one at a time we were pushed out into our individual little prisons. A few of the rats snarled and tried to bite; I did not, and neither did Jenner; it was too obviously futile. When it was finished, the man in the white coat said, 'Sixty-three – good work.' A man from the trolley said, 'Thanks, Dr Schultz.' And we were stacked on the hand truck and wheeled into the building.

Dr Schultz. I did not know it then, but I was to be his prisoner (and his pupil) for the next three years.

We spent the rest of that night in a long white room. It was, in fact, a laboratory, with a lot of equipment at one end that I didn't understand at all then – bottles and shiny metal things and black boxes with wires trailing from them. But our end held only rows of cages on shelves, each cage with a tag on it, and each separated from its neighbours by wooden partitions on both sides. Someone came around with a stack of small jars and fastened one to my cage; a little pipe led through the bars like a sipping straw – drinking water. Then the lights were dimmed and we were left alone.

That cage was my home for a long time. It was not uncomfortable; it had a floor of some kind of plastic, medium soft and warm to the touch; with wire walls and ceiling, it was airy enough. Yet just the fact that it was a cage made it horrible. I, who had always run where I wanted, could go three hops forward, three hops back again, and that was all. But worse was the dreadful feeling – I know we all had it – that we were completely at the mercy of someone we knew not at all, for some purpose we could not guess. What were their plans for us?

As it turned out, the uncertainty itself was the worst suffering we had to undergo. We were treated well enough, except for some very small, very quick flashes of pain, which were part of our training. And we were always well fed, though the food, scientifically compiled pellets, was not what you'd call delicious.

But of course we didn't know that when we arrived, and I doubt that any of us got much sleep that first night. I know I didn't. So, in a way, it was a relief when early the next morning the lights snapped on and Dr Schultz entered. There were two other people with him, a young man and a young woman. Like him, they were dressed in white laboratory coats. He was talking to them as they entered the room and walked towards our cages.

'. . . three groups. Twenty for training on injection series A, twenty on series B. That will leave twenty-three for the control group. They get no injections at all – except, to keep the test exactly even, we will prick them with a plain needle. Let's call the groups A, B, and C for control; tag them and number them A-1 to A-20, B-1 to B-20, and so on. Number the cages the same way, and keep each rat in the same cage throughout. Diet will be the same for all.'

'When do we start the injections?'

'As soon as we're through with the tagging. We'll do that now. George, you number the tags and the cages. Julie, you tie them on. I'll hold.'

So the young woman's name was Julie; the young man was George. They all put gloves on, long, tough plastic ones that came to their elbows. One by one we were taken from our cages, held gently but firmly by Dr Schultz while Julie fastened around each of our necks a narrow ribbon of yellow plastic bearing a number. I learned eventually that mine was number A-10.

They were kind, especially Julie. I remember that when one rat was being tagged, she looked at it and said, 'Poor little thing, he's frightened. Look how he's trembling.'

'What kind of biologist are you?' said Dr Schultz. 'The "poor little thing" is a she, not a he.'

When my turn came, the door of my cage slid open just enough for Dr Schultz to put his gloved hand through. I cowered to the back of the cage, which was just what he expected me to do; one hand pressed me flat against the wire wall; then his fingers gripped my shoulders. The other hand held my head just behind the ears, and I was powerless. I was lifted from the cage and felt the plastic collar clipped around my neck. I was back inside with the door closed in less than a minute. The collar was not tight, but by no amount of tugging, twisting or shaking was I ever able to get it off.

I watched through the wire front of my cage as the others were caught and tagged. About six cages down from me, on the same shelf, I saw them put a collar on Jenner; but once he was back in his cage, I could see him no longer.

A little later in the morning they came around again, this time pushing a table on wheels. It was loaded with a bottle of some clear liquid, a long rack of sharp needles, and a plunger. Once more I was lifted from the cage. This time George did the holding while Dr Schultz fastened one of the needles to the plunger. I felt a sharp pain in my hip; then it was over. We all got used to that, for from then on we got injections at least twice a week. What they were injecting and why, I did not know. Yet for twenty of us those injections were to change our whole lives.

ROBERT C. O'BRIEN, *Mrs Frisby and the Rats of NIMH*

Nicodemus says 'just the fact that it was a cage made it horrible'. Why?

What is the worst suffering of all?

Does this account make you feel any sympathy for the rats? Try to explain why.

If possible, read the rest of the novel. I think you will enjoy it.

More Experiments

What kind of feelings do the following pictures arouse in you?

Are there any other factors we should take into consideration?

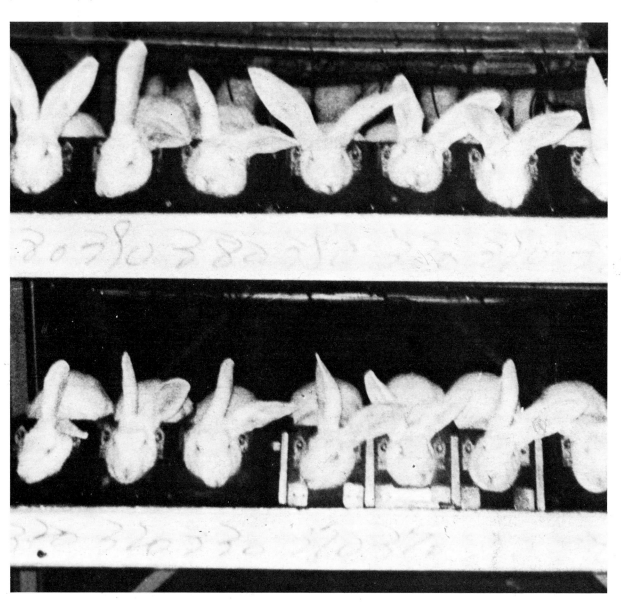

Rabbits undergoing drug tests.

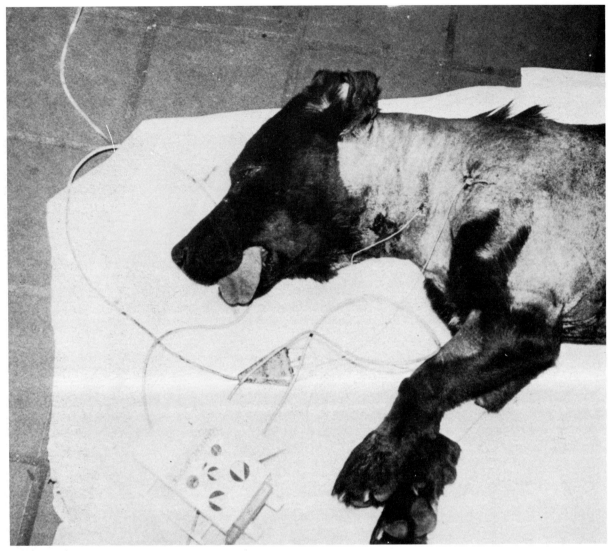

A dog which has just received a heart transplant.

At the Zoo

One of the best ways of observing animals is to visit a zoo. There you can see all kinds of animals that you couldn't possibly come across in ordinary life. This is one of the things zoos do – they enable us to study animals without having to travel all over the world to where the animals normally live. Another thing zoos do is to help to preserve species of animals which are in danger of dying out. Yet some people say that zoos are another example of the way in which man is cruel to animals. Can you think why? The following poems may help to make this clear.

Au Jardin des Plantes

The gorilla lay on his back,
One hand cupped under his head,
Like a man.

Like a labouring man tired with work,
A strong man with his strength burnt away
In the toil of earning a living.

Only of course he was not tired out with work,
Merely with boredom; his terrible strength
All burnt away by prodigal idleness.

A thousand days, and then a thousand days,
Idleness licked away his beautiful strength
He having no need to earn a living.

It was all laid on, free of charge.
We maintained him, not for doing anything,
But for being what he was.

And so that Sunday morning he lay on his back,
Like a man, like a worn-out man,
One hand cupped under his terrible hard head.

Like a man, like a man,
One of those we maintain, not for doing anything,
But for being what they are.

A thousand days, and then a thousand days,
With everything laid on, free of charge,
They cup their heads in prodigal idleness.

JOHN WAIN

Why does the poet say the gorilla is tired out with boredom?

What do you think the poet is trying to say by emphasizing the strength of the gorilla and contrasting it with the kind of life it is leading in the zoo?

The Jaguar

The apes yawn and adore their fleas in the sun.
The parrots shriek as if they were on fire, or strut
Like cheap tarts to attract the stroller with the nut.
Fatigued with indolence, tiger and lion

Lie still as the sun. The boa-constrictor's coil
Is a fossil. Cage after cage seems empty, or
Stinks of sleepers from the breathing straw.
It might be painted on a nursery wall.

But who runs like the rest past these arrives
At a cage where the crowd stands, stares, mesmerized,
As a child at a dream at a jaguar hurrying enraged
Through prison darkness after the drills of his eyes

On a short fuse. Not in boredom –
The eye satisfied to be blind in fire,
By the bang of blood in the brain deaf the ear –
He spins from the bars, but there's no cage to him

More than to the visionary his cell:
His stride is wilderness of freedom:
The world rolls under the long thrust of his heel.
Over the cage floor the horizons come.

TED HUGHES

Describe the impression of the zoo the poet gives in the first two verses.

What is different about the jaguar?

Why does the poet say of the jaguar that 'there's no cage to him'?

What does he mean when he says the jaguar's stride is 'wilderness of freedom'?

Fear

When it comes to dealing with animals, man is not always in control. There are still times when animals can endanger life or man's livelihood. Can you think of examples where animals are a pest or a danger? The following extract describes an incident in the life of a Ugandan boy herding goats for his father.

The sun lowered itself toward the western mountains and the shadows of the hills crept into the valley. It grew cooler in the lowland, and with the sinking of the sun Kabana sat in the shadow of jutting rocks. He decided to read one more page before starting the goats down the valley to reach home by nightfall. It was only a moment later that he heard the scrambling feet of goats running down the sharp rocks.

The young kids squealed as they made for their nannies. Frightened goats stampeded down the valley, bleating and looking back. Kabana jumped up, looking all around at the goats running by him. Some pushed against his legs as they dashed by. He instinctively threw up his hands to stop them, to drive them back and prevent them scattering over the floor of the valley. But they came on. He was surrounded by frightened goats, bleating goats, goats that couldn't be stopped. Some of their terror was transmitted to him. He looked about him. Were there thieves in the hills ahead? Or, perhaps, a leopard in the rocks? What caused them to stampede? Turning, he looked to the hills: there was no leopard. In the valley, ahead, he saw no thieves.

He ran to the nearest rock and bounded up on it to get a better view. His eyes, just removed from the book, were momentarily blinded by the harsh glare of the dying sun flashing on the rocks above. Shielding his eyes with one hand, he was stunned and frightened by what he saw.

Three animals were chasing the goats and leaping about among them. They were big dog-like creatures as high as his chest. Big! Big! Too big to be coyotes, and too agile for hyenas. They were wild dogs! Kabana was really frightened then for he had heard of wild dogs killing whole herds of animals. At that moment one big mangy dog leapt through the herd onto the back of a goat. Kabana saw it sink its long teeth into the neck of the staggering goat. The goat's wild bleating changed to a long scream that quivered in agony and died on the evening air. Still clutching his book, Kabana raced toward the goats – frightened, yet knowing he must do something. But he was too late. The dogs had already killed two of the goats and were dragging them away. Two dogs, holding a goat each in their teeth with the flanks dragging on the grass, moved at a trotting pace towards the rocky hillside. The third dog moved behind, looking back warily.

Kabana followed them, armed only with his book. As he started in pursuit of the dogs, the last one turned to meet him. After every few steps the dog stopped, growled, sat back on its haunches and sprang toward Kabana. A dry, piercing whine escaped its throat. The lips drew back in a snarl, revealing long, dull-brown, dangerous teeth, and a quivering red tongue that sprayed out a white, foamy saliva. It dripped from the sides of the mouth.

Kabana felt a chill race up his spine; his knees grew weak and his eyes seemed to feel larger than they were. Kabana flung out his arm as though he was throwing the book. But the growls grew more fierce and the dog flung its head to the side snapping its jaws. The dog was less than ten feet away now. It came on, the ears stiff and round, the jaws big and powerful. The brown and black spotted mangy coat bristled as the dog set to leap. The body twitched back and forth and the nostrils flared. Kabana froze in his tracks. He glanced about for a weapon – anything. But he saw nothing, except a small stone on the path. Keeping his eyes on the dog, he bent, cautiously, to pick it up. It was a mistake! The dog sprang for his neck. Kabana saw it coming. He threw up his arms and hands to protect his head. Quickly, he leaped aside. The dog's body struck him a glancing blow and knocked him to his knees. He heard the rip of cloth as the dog's teeth tore through the trousers and the skin of his upper leg, and felt a searing pain. The animal's body went on by him, skittered over rocks, regained balance, and ran steadily toward the valley.

Kabana, dazed and frightened but determined to fight, ignored his wound and started uphill behind the two dogs that still dragged the goats. He had gone only a few yards when he again heard the loud bleating of goats. Whirling around, he saw the dog which had attacked him chasing the kids, growling furiously, and looking up the hill toward Kabana. It was as though the dog was trying to get Kabana's attention – to guard the retreat of the other dogs.

Kabana hurried down the hill to protect the goats. He couldn't let any more of them be killed. The dog watched him until he was near, then ran down the

valley a short distance, turned uphill and disappeared into the rocks. Kabana, with a cold feeling of fright and shame in him, watched the dogs go.

As he rounded up the goats to start for home, a heavy load of grief and shame settled upon his shoulders. How would he explain the loss of the goats to his father? This after promising, only that day, to be a dutiful son and try to make him proud. The first task assigned him on the first day had ended in failure.

Perhaps if he hadn't been reading he could have seen the danger earlier and protected the goats. He clenched the book in his hand blaming it for his trouble.

MUSA NAGENDA, *Dogs of Fear*

Why were the dogs able to attack the goats before Kabana was aware of them?

Describe the part played by the third dog in the attack.

Why was Kabana particularly upset by the attack?

 Assignments

Choose several of the following to write about:

1. What kind of animal are you most afraid of? Write about it and explain your choice.
2. Write a story about an encounter with an animal. It might be a bull in a field or a mouse in the kitchen. It could be frightening or funny.
3. Try to describe as accurately as possible an animal you have watched and studied. It might be a rabbit in the countryside or a blackbird in your own garden.
4. Write a story about an animal that works for man. It might be about a carthorse or a police dog.
5. Write a story about helping an animal that is injured. It might be a bird with a broken wing or an animal that has been run over.
6. You hear an animal cry out in pain. You search for it and find it caught in a trap. Describe how you feel and what you do.
7. Give arguments for and against using animals in experiments.
8. Write about a visit to a zoo.

9. Imagine the thoughts of an animal at the zoo about his life and the people who come to look at him. This could be a story or a poem.
10. If you had the choice of being any other animal other than a human being, which animal would you choose to be? Give a full account of the reasons for your choice.
11. Write a story about an occasion when you come across an animal being treated cruelly.

 Language

A. The Semi-colon

Why are punctuation marks important?

You should already be able to use the full stop, the comma, the question mark, the exclamation mark and quotation marks correctly. Can you remember how they are used?

Now we shall look at the remaining punctuation marks: the semi-colon, the colon, brackets and the dash.

The semi-colon (;) is a punctuation mark halfway in force between a comma and a full stop. It is used between statements which are related to each other where a full stop would suggest too abrupt a break. Instead of using a semi-colon, the connection between the two statements might be made by using a conjunction. Compare:

The playground was deserted; only a few pigeons waddled across it pecking at crumbs.

The playground was deserted, and only a few pigeons waddled across it pecking at crumbs.

The semi-colon can also be used instead of commas for items in a list where these items consist of more than one word and confusion could arise, e.g.

These are my favourite foods: bananas and custard; cakes full of cream; those puddings, found in some restaurants, packed with currants and spices; scones dripping with honey.

If commas were used in this example instead of semi-colons, the sense would not be clear.

The semi-colon is a fairly subtle punctuation mark. Often you could use a full stop or a comma instead with little effect on the meaning. In fact, it would be possible never to use a semi-colon in your own writing, but it can be important to know about the semi-colon and how it is used when you study the writing of other people.

Rewrite the following sentences correctly punctuated, using semi-colons.

1. The river was calm and peaceful boats glided smoothly over the surface.
2. Bring me the following objects a pencil sharpened at both ends a ruler marked out in centimetres a pair of compasses and a piece of paper eight inches by five.
3. The right-hand side was laid out with rose beds the left-hand side consisted of herbaceous borders the centre was a lawn of billiard-table smoothness.
4. The lions were lying sleepily watching the passers-by the tiger was prowling up and down its cage.

B. The Colon

This punctuation mark (:) can be used as follows:

(i) **to indicate the balancing of one phrase or idea against another**, e.g.

Man proposes: God disposes.

Another way of expressing the idea without a colon would be:

On the one hand, man proposes, but on the other, God disposes.

Using the colon makes the expression much neater.

(ii) **to introduce an illustration or as a substitute for an expression such as 'namely' or 'in other words' or 'with the result that'**, e.g.

After much discussion, they reached a decision: the man would have to be arrested.

(iii) **to introduce a list.** Sometimes a colon and dash are used, e.g.

You will need the following: (or :-) flour, eggs, sugar and butter.

As with the semi-colon, the colon is a very useful punctuation mark.

Write two sentences illustrating each of the three uses of the colon given above.

Rewrite the following sentences correctly punctuated, using the colon.

1. Remember to get these apples bananas and pears.
2. You go your way I'll go mine.
3. There was no alternative the wounded animal would have to be destroyed.
4. He hadn't practised his driving he would fail his test.
5. Only one thing would satisfy him success.

C. The Dash

This punctuation mark (–) is used to cut off an afterthought or an added example or explanation from the rest of the sentence. Dashes are usually used in pairs when they come in the middle of a sentence, e.g.

He drank his coffee – it was already cold – and hurried into his coat.
He arrived at the station in time – the train was late.

The dash is also used to link a series of disconnected phrases, e.g.

The lion was an extraordinary sight – powerful muscles – tawny eyes – swinging tail – thick ropy mane.

Rewrite the following sentences correctly punctuated, using dashes where appropriate.

1. The smallest elephant last in line swung its tail jauntily.
2. The animals lost interest the food was all gone.
3. The food ten tons of it lasted only a week.
4. The dog was angry all flashing teeth glaring eyes growling throat threatening stance.
5. He bought a fishing-rod the last in the shop.

Note that in some of these examples, a pair of commas would be as effective as a pair of dashes. Sometimes a colon could be used instead of a dash. *Rewrite these sentences using commas and colons instead of dashes.*

D. Brackets

These punctuation marks ( ) can be used like dashes to cut off an afterthought or an extra example or explanation from the rest of the sentence, e.g.

The duck (together with her brood of ducklings) crossed the road safely.

Unlike dashes, brackets are always used in pairs.

Rewrite the following sentences correctly punctuated, using brackets.

1. The discovery it was no business of hers interested her greatly.
2. He was awarded the Gallantry Medal Second Class.
3. He was unlike his sisters a very pleasant person to know.
4. His disguise not a very good one was easy to see through.
5. He always served champagne only the best at his parties.

(Note that in some of these examples, dashes or commas would be just as effective as brackets. This statement illustrates another use of brackets. What is it?)

E. Paragraphs

Remember to divide any extended piece of writing you do into paragraphs, that is, subsections, each dealing with a particular aspect of the subject you are writing about. Each new paragraph should be indented from the margin. By using paragraphs, you break up your work so that it is easier for a reader to follow what you are writing.

Often in paragraphs there is one particular sentence which acts as a kind of key to what the paragraph is about. This sentence makes a general statement which the rest of the paragraph goes on to illustrate or expand upon. This sentence is called the topic sentence. Sometimes, if you are not sure what a particular paragraph is about or where it is leading, it can help to look for the topic sentence, the sentence which seems to summarize what the paragraph is about, and then the point of the paragraph becomes clearer. Often the topic sentence is the first sentence of the paragraph.

What are the topic sentences of the following paragraphs?

1. The car gave me nothing but trouble. First, there was the difficulty of starting it. It was not just on cold mornings that I had this problem: it happened in the summer as well. Then there was the fact that the car wouldn't accelerate properly. I would get to about twenty-five miles an hour and then the car would judder and hesitate and it was only with great reluctance that it would go above that speed. Finally, the radiator kept getting hot, and it was only later that I discovered that it was leaking. The last straw was when I found clouds of smoke rising from the bonnet and had to take refuge on the hard-shoulder of the motorway: the radiator had run out of water.

2. You have to make sure the tyres are properly pumped up. The chain has to be lubricated and checked. It is essential that the lights and brakes are in good working order. If the saddle is at the wrong height, you can have a very uncomfortable journey. The handle-bars and hand-grips too should be the right size and at the right angle. These are some of the things you have to make sure of before setting out on a long bicycle run.

3. The train was ready to start. A great puff of smoke warned the passengers. Doors were slammed. Porters hurried along the platform checking that all was ready. Windows were lowered and heads poked out to catch the last sight of friends left behind. The driver looked from his cabin, his eyes surveying the platform, ready to catch the guard's signal that meant that all was clear and that the great monster could start on its journey.

Choose one of the following. Write a paragraph about it. Don't try to cover too much ground. Just take one aspect of the subject. Make sure your paragraph contains a topic sentence. Underline the topic sentence.

1. The boat race
2. The mill
3. The steel foundry
4. The clockwork toy
5. The watch

 # Vocabulary

A. Animals

How many different animals belonging to the cat family can you name?

How many different animals belonging to the antelope family can you name?

How many animals can you name which are mammals?

How many different kinds of sea creatures can you name?

B. Acronyms

An acronym is a word formed from the first letter or letters of a number of words. For instance, the word 'radar' comes from the initial letters of '*r*adio *d*etection *a*nd *r*anging'. Here are some more examples. Can you say what they refer to and what the full versions are?

Naafi
Wrens
Anzac

Can you find any more examples of acronyms?

C. Extending your Vocabulary

Are you keeping up your vocabulary notebook? Try to look up in your dictionary the meaning of any word in your reading that you don't understand. Copy it together with its meaning into your vocabulary notebook. Try to use it in your own writing. For instance, look again at the extract from *The Call of the Wild* in the 'Reading and Understanding' section. What do the following words mean, taking into account their context?

callous	honked
galvanized	fissures
innutrious	rending

indigestible innocuously
perambulating wistfully
insensible painstakingly
malignant monosyllable
malinger irresolutely
fraught

Use these words in sentences of your own.

 Spelling

A. Plurals

The plural of 'man' is 'men'. The plural of 'beast' is 'beasts'. If you didn't know, it would be difficult to guess how the plural of a noun is formed. There are certain rules which we studied in Book One. Here is a chance for you to revise them.

1. The plural of 'beast' is 'beasts'. What is the most common way of forming the plural? *Give ten examples.*
2. The plural of 'fox' is 'foxes'. How do we form the plural of words ending in -ch, -s, -sh, -ss and -x? *Give ten more examples.*
3. The plural of 'lady' is 'ladies'. What is the rule for forming the plural of words ending in -y? *Give ten examples.*
4. The plural of 'calf' is 'calves'. What is the rule for forming the plural of words ending in -f or -fe? *Give five examples. Give five examples of exceptions to this rule.*
5. The plural of 'man' is 'men'. How do words like this form their plural? *Give five examples.*
6. The plural of 'radio' is 'radios'. What is the rule for forming the plural of words ending in -o? *Give five examples. Give five examples of exceptions.*
7. The plural of 'passer-by' is 'passers-by'. What is the rule for forming the plural of compound nouns? *Give five examples.*
8. The plural of 'sheep' is 'sheep'. *Give five examples of words which have the same form in the singular and the plural.*
9. *Give five examples of words almost always used in the plural.*

B. Soft 'c' and 'g'

Pronunciation can sometimes be a guide to spelling. The letter 'c', for instance, is always pronounced soft (that is, the same as 's') if it appears before the vowels 'e', 'i' and 'y'. Before other vowels, 'c' is pronounced hard (that is, the same as 'k').

Compare	cellar	*with*	card
	circle		cord
	icy		cut

In order to keep the 'c' soft, 'e' has to be retained when a suffix beginning with 'a', 'o' or 'u' is added.

Compare	noticing	*with*	noticeable
	inextricable		ineffaceable

The same is true of the letter 'g' which can be pronounced soft or hard. It is pronounced soft (that is, like 'j') before the vowels 'e' and 'i'. Before other vowels, 'g' is often hard (that is, the same as in 'garden').

Compare	gem	*with*	god
	giant		gun
			gay

There are, however, many exceptions to this, e.g.

goal	give
margarine	giggle
girl	gear

and many others.

Nevertheless, the tendency is worth remembering. When 'g' is pronounced soft, an 'e' is sometimes required to keep it soft.

Compare	manager	*and*	manageable
	languorous		courageous
	changing		changeable

Divide the following words into columns according to whether the 'c' or 'g' is soft or hard. Learn the spellings.

exchange	interchangeable
grind	cypher
circle	gasp

ranger	giraffe
cabbage	serviceable
chancy	gild
clergy	enforceable
marriageable	gin
content	girder
custard	comic
knowledgeable	chargeable
centre	cylinder
giddy	peaceable
cement	cymbal
damageable	gate
gift	traceable
pronounceable	forgeable
citadel	gulf

4. Find out about new methods of farm production involving animals, for example battery hens, milk-fed calves. Lead a discussion with the rest of the class on whether these new methods are good or bad.

5. Make a list of all the different kinds of animals and birds you have seen in your area (excluding those you have seen at the zoo or the circus). Compare your list with lists made by other pupils in your class.

6. Find out about animals which are extinct or in danger of becoming extinct. Discuss your findings with the rest of the class.

7. If you can, visit a zoo and write down or talk about your impressions.

8. Try to listen to *The Carnival of the Animals* by Saint-Saëns or *Peter and the Wolf* by Prokofiev. Write down or talk about your impressions.

 Activities

A. 1. Think about, talk about and demonstrate the different ways animals stand and move. In groups, work out a scene at the zoo with a crowd of spectators in front of a cage. Suppose one of the spectators gets his hand or his head caught between the bars ... Or teases the animal with a piece of biscuit which he offers and withdraws ...

2. Can you use the extract from *The Call of the Wild* as a basis for improvising a dramatic situation?

3. In groups, work out what happens when the hero of the extract from *Dogs of Fear* returns home to his father and family.

B. 1. Find out about the R.S.P.C.A. Try to obtain some of its literature. Make a display of it. Give a talk to the rest of the class about the Society's work.

2. Find out as much as you can about the Anti-Vivisection Society. Try to obtain some of its literature. Make a display of it. Give a talk to the rest of the class about the Society's work.

3. Discuss the pros and cons of experiments on animals. Perhaps you could do this as a formal debate.

Reading List

Try to read some of the following novels which involve man and his relationship with animals.

D. R. Sherman, *Old Mali and the Boy*
Catherine Cookson, *Joe and the Gladiator*
John Steinbeck, *The Red Pony*
René Guillot, *Grishka and the Bear*
Jack London, *White Fang*
   The Call of the Wild
Gerald Durrell, *My Family and Other Animals*
   The Bafut Beagles
   The New Noah
Musa Nagenda, *Dogs of Fear*
Robert C. O'Brien, *Mrs Frisby and the Rats of NIMH*
Anna Sewell, *Black Beauty*

For further poems about animals, see
Men and Beasts (Themes), edited by Rhodri Jones.

UNIT 9

The Senses

 ### Reading and Understanding

Impressions

What are the five senses? Some people claim that they have a sixth sense. What do you think this is?

But let's concentrate on the five senses. Most of the impressions we get of the world come to us through our senses. Our eyes, our ears, our noses, our sense of taste and our sense of touch tell us a great deal about the world around us. For a moment, imagine what it would be like to be without one of these senses. Supposing, for instance, you lost the use of your eyes, how would this affect you? Or, supposing you were deaf, how do you think you would cope? Just out of interest, name five things that give you pleasure to look at, to hear, to smell, to taste and to touch.

In the following extract, Mark Twain remembers his boyhood. See how many of his memories depend upon the feelings his senses experienced.

I spent some part of every year at the farm until I was twelve or thirteen years old. The life which I led there with my cousins was full of charm, and so is the memory of it yet. I can call back the solemn twilight and mystery of the deep woods, the earthy smells, the faint odours of the wild flowers, the sheen of rain-washed foliage, the rattling clatter of drops when the wind shook the trees, the far-off hammering of woodpeckers and the muffled drumming of wood pheasants in the remoteness of the forest, the snapshot glimpses of disturbed wild creatures scurrying through the grass – I can call it all back and make it as real as it ever was, and as blessed. I can call back the prairie, and its loneliness and peace, and a vast hawk hanging motionless in the sky, with his wings spread wide and the blue of the vault showing through the fringe of their end-feathers. I can see the woods in their autumn dress, the oaks purple, the hickories washed with gold, the maples and the sumachs[1] luminous with crimson fires, and I can hear the rustle made by the fallen leaves as we plowed through them. I can see the blue clusters of wild grapes hanging among the foliage of the saplings, and I remember the taste of them and the smell. I know how the wild blackberries looked, and how they tasted, and the same with the paw-paws,[2] the hazelnuts, and the persimmons;[3] and I can feel the thumping rain, upon my head, of hickory[4] nuts and walnuts when we were out in the frosty dawn to scramble for them with the pigs, and the gusts of wind loosed them and sent them down. I know the stain of blackberries, and how pretty it is, and I know the stain of walnut hulls, and how little it minds soap and water, also what grudged experience it had of either of them. I know the taste of maple sap, and when to gather it, and how to arrange the troughs and the delivery tubes, and how to boil down the juice, and how to hook the sugar after it is made, also how much better hooked sugar tastes than any that is honestly come by, let bigots say what they will. I know how a prize watermelon looks when it is sunning its fat rotundity among pumpkin vines and 'simblins'; I know how to tell when it is ripe without 'plugging' it; I know how inviting it looks when it is cooling itself in a tub of water under the bed, waiting; I know how it looks when it lies on the table in the sheltered great floor space between house and kitchen, and the children gathered for the sacrifice and their mouths watering; I know the crackling sound it makes when the carving knife enters its end, and I can see the split fly along in front of the blade as the knife cleaves its way to the other end; I can see its halves fall apart and display the rich red meat and the black seeds, and the heart standing up, a luxury fit for the elect; I know how a boy looks behind a yardlong slice of that melon, and I know how he feels; for I have been there. I know the taste of the

---

[1] Kind of shrub or small tree. [3] Date plums.
[2] Fruit of South American tree. [4] Tree of walnut family.

watermelon which has been honestly come by, and I know the taste of the watermelon which has been acquired by art. Both taste good, but the experienced know which tastes best. I know the look of green apples and peaches and pears on the trees, and I know how entertaining they are when they are inside of a person. I know how ripe ones look when they are piled in pyramids under the trees, and how pretty they are and how vivid their colours. I know how a frozen apple looks, in a barrel down cellar in the wintertime, and how hard it is to bite, and how the frost makes the teeth ache, and yet how good it is, notwithstanding. I know the disposition of elderly people to select the speckled apples for the children, and I once knew ways to beat the game. I know the look of an apple that is roasting and sizzling on a hearth on a winter's evening, and I know the comfort that comes of eating it hot, along with some sugar and a drench of cream. I know the delicate art and mystery of so cracking hickory nuts and walnuts on a flatiron with a hammer that the kernels will be delivered whole, and I know how the nuts, taken in conjunction with winter apples, cider and doughnuts, make old people's old tales and old jokes sound fresh and crisp and enchanting, and juggle an evening away before you know what went with the time. I know the look of Uncle Dan'l's kitchen as it was on the privileged nights, when I was a child, and I can see the white and black children grouped on the hearth, with the firelight playing on their faces and the shadows flickering upon the walls, clear back toward the cavernous gloom of the rear, and I can hear Uncle Dan'l telling the immortal tales which Uncle Remus Harris was to gather into his books and charm the world with, by and by; and I can feel again the creepy joy which quivered through me when the time for the ghost story of the 'Golden Arm' was reached – and the sense of regret, too, which came over me, for it was always the last story of the evening and there was nothing between it and the unwelcome bed.

I can remember the bare wooden stairway in my uncle's house, and the turn to the left above the landing, and the rafters and the slanting roof over my bed, and the squares of moonlight on the floor, and the white cold world of snow outside, seen through the curtainless window. I can remember the howling of the wind and the quaking of the house on stormy nights, and how snug and cosy one felt, under the blankets, listening; and how the powdery snow used to sift in, around the sashes, and lie in little ridges on the floor and make the place look chilly in the morning and curb the wild desire to get up – in case there was any. I can remember how very dark that room was, in the dark of the moon, and how packed it was with ghostly stillness when one woke up by accident away in the night, and forgotten sins came flocking out of the secret chambers of the memory and wanted a hearing; and how ill chosen the time seemed for this kind of business; and how dismal was the hoo-hooing of the owl and the wailing of the wolf, sent mourning by on the night wind. I remember the raging of the rain on that roof, summer nights, and how pleasant it was to lie and listen to it, and enjoy the white splendour of the lightning and the majestic booming and crashing of the thunder. It was a very satisfactory room, and there was a lightning rod which was reachable from the window, an adorable and skittish thing to climb up and down, summer nights, when there were duties on hand of a sort to make privacy desirable.

I remember the 'coon and 'possum hunts, nights, with the negroes, and the long marches through the black gloom of the woods, and the excitement which fired everybody when the distant bay of an experienced dog announced that the game was treed; then the wild scramblings and stumblings through briers and bushes and over roots to get to the spot; then the lighting of a fire and the felling of the tree, the joyful frenzy of the dogs and the negroes, and the weird picture it all made in the red glare – I remember it all well, and the delight that everyone got out of it, except the 'coon.

I remember the pigeon seasons, when the birds would come in millions and cover the trees and by their weight break down the branches. They were clubbed to death with sticks; guns were not necessary and were not used. I remember the squirrel hunts, and prairie-chicken hunts, and wild-turkey hunts, and all that; and how we turned out, mornings, while it was still dark, to go on these expeditions, and how chilly and dismal it was, and how often I regretted that I was well enough to go. A toot on a tin horn brought twice as many dogs as were needed, and in their happiness they raced and scampered about, and knocked small people down, and made no end of unnecessary noise. At the word, they vanished away toward the woods, and we drifted silently after them in the melancholy gloom. But presently the grey dawn stole over the world, the birds piped up, then the sun rose and poured light and comfort all around, everything was fresh and dewy and fragrant, and life was a boon again. After three hours of tramping we arrived back wholesomely tired, overladen with game, very hungry, and just in time for breakfast.

MARK TWAIN, *Autobiography*

The particular words writers choose can appeal to the senses. For instance, Mark Twain talks about 'the sheen of rain-washed foliage'. The word 'sheen' appeals to the sense of sight. We can see the shininess of the wet leaves. But it also appeals to our sense of touch. The word suggests the smoothness of the leaves as well. *Examine the author's use of the following words and say precisely what senses each appeals to:*

clatter	crisp
scurrying	flickering
washed	creepy
luminous	quivered
thumping	howling
frosty	quaking
stain	wailing
watering	raging
cleaves	bay
ache	glare
sizzling	scampered
drench	poured

Pick out two details from the extract which appeal to each of the senses of sight, hearing, taste, smell and touch.

Being Able to See

In the previous section, you were asked how you would feel if you lost the use of your eyes. Recently in the news someone had his sight suddenly restored to him after many years of blindness when he was travelling in an aeroplane. How do you think he felt? What things do you think he would be most pleased or most surprised to see?

In the following extract Richard Church tells how acquiring a pair of spectacles transformed his whole view of the world he lived in.

A medical examination at school had revealed the fact that I was short-sighted. The doctor took me solemnly between his knees, looked into my face, and said, 'If you don't get some glasses, you'll be blind by the time you are fifteen, and I shall tell your parents so.'

I was rather proud of this distinction. Fifteen! That was so far ahead that it meant nothing to me, except a sort of twilight at the end of life. My parents thought otherwise, and one Saturday afternoon I was taken, via a steep road called Pig Hill, to a chemist's shop on Lavender Hill, Clapham. Behind the shop was a room where my eyes were tested in the rough and ready way customary in those days. The chemist hung an open framework that felt like the Forth Bridge around my ears and on my nose. Lenses were slotted into this, and twisted about, while I was instructed to read the card of letters beginning with a large E.

I remember still the astonishment with which I saw the smaller letters change from a dark blur into separate items of the alphabet. I thought about it all the following week, and found that by screwing up my eyes when I was out of doors I could get to some faint approximation of that clarity, for a few seconds at a time.

This made me surmise that the universe which hitherto I had seen as a vague mass of colour and blurred shapes might in actuality be much more concise and defined. I was therefore half prepared for the surprise which shook me a week later when, on the Saturday evening, we went again to the shop on Lavender Hill, and the chemist produced the bespoken pair of steel-rimmed spectacles through which I was invited to read the card. I read it, from top to bottom! I turned, and looked in triumph at Mother, but what I saw was Mother intensified. I saw the pupils of her eyes, the tiny feathers in her boa necklet; I saw the hairs in Father's moustache, and on the back of his hand. Jack's cap might have been made of metal, so hard and clear did it shine on his close-cropped head, above his bony face and huge nose. I saw *his* eyes too, round, inquiring, fierce with a hunger of observation. He was studying me with a gimlet sharpness such as I had never before been able to perceive.

Then we walked out of the shop, and I stepped on to the pavement, which came up and hit me, so that I had to grasp the nearest support – Father's coat. 'Take care, now, take care!' he said indulgently (though he disapproved of all these concessions to physical weakness). 'And mind you don't break them!'

I walked still with some uncertainty, carefully placing my feet and feeling their impact on the pavement whose surface I could see sparkling like quartz in the lamplight.

The lamplight! I looked in wonder at the diminishing crystals of gas-flames strung down the hill. Clapham was hung with necklaces of light, and the horses pulling the glittering omnibuses struck the granite road with hooves of iron and ebony. I could see the skeletons inside the flesh and blood of the Saturday-night shoppers. The garments they wore were made of separate threads. In this new world, sound as well as sight was changed. It took on hardness and definition, forcing itself upon my hearing, so that I was besieged simultaneously through the eye and through the ear.

How willingly I surrendered! I went out to meet this blazing and trumpeting invasion. I trembled with the excitement, and had to cling to Mother's arm to prevent myself being carried away in the flood as the pavements rushed at me, and people loomed up with their teeth like tusks, their lips luscious, their eyes bolting out of their heads, bearing down on me as they threw out spears of conversation that whizzed loudly past my ears and bewildered my wits.

'Is it any different?' asked Jack, in his proprietary voice. He was never satisfied until he had collected all possible information on everything which life brought to his notice.

'It makes things clearer,' I replied, knowing that I had no hope of telling him what was happening to me. I was only half-aware of it myself, for this urgent demand upon my attention made by the multitudinous world around me was the beginning of a joyous imposition to which I am still responding today, breathless and enraptured, though the twilight of the senses begins to settle.

My excitement must have communicated itself to the rest of the family, for Father proposed that, instead of our going home to supper, we should have the meal at 'The Creighton', an Italian restaurant near Clapham Junction. This was the first time in my life that I ate in public, and I remember it so clearly because the tablecloth appeared to be made of white ropes in warp and woof, and the cutlery had an additional hardness, beyond that of ordinary steel and plate. When the food came to the table, the steam rising from it was as coarse as linen. I saw the spots of grease on the waiter's apron, and the dirt under his finger-nails.

All this emphasis made me shy, as I would have been, indeed, without this optical exaggeration that had the effect of thrusting me forward, to be seen as conspicuously as I now saw everything and everybody around me. But I ate my fried plaice, dissecting it with a new skill, since every bone was needle-clear. Our parents drank stout, their usual supper glass. Jack and I had ginger-beer, a rare luxury that added to the formality of the feast.

By the time we reached the darker streets near home, my head ached under the burden of too much seeing. Perhaps the grease of the fried fish, and the lateness of the hour, had something to do with the exhaustion that almost destroyed me as we trailed homeward. The new spectacles clung to my face,

eating into the bridge of my nose and behind the ear-lobes. I longed to tear them off and throw them away into the darkness. I tried to linger behind, so that at least I might secrete them in the pocket of my blouse.

But before I could further this purpose, something caught my attention. I realized that, after all, the side-streets were not quite dark; that the yellow pools round each gas-lamp, now as clearly defined as golden sovereigns, were augmented, pervaded, suffused by a bluish-silver glory. I looked upward, and saw the sky. And in that sky I saw an almost full moon, floating in space, a solid ball of roughened metal, with an irregular jagged edge. I could put up my hand and take it, ponder its weight, feel its cold surface.

I stopped walking, and stared. I turned up my face, throwing back my head to look vertically into the zenith. I saw the stars, and I saw them for the first time, a few only, for most were obscured by the light of the moon; but those I saw were clean pin-points of light, diamond-hard, standing not upon a velvet surface, but floating in space, some near, some far, in an awe-striking perspective that came as a revelation to my newly educated eyes. I felt myself swept up into that traffic of the night sky. I floated away, and might have disappeared into space had not a cry recalled me.

It was Mother's voice, in alarm, for she had looked round, perhaps impatiently, to urge me along, only to see me lying on my back on the pavement, in a state of semi-coma. Father picked me up, and I was still too far gone to resent being carried like a baby.

RICHARD CHURCH, *Over the Bridge*

What is the difference between being short-sighted and long-sighted?

Why was the author 'rather proud of this distinction'?

Describe how the author was tested for his spectacles.

What was the first sign the author had of the wonders of being able to see properly?

What does he mean when he says that what he saw was 'Mother intensified'?

Why does he say 'Jack's cap might have been made of metal'?

Why does he describe the pavement as coming up and hitting him?

Describe some of the ways in which the author found his sight and hearing sharpened.

What do you think the author means by

describing Jack's voice as 'proprietary'?

Describe the author's feelings on being able to see more clearly.

Why did the ginger-beer add to 'the formality of the feast'?

Describe the way the new spectacles intensified the author's impression of the moon and the stars.

 ## Writing

Looking at Things

Often, we are so used to looking at things that we no longer really notice them. For instance, think of a picture you have hanging on the wall at home or at school. You know it is there and you have seen it day after day, but can you really describe in detail what the picture is about? This is one of the things which writers do: they describe ordinary everyday things in such a way that we see them as though for the first time; we see them as something fresh and new. And this is something which you should be trying to do in your own writing. You should really look at the things you are writing about, in fact or in your mind's eye, and describe them as exactly and precisely as you can so that the reader gains a new understanding of them. This is what the writer of this poem is doing. 'Glass' seems a very ordinary and boring thing to write about. See whether the poet makes his subject interesting and alive.

Glass

Will not bleed
but wounds when itself wounded,
outlives a generation, cracks
at a blow, sharp sound.
Older than the Pharoahs, bends
with furnace heat, polishes to ice surface,
screams at engraver's knife.
Backcloth for raindrops, frost crystals,
flying angels, saints in carmine,
all colours, and none,
will keep out angry voices, snow-drifts.

Married to light, holds rainbows
in chandeliers, broken bottles, or shows
delicate architecture of wasp's wing,
fault in bone, diamond;
can be a false jewel.
Glass gives new eyes, photographs of eyes,
prospect of life through an inch of it,
telescopes a dead star;
in league with sun will burn
forests and fields to loose ashes.
Milky, clear, solid as rock,
flowers to Venetian stem, gilt goblet,
hour-glass on the run, bauble for Christmas,
dancing float, witches' ball.
The whole world is a house of glass;
we breathe our frail names on its cold face.

LEONARD CLARK

What does the poet mean when he says glass 'wounds when itself wounded'?

Pick out some of the uses of glass the poet mentions.

What do you think the poet means when he says 'we breathe our frail names on its cold face'?

Colours

One of the things which makes being able to see such a joy is colour. It gives such a richness to everything we see, whether it is the blue of a summer sky or the reds and golds and browns of leaves in autumn. Think about the difference between black-and-white television and colour television. Which do you prefer and why?

Here are two poems about colours.

What is Pink?

What is pink? A rose is pink
By the fountain's brink.

What is red? A poppy's red
In its barley bed.

What is blue? The sky is blue
Where the clouds float through.

What is white? A swan is white
Sailing in the light.

What is yellow? Pears are yellow,
Rich and ripe and mellow.

What is green? The grass is green
With small flowers between.

What is violet? Clouds are violet
In the summer twilight.

What is orange? Why, an orange,
Just an orange!

CHRISTINA ROSSETTI

Black

To me black means
Tree trunks tall and slender,
The mud that comes after the rain.
Some stones are big and black.

Black is better than brown,
Some metal is black but very hard.
At night the sky is black,
And when a storm's on its way,
You can see black thunder-clouds
In the sky.

ANGELA LAST

Choose a colour and name five things that you associate with that colour.

Sounds

Nearly everywhere today we are surrounded by sounds and noises. Name some of the sounds you might expect to hear in a busy town centre or a school or at a football match. Sometimes, we get moments of peace, and then because it is so quiet someone might say you can hear the silence. What would he mean?

Here are two poems by pupils of your own age describing the sounds they hear in different situations.

In the Night

I rustle the sheets and jump into bed.
I lie there, eyes closed, and listen.
I hear the wind howling at the window,
And the creaking of the door as it sways to and fro.
I hear the rumbling of cars outside,
And the tapping of the cat trying to draw my
     attention to the window.
Soon the night train will pass making a clattering
     sound,
While down in the street people are chattering as
     they pass by.
Then my ears start to tingle as the church bells
     begin to ring,
And car doors bang as neighbours come home from
     a party.
Just at that moment the stairs start to creak –

My parents are coming to bed.
And I know I should be asleep!

PAT ARNOLD

What sounds do you hear when you are lying in bed at night?

Town Noises

Saturday morning
Going shopping
High Road
Lorries rumbling
People talking
Workmen working
Pneumatic drills
Trembling quaking
Traffic shaking
Lights red
Cars hooting
Shop aflame
Treble nine
Fire engine
Coming ringing
Brakes shriek
Firemen ready
Ladder extended
Water jet
Whoosh swish
Fire out
Ruined apartment
Firemen home
Insurance bankrupt

DAVID COLEMAN

What noises other than those mentioned in the poem would you expect to hear in a town?

Taste

Have you ever had a dish placed before you at dinner that you have never had before, or been given a fruit or a sweet that you have never tasted before. Can you remember how you experienced it and what your impressions were? Talk about it.

In this extract, David, who has spent his life in a camp for political prisoners, has escaped. He has not been in the free world before and everything is new and fresh to him. He has never eaten an orange before and doesn't even know what it is.

Right down by the edge of the water he was sheltered from the road, and the nearest house was some way off. David did not think anyone would be able to see him from there, but he was not sure – and it was necessary to be sure. If he could get over to that rock, he would be in a kind of cave with two walls and a bit of a roof. But it was too far for him to jump across. David put his bundle down and stretched his leg over the edge, feeling about with his foot for some support; but it was very steep and slippery. Only a yard separated him from the best hiding-place he had ever seen!

'I *will* get over!' he said to himself. It must be possible, there must be some way ... Perhaps he could find a big stone and drop it into the cleft so that he could clamber across? But struggle as he would, he could not budge the only boulder that looked big enough. If he had a rope ... but there was nothing he could make it fast to on the other side, and the only thing he had that at all resembled a rope was the bit of string round his trousers.

Then something brown caught his eye a little farther down on his own side of the cleft. A wooden packing-case – or rather a bit of one: a plank.

David suppressed his excitement. It was not big enough, he told himself. But he ought to try, just to make sure. When his heart was beating normally again, he set off after it. The plank was long enough! He could lay it across like a bridge, and lift it away after he had crossed over it so that no one could follow him!

But was it stout enough? He found two smaller stones and laid them one under each end of the plank: then he stepped carefully on to it. It creaked a little, but it would take his weight.

It was very bare on the other side. Bare but safe, and there was room enough to lie down; and owing to the formation of the projecting rock, he would be in shadow most of the time. He could see a short stretch of the road above from where he was without being seen himself and he could see the whole coastline towards the east.

David took his wet trousers off and spread them and his shirt out to dry in the sun, and then he unpacked his bundle and arranged his possessions neatly by his side – his compass, his knife, his bottle, the bit of bread the man on board the ship had given

him, and finally the round yellow thing. He held it firmly but carefully while he scratched it with his finger-nail and bored his finger right through the skin. It was moist inside. He sniffed his finger and licked it – it smelled good and had a bitter-sweet taste. So he took the peel right off and pulled the inside apart. It was quite easy to separate into small pieces, each like a half moon. He was hungry, and he had a bit of bread as well. He wondered if that round thing were fit to eat.

Taking a bite, he chewed and swallowed and waited to see what would happen. But nothing happened, nothing except that it tasted good. It did not make him ill.

David ate half the pieces and chewed a bit of bread. Then he tried the orange-coloured peel, but that tasted sharp and unpleasant. He tried to push the thought away but it kept returning: 'I don't *know* anything! How can I stay free when I don't know what everybody else knows? I don't even know what's good to eat and what's poisonous. The only food I know about is porridge and bread and soup.'

For a little while he lost courage. Why had he not talked to the others in the camp, listened to their conversation and asked about the world outside? Not about food, of course, for there was a rule in the camp that no one might talk about food: for once in a way, it was not one of *their* rules, but one made by the prisoners themselves. When you had nothing but bread and porridge, and not enough of that, you did not want to talk about the kind of food you used to have when you were free. But there were other things he could have asked about. As long as Johannes had been with him, he had asked questions all the time, but he was only a little boy then and had asked about all sorts of things he had no use for now.

ANNE HOLM, *I am David*

Tell in your own words how David investigates the orange and finds that it is good to eat.

Why did the prisoners not talk about food?

Describe how you would examine and eat an everyday example of food as though it were something you had never seen before.

Smells

Smells can be pleasant or unpleasant. Name some that you like and some that you object to. Sometimes smells can be very evocative, that is they can bring back experiences and places from the past. Can you think of any smells that recall events or memories in your own life? Here is Keith Waterhouse remembering smells from his childhood.

Golden Days Of Rubbish

For some people it's the smell of apples on the bough or newly-baked bread. For me it has always been the smell of freshly-mixed cement, wet mortar and boiling tar.

I'm talking about those delicate, elusive, siren odours that waft you back into childhood. I walked past a building site on a hot afternoon last week and at once I was transported thirty-five years back in time.

Some of the happiest days of my life were spent pouring buckets of water into a pile of builder's sand and pretending I was at the seaside.

I've never regretted that mine was a city child-hood. We never knew the delights of swimming in a river or riding in hay-carts. But there were newts to be caught in the corporation reservoir, and dams to be built across the festering stream that carried effluent from the dye-works.

We stole nails by the hundredweight from the clerk of works' yard. We became bronze-tanned in the equatorial heat of the watchman's brazier where we melted down strips of purloined lead. The scent of hot tar, putty and cement, all mingled, was heady as May blossom.

There were expeditions to the slag heaps where, equipped with a dustbin lid, you could slide down a Cresta Run of smouldering ash.

There was a limestone quarry from which we emerged after a morning's reconnaissance looking like the Homepride flour graders.

There were the indoor swimming baths, smelling pungently of carbolic and Bovril.

And there were always golf balls to be 'found' on the municipal links. Scooping a golf ball out of a bunker and disappearing at the speed of light into the sanctuary of the rhododendron bushes was one excitement. The other was cutting into your loot with a sharp penknife and seeing what came out.

If you were unlucky, it was a putrescent, sticky, white fluid that was said to be liable to burn your hand off if you touched it. If you were fortunate, it was a tightly-bound ball of elastic with easily a thousand uses if only you could think of them.

There were raids to be carried out on the local rubbish dump which, at that time of year, had the languorous, heavy atmosphere of a tropical swamp.

Bluebottles hovered lazily over the clumps of deadly nightshade that flourished in a compost of rotting cardboard; city-orientated bees carried rust-like pollen from one abandoned bicycle frame to another.

We risked typhoid and cholera, but there were valuable trophies in that steaming urban jungle. One week we bore home a bus tyre, taking it in turns to roll along the main road curled up inside it.

Another time we found an enormous cache of used typewriter ribbons, and for weeks they fluttered from the telegraph wires like streamers after the biggest Mardi Gras in history.

We preferred marbles in the dustbowl of the school playground to climbing trees in the bluebell woods, and the asphalt perimeter of the park band-stand to the treacherous grass beyond it.

Which is not to say that we were ignorant of the lore of the countryside. We knew that all red berries are poisonous, that ladybirds bring you luck and picking dandelions makes you wet the bed. But at the end of the day we were urban creatures by instinct and inclination.

At harvest time we liked to forage for used tram tickets around the terminus. If it had been a good summer they lay clean and thick on the ground, all sky-blue or deep green, or white with a broad red band signifying a workman's return – as rare and precious as a thrush's egg.

The sun blazed, the unidentified birds sang, and all the anonymous flowers bloomed.

For us, the true, deep joy of summer was playing whip-and-top on the melting tarmac, drinking Tizer straight from the bottle, and the welcome bell of the Walls' ice cream man. And the limestone quarry, the golf links, the rubbish dump and the corporation reservoir.

Huckleberry Finn, you may believe me, didn't have it any more golden.

KEITH WATERHOUSE, *Mondays, Thursdays*

What does the author mean when he says 'the scent of hot tar, putty and cement was as heady as May blossom'?

Why is the word 'found' in quotation marks?

The author says the swamp 'had the languorous, heavy atmosphere of a tropical swamp'. What does he mean?

Why do you think the author preferred the town to the country as a child?

What does he mean by the last sentence?

Touch

Describe what it would feel like to touch each of the objects in the pictures on the next page.

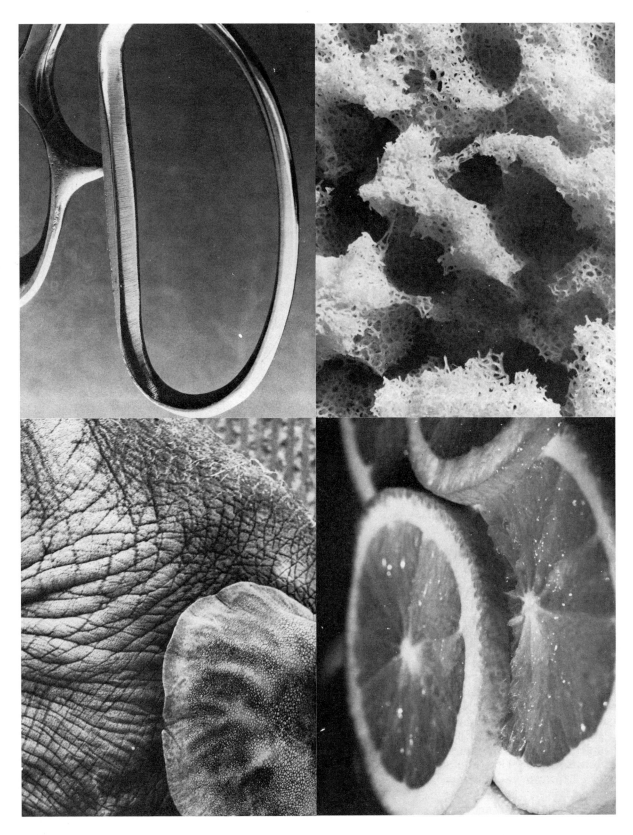

140

Learning through Touch

Helen Keller was not just blind, she was also deaf and dumb. Almost the only sense left to her was her sense of touch. Yet through the determination of a gifted teacher and finally her own will-power, Helen learned how to communicate. Part of this true story is told in this extract from the play *The Miracle Worker*.

If we were watching the play in a theatre (or looking at the film version of the play), the fact that the main character cannot speak would present no problems. We would be able to see what was happening. But if we are reading the play, a great number of stage directions are needed to indicate what is happening. Try reading this extract aloud with different people taking the different parts and with someone reading the stage directions.

Annie has been hired to look after Helen and to try to teach her. Helen is an unruly child who has always had her own way and is pampered by the family because she is blind. Annie thinks that this is part of the problem with Helen. She believes that she has to be firm – even cruel – if Helen is to be made to learn how to behave properly and how to communicate.

ANNIE: She's testing you. You realize?

JAMES (*to* ANNIE): She's testing you.

KELLER: Jimmie, be quiet. (JAMES *sits, tense.*) Now she's home, naturally she ——

ANNIE: And wants to see what will happen. At your hands. I said it was my main worry, is this what you promised me not half an hour ago?

KELLER (*reasonably*): But she's *not* kicking, now—

ANNIE: And not learning not to. Mrs Keller, teaching her is bound to be painful, to everyone. I know it hurts to watch, but she'll live up to just what you demand of her, and no more.

JAMES (*palely*): She's testing *you.*

KELLER (*testily*): Jimmie.

JAMES: I have an opinion, I think I should—

KELLER: No one's interested in hearing your opinion.

ANNIE: *I'm* interested, of course she's testing me. Let me keep her to what she's learned and she'll go on learning from me. Take her out of my hands and it all comes apart. (KATE *closes her eyes, digesting it;* ANNIE *sits again, with a brief comment for her.*) *Be* bountiful, it's at her expense. (*She turns to* JAMES, *flatly.*) Please pass me more of – her favorite foods.

(*Then* KATE *lifts* HELEN'S *hand, and turning her toward* ANNIE, *surrenders her;* HELEN *makes for her own chair.*)

KATE (*low*): Take her, Miss Annie.

ANNIE (*then*): Thank you.

(*But the moment* ANNIE *rising reaches for her hand,* HELEN *begins to fight and kick, clutching to the tablecloth and uttering laments.* ANNIE *again tries to loosen her hand, and* KELLER *rises.*)

KELLER (*tolerant*): I'm afraid you're the difficulty, Miss Annie. Now I'll keep her to what she's learned, you're quite right there—(*He takes* HELEN'S *hands from* ANNIE, *pats them;* HELEN *quiets down.*)—but I don't see that we need send her from the table, after all, she's the guest of honor. Bring her plate back.

ANNIE: If she was a seeing child, none of you would tolerate one—

KELLER: Well, she's not, I think some compromise is called for. Bring her plate, please. (ANNIE'S *jaw sets, but she restores the plate, while* KELLER *fastens the napkin around* HELEN'S *neck; she permits it.*) There. It's not unnatural, most of us take some aversion to our teachers, and occasionally another hand can smooth things out. (*He puts a fork in* HELEN'S *hand;* HELEN *takes it. Genially.*) Now. Shall we start all over?

(*He goes back around the table, and sits.* ANNIE *stands watching.* HELEN *is motionless, thinking things through, until with a wicked glee she deliberately flings the fork on the floor. After another moment she plunges her hand into her food, and crams a fistful into her mouth.*)

JAMES (*wearily*): I think we've started all over—

(KELLER *shoots a glare at him, as* HELEN *plunges her other hand into* ANNIE'S *plate.* ANNIE *at once moves in, to grasp her wrist, and* HELEN, *flinging out a hand, encounters the pitcher; she swings with it at* ANNIE; ANNIE, *falling back, blocks it with an elbow, but the water flies over her dress.* ANNIE *gets her breath, then snatches the pitcher away in one hand, hoists* HELEN *up bodily under the other arm, and starts to carry her out, kicking.* KELLER *stands.*)

ANNIE (*savagely polite*): Don't get up!

KELLER: Where are you going?

ANNIE: Don't smooth anything else out for me, don't interfere in any way! I treat her like a seeing child because I *ask* her to see, I *expect* her to see, don't undo what I do!

KELLER: Where are you taking her?

ANNIE: To make her fill this pitcher again!

(*She thrusts out with* HELEN *under her arm, but* HELEN *escapes up the stairs and* ANNIE *runs after her.* KELLER *stands rigid.* AUNT EV *is astounded.*)

AUNT EV: You let her speak to you like that, Arthur? A creature who *works* for you?

KELLER (*angrily*): No, I don't.

(*He is starting after* ANNIE *when* JAMES, *on his feet with shaky resolve, interposes his chair between them in* KELLER'S *path.*)

JAMES: Let her go.

KELLER: What!

JAMES (*a swallow*): I said – let her go. She's right. (KELLER *glares at the chair and him.* JAMES *takes a deep breath, then headlong:*) She's right, Kate's right, I'm right, and you're wrong. If you drive her away from here it will be over my dead – chair, has it never occurred to you that on one occasion you might be consummately wrong?

(KELLER'S *stare is unbelieving, even a little fascinated.* KATE *rises in trepidation, to mediate.*)

KATE: Captain.

KELLER (*he stops her with his raised hand; his eyes stay on* JAMES' *pale face, for a long hold. When he finally finds his voice, it is gruff*): Sit down, everyone. (*He sits.* KATE *sits.* JAMES *holds onto his chair.* KELLER *speaks mildly.*) Please sit down, Jimmie. (JAMES *sits, and a moveless silence prevails;* KELLER'S *eyes do not leave him.*)

(ANNIE *has pulled* HELEN *downstairs again by one hand, the pitcher in her other hand, down the porch steps, and across the yard to the pump. She puts* HELEN'S *hand on the pump handle, grimly.*)

ANNIE: All right. Pump. (HELEN *touches her cheek, waits uncertainly.*) No, she's not here. Pump! (*She forces* HELEN'S *hand to work the handle, then lets go. And* HELEN *obeys. She pumps till the water comes, then* ANNIE *puts the pitcher in her other hand and guides it under the spout, and the water tumbling half into and half around the pitcher douses* HELEN'S *hand.* ANNIE *takes over the handle to keep water coming and does automatically what she has done so many times before, spells into* HELEN'S *free palm:*) Water. W, a, t, e, r. *Water.* It has a – *name*——

(*And now the miracle happens.* HELEN *drops the pitcher on the slab under the spout, it shatters. She stands transfixed.* ANNIE *freezes on the pump handle: there is a change in the sundown light, and* with it a change in HELEN'S *face, some light coming into it we have never seen there, some struggle in the depths behind it; and her lips tremble, trying to remember something the muscles around them once knew, till at last it finds its way out, painfully, a baby sound buried under the debris of years of dumbness.*)

HELEN: Wah. (*And again, with great effort.*) Wah. Wah. (HELEN *plunges her hand into the dwindling water, spells into her own palm. Then she gropes frantically,* ANNIE *reaches for her hand, and* HELEN *spells into* ANNIE'S *hand.*)

ANNIE (*whispering*): Yes. (HELEN *spells into it again.*) Yes! (HELEN *grabs at the handle, pumps for more water, plunges her hand into its spurt and grabs* ANNIE'S *to spell it again.*) Yes! Oh, my dear—(*She falls to her knees to clasp* HELEN'S *hand, but* HELEN *pulls it free, stands almost bewildered, then drops to the ground, pats it swiftly, holds up her palm, imperious.* ANNIE *spells into it:*) Ground. (HELEN *spells it back.*) Yes! (HELEN *whirls to the pump, pats it, holds up her palm, and* ANNIE *spells into it.*) Pump. (HELEN *spells it back.*) Yes! Yes! (*Now* HELEN *is in such an excitement she is possessed, wild, trembling, cannot be still, turns, runs, falls on the porch step, clasps it, reaches out her palm, and* ANNIE *is at it instantly to spell:*) Step. (HELEN *has no time to spell back now, she whirls groping, to touch anything, encounters the trellis, shakes it, thrusts out her palm, and* ANNIE *while spelling to her, cries wildly at the house.*) Trellis. Mrs Keller! *Mrs Keller!* (*Inside,* KATE *starts to her feet.* HELEN *scrambles back onto the porch, groping, and finds the bell string, tugs it: the bell rings, the distant chimes begin telling the hour, all the bells in town seem to break into speech while* HELEN *reaches out and* ANNIE *spells feverishly into her hand.* KATE *hurries out, with* KELLER *after her;* AUNT EV *is on her feet, to peer out the window; only* JAMES *remains at the table, and with a napkin wipes his damp brow. From Up Right and Left the* SERVANTS – VINEY, *the two* NEGRO CHILDREN, *the other* SERVANT – *run in, and stand watching from a distance as* HELEN, *ringing the bell, with her other hand encounters her mother's skirt; when she throws a hand out,* ANNIE *spells into it:*) Mother. (KELLER *now seizes* HELEN'S *hand, she touches him, gestures a hand, and* ANNIE *again spells:*) Papa – She *knows!* (KATE *and* KELLER *go to their knees, stammering, clutching* HELEN *to them, and* ANNIE *steps unsteadily back to watch the threesome,* HELEN *spelling wildly into* KATE'S *hand, then into* KELLER'S, KATE *spelling back into* HELEN'S; *they cannot keep their hands off her, and rock her in their clasp. Then* HELEN *gropes, feels nothing, turns all around, pulls free, and comes with both hands groping, to find* ANNIE. *She encounters* ANNIE'S *thighs,* ANNIE *kneels to her,* HELEN'S *hand pats* ANNIE'S *cheek impatiently, points a finger, and waits; and* ANNIE *spells into it:*) Teacher. (HELEN *spells it back, slowly,* ANNIE *nods.*) Teacher.

William Gibson, *The Miracle Worker*

What do you think Annie was going to say when she began 'If she was a seeing child, none of you would tolerate one——'?

Why do you think Helen behaves the way she does – fighting and kicking, throwing the fork on the floor?

Why does James swallow before his speech 'I said – let her go'?

Why do you think the feel of water is important in bringing about Helen's change of attitude?

How would you describe what Helen is feeling as she learns word after word?

 ## Assignments

Choose several of the following to write about:

1. You hear a mysterious bang in the sky every night at the same time. Write about what different people think it is and what they do about it.
2. Write about smells that you find pleasant or unpleasant. Perhaps this could be a poem.
3. Write a poem about pleasant and unpleasant sounds.
4. Write a story about someone who is blind.
5. Write a poem about all the different things suggested to you by a particular colour.
6. Choose two or three everyday objects (such as a safety pin, a typewriter, a screwdriver or an electric kettle) and try to describe them as exactly as possible. Imagine you are explaining what they look like and how they work to someone blind who has never come across them before.

7. Write about the taste of different things, some pleasant, some strange, some nasty. Perhaps this could be a poem.
8. Write a story about someone who loses his spectacles or has them broken.
9. Choose an ordinary everyday object (such as grass, sand, water or leaves) and try to write about it in an interesting way.
10. Write about each of the senses in turn and say what it is about each that gives you pleasure.
11. Write about what it must be like to be blind, deaf or dumb. Which do you think is the greatest deprivation? Why?

 ## Language

Agreement

A verb must agree in number with its subject. That is, if the subject is singular, the verb must be singular; if the subject is plural, the verb must be plural, e.g.

He is watching the procession. ('he' is singular; 'is watching' is singular.)

They are watching the procession. ('they' is plural; 'are watching' is plural.)

The same is true of person.

Care should be taken with the following cases:

1. The verb 'to be' agrees with the subject regardless of the number of the complement, e.g.

The *answer* (subject) to the problem *is* (verb) more workers (both singular).

2. Or, either ... or, neither ... nor, when they join singular nouns or pronouns take a singular verb, and the verb agrees in person with the noun or pronoun nearest to it, e.g.

Neither *he* (singular) nor *I am* (first person singular) to be present (first person singular).

Either *she* (singular) or *you are* (second person singular) quite wrong (second person singular).

3. Don't be misled when a phrase comes between the subject and the verb, e.g.

The *results* (plural) of the competition in last week's newspaper *are* (plural) to be published today.

4. Pronouns like everyone, everybody, neither, either, require a singular verb, e.g.

Neither (singular) *was* (singular) present yesterday.

Everybody (singular) *is* (singular) very grateful.

5. In sentences containing phrases like 'one of those who', the following verb should be plural agreeing with 'who' which in turn agrees with 'those' (plural), e.g.

That pupil is one of those *who* (plural) never *let* (plural) anything ruffle them (plural).

6. Collective nouns take a singular or plural verb depending on the meaning. They are normally singular when we consider all the members contained in the collective noun as doing the same thing, e.g.

The crew *was working* (singular) hard.

But if we think of the collective noun as the sum of a number of individuals doing different things, the verb could well be plural, e.g.

The police *were divided* (plural) about the best way to proceed.

Note that whether you decide that the verb is singular or plural, you must be consistent when it comes to words like possessive adjectives, e.g.

The *jury* (singular) *is taking* (singular) *its* (singular) time.
NOT
The *jury* (singular) *is taking* (singular) *their* (plural) time.

The same is true of words like 'each', 'everyone', 'everybody', 'anyone', 'anybody', 'no one', etc. These are singular and must be followed by singular pronouns and possessives, e.g.

Everyone (singular) *has* (singular) to work *his* (singular) hardest.
NOT
Everyone (singular) *has* (singular) to work *their* (plural) hardest.

There are some difficult points here. *Re-read the notes and make sure you have understood them.*

Rewrite the following sentences, using the appropriate forms of the verbs and other words.

1. Neither brother ... going to the party.
2. She is one of those people who ... never upset by examinations.
3. Everyone ... looking forward to ... exhibit winning the prize.
4. Angela, together with her parents and her two small brothers, ... going to the seaside.
5. Either you or I ... win the competition.
6. Man ... many characters in one.
7. The class ... not able to make up ... mind who should be captain.
8. He is one of those artists who ... not willing to compromise ... art.
9. The government ... not able to reach a decision about ... policy.
10. Neither John nor you ... going to be allowed to come.

Vocabulary

A. Sensible/Sensitive/Sensual/Sensuous

These four words have similarities in meaning, but there are very clear distinctions between them. *Look them up in your dictionary. Explain the differences in meaning. Use each of them in a sentence.*

B. Colours

Everyone knows more or less what colour we are referring to when we use words like 'red' or 'green' or 'brown'. But what colours do the following words indicate?

puce maroon
khaki crimson
magenta ochre
ultramarine saffron
mahogany aquamarine
emerald auburn

Even with ordinary 'red' or 'green', there are many variations and gradations, and sometimes these words are qualified to give a more precise impression. *Can you distinguish between the following?*

pillar box red
carnation red
cardinal red
Lovat green
sea-green
bottle-green
pea-green
battleship-grey
dove-grey
chocolate brown
chestnut brown
plum-coloured
bishop's purple

C. Smells

There are a number of words which name smells of different kinds. Can you say under what circumstances each of the following would be appropriate?

odour perfume
smell fume
scent bouquet
whiff stench
stink fragrance
aroma

Use these words in sentences.

 Spelling

A. More Homophones

Here are some more homophones (or near homophones) for you to distinguish between. Make sure you know what each word means so that you can use the correct spelling when you come to use the word.

tail, tale
tea, tee
team, teem
their, there, they're
threw, through
throne, thrown
to, too
troop, troupe
vain, vein
vale, veil
villain, villein
wain, wane
waist, waste
waive, wave
weak, week
weather, whether
were, where
who's, whose
wont, won't
yoke, yolk

Use some of these words in sentences.

B. Double 'l'

Care has to be taken with words containing double 'l'. When forming a compound word, a double 'l' often becomes single, e.g.

joy+full joyful
un+till until
spoon+full spoonful
full+fill fulfil
well+come welcome
all+ready already
all+ways always
all+together altogether
all+though although
all+most almost
skill+full skilful
all+mighty almighty

Note the following exceptions:

smallness
tallness
shrillness
stillness
illness

fullness
dullness
wellbeing (or well-being)
well-doer
well-wisher
well-nigh
all-round
all-consuming
all-in
overall
chockfull (or chock-full)

Find more examples of words where double 'l' becomes single in compound words.

Use some of these words in sentences. (Remember that the opposite process often happens as well, that is, single 'l' is doubled when a suffix is added.)

 Activities

A. 1. Spread yourselves out in a large open space, perhaps the playground. With eyes tightly shut, start to move. Afterwards, discuss what your feelings were.

2. Collect some unusual objects (such as a sheep's skull, a large shell, a piece of silk, a piece of plastic) which have interesting shapes or textures. Don't let anyone know what they are. Now blindfold one of your classmates and get him to say as much as he can about an object just by feeling it.

3. Do the same with objects that smell differently. Blindfold one of your classmates and don't let him touch the object. Just let him smell it and describe the kind of smell and what he thinks the object might be. (Try a bottle of after-shave or disinfectant or a piece of leather or a pot of damp earth.)

4. The same thing can be done with tastes. Try a tiny pinch of salt or yoghurt or health salts or vinegar.

B. 1. Make a list of as many different objects as you can that have different textures and arrange them into different categories such as smooth, rough, lumpy, jagged, etc.

2. Find out about the Royal National Institute for the Blind or the Royal National Institute for the Deaf and tell the rest of the class what you have learned about it.

3. Try to see the film version of *The Miracle Worker.*

4. Find out about the work of the Noise Abatement Society. Tell the rest of the class about it.

5. What do you know about Muzak? Make a survey of the rest of the class to find out whether they approve of it or not.

6. One of the arguments against Concorde is that it makes too much noise. Have a debate for and against the amount of noise there is in the world today.

Reading List

CONSOLIDATION III

Revise the 'Language', 'Vocabulary' and 'Spelling' sections of Units 7, 8 and 9, and then see if you can answer these questions. If you find there are questions you can't answer, re-study the appropriate section.

A. Language

1. Give two ways of defining what a sentence is.
2. Give two uses of the full stop.
3. What is a paragraph?
4. Why do we use paragraphs?
5. What is a topic sentence?
6. What form of nouns and pronouns do prepositions govern?
7. Write sentences using the word 'in' first as a preposition, then as an adverb.
8. When do we use the semi-colon?
9. When do we use the colon?
10. Write a sentence containing a colon and a semi-colon.
11. When do we use the dash?
12. When do we use brackets?
13. Give an example of a sentence where dashes, brackets or commas could be used as alternatives.
14. What do we mean by 'agreement'?
15. How do we decide whether a collective noun has a singular or a plural verb?
16. Does 'everybody' have a singular or a plural verb?
17. Is the verb following phrases like 'one of those who' singular or plural?
18. What parts of speech do adverbs modify?
19. Give examples in sentences of adverbs modifying each of these parts of speech.
20. Name three adverbs which have the same form as their adjectives.
21. Name three words ending in '-ly' which are not adverbs.
22. Name three adverbs which indicate time.
23. Name three adverbs which indicate manner.
24. What question would you expect after a verb if the answer is an adverb indicating reason?
25. What are the comparative and superlative forms of the adverb 'well'?

B. Vocabulary

1. What is the origin of the word 'television'?
2. Where does the word 'skinhead' come from?
3. What is the difference in meaning between 'jump on' and 'jump at'?
4. Write sentences containing the words 'stand for' and 'stand up to'.
5. What is an acronym?
6. Give an example of an acronym and say what the full version is.
7. What is the difference in meaning between 'sensible' and 'sensitive'?
8. What colour is 'khaki'?
9. What colour is 'saffron'?
10. What words would you use instead of 'smell' to indicate an unpleasant smell?

C. Spelling

1. What is the difference between 'quiet' and 'quite'?
2. What is the difference between 'sight' and 'site'?

3. Write a sentence containing the word 'storey'.
4. Write a sentence containing the word 'sort'.
5. What is the most common way of forming the plural of a noun?
6. Write down the plural form of 'bus'.
7. Write down the plural form of 'knife'.
8. Write down the plural form of 'piano'.
9. Write down the plural form of 'baby'.
10. Before what letters is 'c' pronounced the same as 's'?
11. Write down the word you get when you add the suffix 'able' to 'pronounce'.
12. Write down the word you get when you add the suffix 'able' to 'change'.
13. Before what vowels is 'g' often pronounced the same as 'j'?
14. Distinguish between 'tail' and 'tale'.
15. Distinguish between 'weather' and 'whether'.
16. Write sentences containing 'their', 'there', and 'they're'.
17. Write sentences containing 'were' and 'where'.
18. What happens to the suffix '-full' when you add it to a word?
19. Give five examples of words to which the suffix '-full' has been added.
20. Write down the past tense of the verb 'to fulfil'.